Yanmar

YANMAR MARINE ENGINES SY SERIES –
6SY-STP2/6SY655/8SY-STP

Service Manual

Yanmar

YANMAR MARINE ENGINES SY SERIES – 6SY-STP2/6SY655/8SY-STP

Service Manual

ISBN/EAN: 9783954273454
Erscheinungsjahr: 2013
Erscheinungsort: Bremen, Deutschland

© maritimepress in Europäischer Hochschulverlag GmbH & Co. KG, Fahrenheitstr. 1, 28359 Bremen. Alle Rechte beim Verlag und bei den jeweiligen Lizenzgebern.

www.maritimepress.de | office@maritimepress.de

Bei diesem Titel handelt es sich um den Nachdruck eines historischen, lange vergriffenen Buches. Da elektronische Druckvorlagen für diese Titel nicht existieren, musste auf alte Vorlagen zurückgegriffen werden. Hieraus zwangsläufig resultierende Qualitätsverluste bitten wir zu entschuldigen.

TABLE OF CONTENTS

	Page
Table of Contents	2-i
Introduction	1-1
Safety	2-1
General Service Information	3-1
Periodic Maintenance	4-1
Engine	5-1
Fuel System	6-1
Cooling System	7-1
Lubrication	8-1
Turbocharger	9-1
Starter Motor	10-1
Alternator	11-1
EMS	12-1
Troubleshooting	13-1

TABLE OF CONTENTS

This Page Intentionally Left Blank

Section 1

INTRODUCTION

This manual gives specific instructions for the proper repair of Yanmar SY series marine engines.

Please follow the procedures carefully to ensure quality service.

Yanmar recommends that you read this *Service Manual* completely before starting with repairs.

Along with standard tools, Yanmar recommends the use of special tools, necessary to perform repairs correctly.

Yanmar products are continuously undergoing improvement. This *Service Manual* has been checked carefully in order to avoid errors. However Yanmar is not liable, for any misrepresentations, errors of description or omissions. Contact an authorized Yanmar marine dealer or distributor for any questions you have regarding this *Service Manual*.

INTRODUCTION
Revision History
REVISION HISTORY

This manual is a living document. Periodic manual revisions are published to document product improvements and changes. This practice ensures the manual has the most current information.

As manual revisions become necessary, individual pages are prepared and sent to those who need the information. If a page, or number of pages should be replaced, the replacement information is sent along with a revised Revision Control Table. Discard the older, obsolete information.

At times, the revision involves inserting additional pages in one or more sections. Replace the Revision Control Table and insert the new pages.

This method of revision control represents the most cost-effective solution to providing current, updated information as needed.

Revision Control Table

Revision Date Revision Number	New Page Numbers Involved	Remarks	Initiating Dept.
DEC 2006 Rev. 01	All	Re-release	YMU
JAN 2007 Rev. 02	7-4 7-28	Corrected torque value for seawater pump gear nut	YMU

Section 2

SAFETY

Yanmar is concerned for your safety and the condition of your marine engine. Safety statements are one of the primary ways to call your attention to the potential hazards associated with Yanmar marine engines. Follow the precautions listed throughout the manual before operation, during operation and during periodic maintenance procedures for your safety, the safety of others and to protect the performance of your marine engine. Keep the decals from becoming dirty or torn and replace them if they are lost or damaged. Also, if you need to replace a part that has a decal attached to it, make sure you order the new part and decal at the same time.

 This safety alert symbol appears with most safety statements. It means attention, become alert, your safety is involved! Please read and abide by the message that follows the safety alert symbol.

⚠ DANGER

Indicates a hazardous situation which, if not avoided, *will* result in death or serious injury.

⚠ WARNING

Indicates a hazardous situation which, if not avoided, *could* result in death or serious injury.

⚠ CAUTION

Indicates a hazardous situation which, if not avoided, *could* result in minor or moderate injury.

NOTICE

Indicates a situation which can cause damage to the machine, personal property and / or the environment or cause the equipment to operate improperly.

SAFETY

SAFETY PRECAUTIONS

⚠ DANGER

The safety messages that follow have DANGER level hazards.

There is no substitute for common sense and careful practices. Improper practices or carelessness can cause burns, cuts, mutilation, asphyxiation, other bodily injury or death. This information contains general safety precautions and guidelines that must be followed to reduce risk to personal safety. Special safety precautions are listed in specific procedures. Read and understand all of the safety precautions before operation or performing repairs or maintenance.

Avoid injury or equipment damage due to engine falling. ALWAYS secure the engine solidly to prevent the engine from falling during maintenance.

NEVER permit anyone to install or operate the engine without proper training.

♦ Read and understand this *Operation Manual* before you operate or service the engine to ensure that you follow safe operating practices and maintenance procedures.
- Safety signs and decals are additional reminders for safe operating and maintenance techniques.
- See your authorized Yanmar marine dealer or distributor for additional training.

⚠ WARNING

The safety messages that follow have WARNING level hazards.

Explosion Hazard

Avoid serious personal injury or equipment damage. While the engine is running or the battery is charging, hydrogen gas is being produced and can be easily ignited. Keep the area around the battery well-ventilated and keep sparks, open flame and any other form of ignition out of the area.

Avoid serious personal injury or equipment damage. ALWAYS turn off the battery switch (if equipped) or disconnect the negative battery cable before servicing the equipment.

Avoid unexpected equipment movement. Shift the marine gear NEUTRAL any time the engine is at idle.

Fire Hazard

Avoid personal injury or equipment damage. Have appropriate safety equipment available.

- Keep fire extinguishers handy in case of fire. Clearly indicate the location of the fire extinguishers with a safety sign.
- Ensure that the type of fire extinguishers are appropriate for material that might catch fire. Check with local authorities.
- Have all fire extinguishers checked periodically for proper operation and / or readiness.
- Post evacuation routes prominently. Periodically conduct fire drills.

Avoid personal injury. ALWAYS read and follow safety-related precautions found on containers of hazardous substances like parts cleaners, primers, sealants and sealant removers.

Wipe up all spills immediately.

Safety Precautions

SAFETY

⚠ WARNING

Entanglement Hazard

Rotating parts can cause severe injury or death. NEVER wear jewelry, unbuttoned cuffs, ties or loose fitting clothing and ALWAYS tie long hair back when working near moving / rotating parts such as the flywheel or PTO shaft. Keep hands, feet and tools away from all moving parts.

Avoid personal injury. ALWAYS stop the engine before beginning service.

Avoid personal injury. NEVER leave the key in the key switch when servicing the engine. Attach a "Do Not Operate" tag near the key switch while performing maintenance on the equipment.

Sever Hazard

Avoid personal injury. The propeller may rotate during towing or if the engine is running at idle speed. NEVER service the marine gear while being towed or when the engine is running.

Avoid personal injury. If the vessel has more than one engine, NEVER service a marine gear if either of the engines are running. In multi-engine configurations the propeller for an engine that is shut down may rotate if any of the other engines are running.

Rotating parts can cause severe injury or death. NEVER operate the engine without the guards in place.

Avoid personal injury. NEVER operate the engine while wearing a headset to listen to music or radio because it will be difficult to hear the warning signals.

Electrical Hazard

Make welding repairs safely.

♦ ALWAYS turn off the battery switch (if equipped) or disconnect the negative battery cable and the leads to the alternator when welding on the equipment.
♦ Remove the multi-pin connector to the engine control unit. Connect the weld clamp to the component to be welded and as close as possible to the welding point.
♦ NEVER connect the weld clamp to the engine or in a manner which would allow current to pass through a mounting bracket.
♦ When welding is completed, reconnect the leads to the alternator and engine control unit prior to reconnecting the batteries.

Exhaust Hazard

Avoid serious injury or death. NEVER block windows, vents, or other means of ventilation if the engine is operating in an enclosed area. All internal combustion engines create carbon monoxide gas during operation and special precautions are required to avoid carbon monoxide poisoning.

Burn Hazard

Avoid serious injury. Some of the engine surfaces become very hot during operation and shortly after shut down. Keep hands and other body parts away from hot engine surfaces.

Handle hot components with heat-resistant gloves.

Sudden Movement Hazard

Avoid personal injury or equipment damage. The engine lifting eyes are engineered to lift the weight of the marine engine only. ALWAYS use the engine lifting eyes when lifting the engine.

To prevent accidental equipment movement, NEVER start the engine in gear.

SAFETY

Safety Precautions

⚠ WARNING

Lifting Hazard

Avoid serious personal injury. Additional equipment is necessary to lift the marine engine and marine gear together. ALWAYS use lifting equipment with sufficient capacity to lift the marine engine.

If you need to transport an engine for repair have a helper assist you attach it to a hoist and load it on a truck.

Alcohol and Drug Hazard

NEVER operate the engine while you are under the influence of alcohol or drugs or are feeling ill.

Exposure Hazard

To avoid injury, ALWAYS wear personal protective equipment including appropriate clothing, gloves, work shoes, eye and hearing protection as required by the task at hand.

Tool Hazard

Avoid personal injury or equipment damage. Always remove any tools or shop rags used during maintenance from the area before operation.

⚠ CAUTION

The safety messages that follow have CAUTION level hazards.

Avoid personal injury. ALWAYS wear eye protection when servicing the engine or when using compressed air or high-pressure water. Dust, flying debris, compressed air, pressurized water or steam may injure your eyes.

Poor Lighting Hazard

Avoid personal injury or equipment damage. Ensure that the work area is adequately illuminated. ALWAYS install wire cages on portable safety lamps.

Tool Hazard

Avoid personal injury or equipment damage. ALWAYS use tools appropriate for the task at hand and use the correct size tool for loosening or tightening machine parts.

Safety Precautions

SAFETY

NOTICE

The safety messages that follow have NOTICE level hazards.

Any part which is found defective as a result of inspection or any part whose measured value does not satisfy the standard or limit must be replaced.

ALWAYS tighten components to the specified torque. Loose parts can cause equipment damage or cause it to operate improperly.

Only use replacement parts specified. Other replacement parts may affect warranty coverage.

NEVER attempt to modify the engine design or safety features such as defeating the engine speed limit control or the diesel fuel injection quantity control.

Modifications may impair the engine's safety and performance characteristics and shorten the engine's life. Any alterations to this engine may void its warranty. Be sure to use Yanmar genuine replacement parts.

ALWAYS be environmentally responsible.

Follow the guidelines of the EPA or other governmental agencies for the proper disposal of hazardous materials such as engine oil, diesel fuel and engine coolant. Consult the local authorities or reclamation facility.

NEVER dispose of hazardous materials by dumping them into a sewer, on the ground or into ground water or waterways.

If any indicator illuminates during engine operation, stop the engine immediately. Determine the cause and repair the problem before you continue to operate the engine.

Make sure the engine is installed on a level surface. If a Yanmar Marine Engine is installed at an angle that exceeds the specifications stated in the Yanmar Marine Installation manuals, engine oil may enter the combustion chamber causing excessive engine speed, white exhaust smoke and serious engine damage. This applies to engines that run continuously or those that run for short periods of time.

SAFETY
Safety Precautions

This Page Intentionally Left Blank

Section 3

GENERAL SERVICE INFORMATION

	Page
Safety Precautions	3-3
Engine Outline Drawings	3-4
6SY-STP2 X ZF325-1	3-4
8SY-STP X MG5114 IV	3-5
Engine Piping Diagrams	3-6
Location of Nameplates	3-9
Engine Nameplate (Typical)	3-9
Diesel Fuel	3-10
Diesel Fuel Specifications	3-10
Filling the Fuel Tank	3-11
Bleeding the Fuel System	3-11
Engine Oil	3-12
Engine Oil Specifications	3-12
Engine Oil Viscosity	3-12
Selection of Marine Gear Oil	3-13
Engine Coolant	3-13
Engine Coolant Specifications	3-13
Coolant (Closed Cooling System)	3-13
Principal Engine Specifications	3-15
Engine Service Standards	3-17
Tightening Torques for Standard Bolts and Nuts	3-18
Tightening Fasteners	3-18
Abbreviations and Symbols	3-19
Abbreviations	3-19
Symbols	3-19

GENERAL SERVICE INFORMATION

Unit Conversions 3-20
    Unit Prefixes 3-20
    Units of Length 3-20
    Units of Volume 3-20
    Units of Mass 3-20
    Units of Force 3-20
    Units of Torque 3-20
    Units of Pressure 3-20
    Units of Power 3-20
    Units of Temperature 3-20

SAFETY PRECAUTIONS

⚠ WARNING

Fire Hazard

Avoid injury or equipment damage from fire. Undersized wiring systems can cause an electrical fire.

Electrical Hazard

Avoid personal injury or equipment damage. ALWAYS keep the electrical connectors and terminals clean. Check the electrical harnesses for cracks, abrasions, and damaged or corroded connectors.

NEVER turn off the battery switch (if equipped) or short the battery cables during operation. Damage to the electrical system will result.

GENERAL SERVICE INFORMATION

Engine Outline Drawings

ENGINE OUTLINE DRAWINGS

6SY-STP2 X ZF325-1

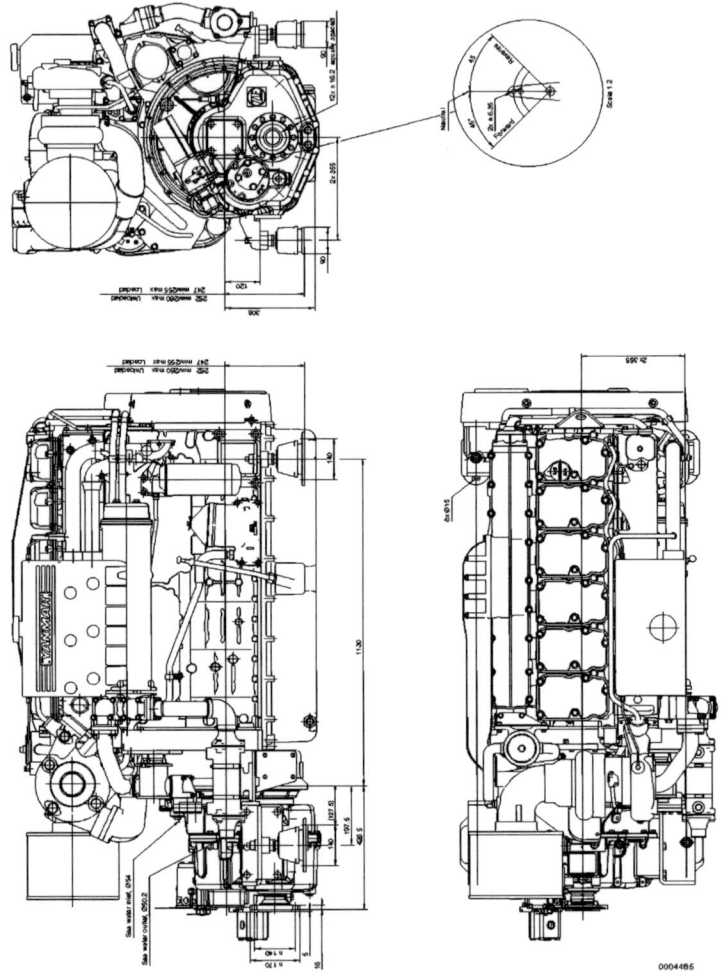

Figure 3-1

Engine Outline Drawings

8SY-STP X MG5114 IV

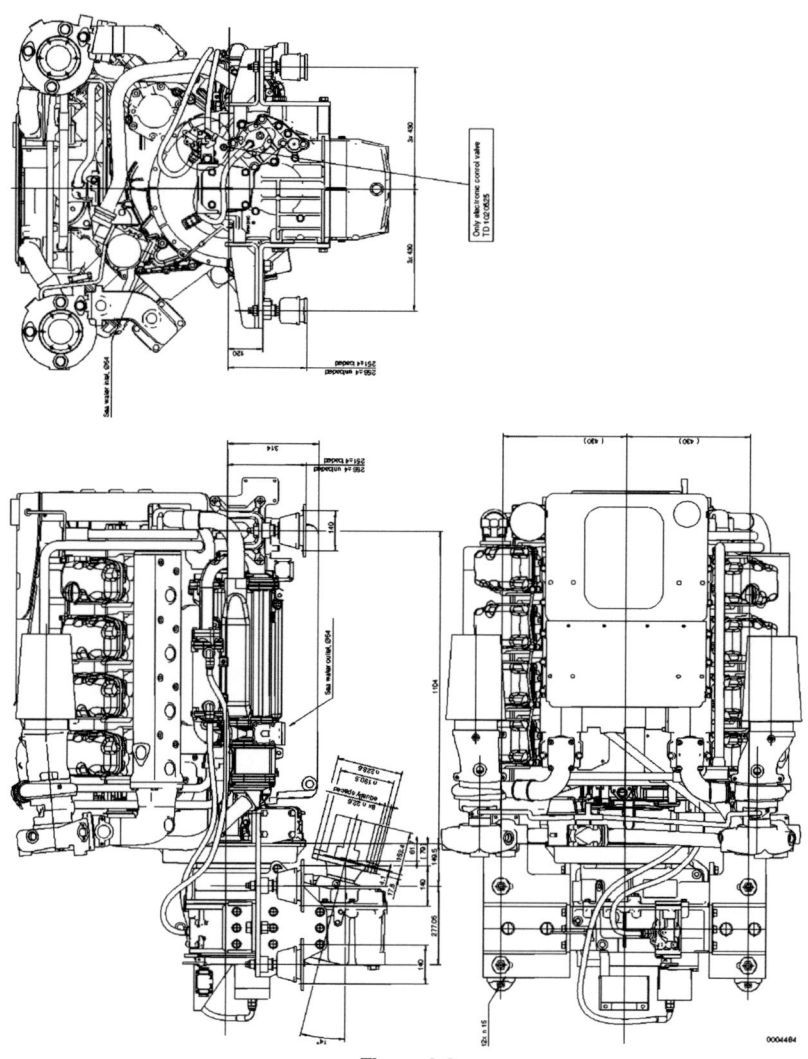

Figure 3-2

GENERAL SERVICE INFORMATION

ENGINE PIPING DIAGRAMS

6SY Fuel Flow

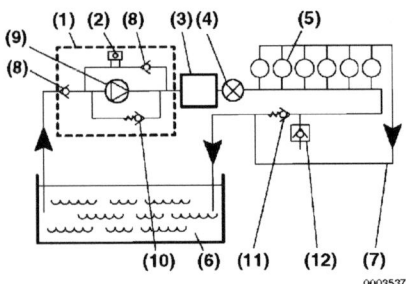

1 – Fuel Feed Pump Assembly
2 – Hand Pump
3 – EMS Control Unit
4 – Fuel Filter
5 – Cylinders
6 – Fuel Tank
7 – Fuel Return Line
8 – Check Valve
9 – Feed Pump Gear Set
10 – Safety Valve
11 – Pressure Relief Valve
12 – Bleeder Valve

Figure 3-3

8SY Fuel Flow

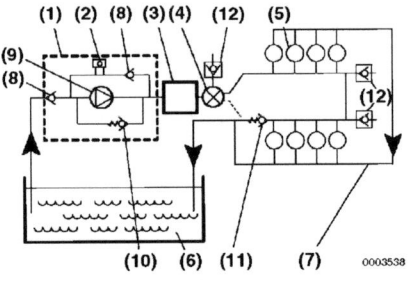

1 – Fuel Feed Pump Assembly
2 – Hand Pump
3 – EMS Control Unit
4 – Fuel Filter
5 – Cylinders
6 – Fuel Tank
7 – Fuel Return Line
8 – Check Valve
9 – Feed Pump Gear Set
10 – Safety Valve
11 – Pressure Relief Valve
12 – Bleeder Valve

Figure 3-4

Engine Piping Diagrams

GENERAL SERVICE INFORMATION

6SY Cooling Flow

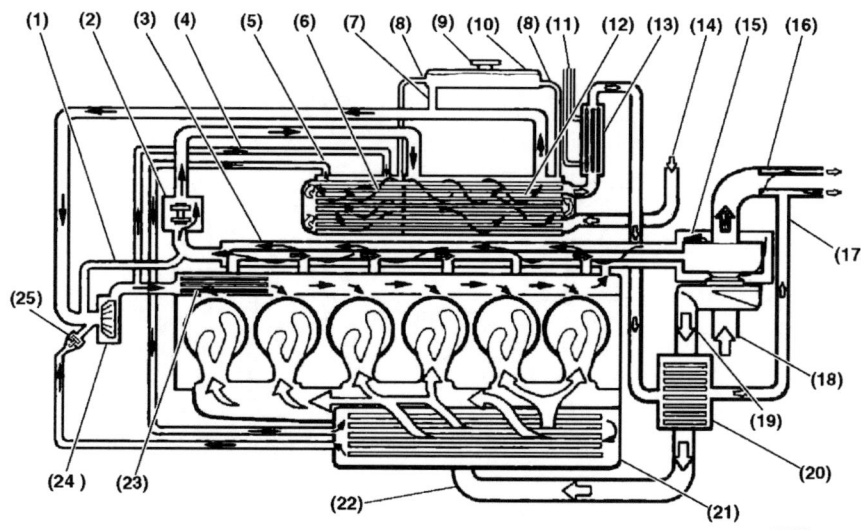

1 – Bypass Channel
2 – Main Thermostat
3 – Water-Cooled Exhaust Manifold
4 – Charge Air Coolant
5 – Charge Air Coolant Supply
6 – Heat Exchanger Element, Charge Air Cooler Section
7 – Static Line
8 – Venting
9 – Pressure Cap
10 – Coolant Recovery Tank (integrated with heat exchanger)
11 – Oil To and From Gearbox
12 – Heat Exchanger Element, Main Section
13 – Cooler for Gearbox Oil
14 – Seawater Intake
15 – Water-Cooled Turbocharger
16 – Raiser with Seawater Outlet
17 – Seawater Outlet
18 – Air Supply to Turbocharger
19 – Air Inlet to Seawater Cooled Charge Air Cooler
20 – Charge Air Cooler with Seawater Cooling
21 – Charge Air Cooler with Coolant Cooling
22 – Air Inlet to Charge Air Cooler with Coolant Cooling
23 – Engine Oil Cooler
24 – Coolant Pump
25 – Thermostat Housing with Thermostat for Charge Air Circuit

Figure 3-5

GENERAL SERVICE INFORMATION

Engine Piping Diagrams

8SY Cooling Flow

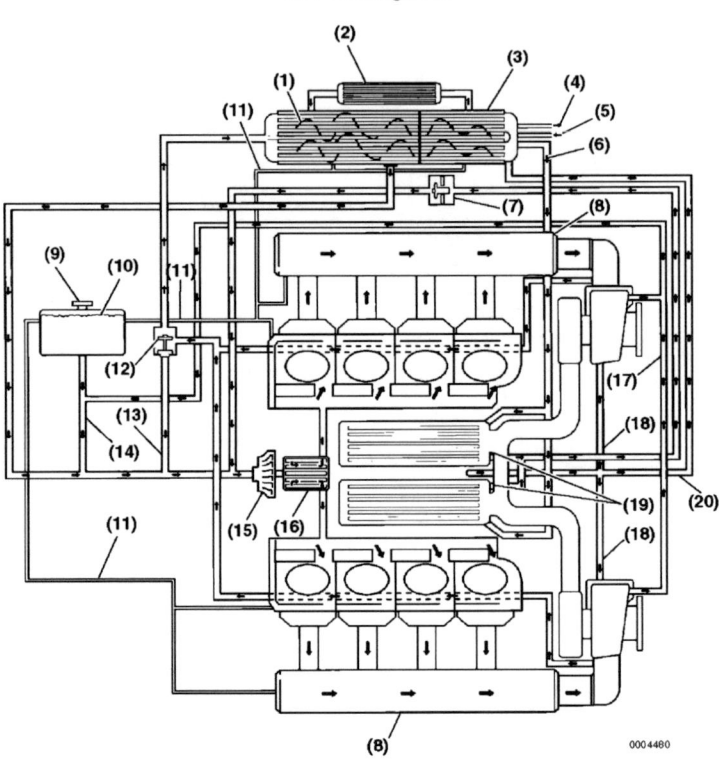

1 – Heat Exchanger Element, Main Section
2 – Reverse Gear Oil Cooler (Optional)
3 – Heat Exchanger Element, Charge Air Section
4 – Seawater Outlet
5 – Seawater Inlet
6 – Coolant to Charge Air Coolers
7 – Thermostat, Charge Air Section
8 – Water-Cooled Exhaust Manifolds
9 – Pressure Cap
10 – Coolant Recovery Tank
11 – Ventilation Line
12 – Thermostats, Main Cooling Circuit
13 – Bypass Lines
14 – Static Line
15 – Coolant Pump
16 – Engine Oil Cooler
17 – Coolant from Turbochargers
18 – Coolant to Turbochargers
19 – Outlet from Charge Air Coolers
20 – Coolant from Block to Charge Air Section of Heat Exchanger

Figure 3-6

GENERAL SERVICE INFORMATION

LOCATION OF NAMEPLATES

The following figures show the location of regulatory and safety nameplates on Yanmar SY marine engines.

Engine Nameplate (Typical)

6SY Engines

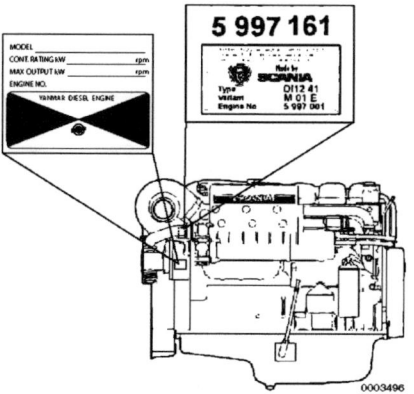

Figure 3-7

The typical location of the engine nameplates is shown for Yanmar 6SY Series marine engines **(Figure 3-7)**.

8SY Engines

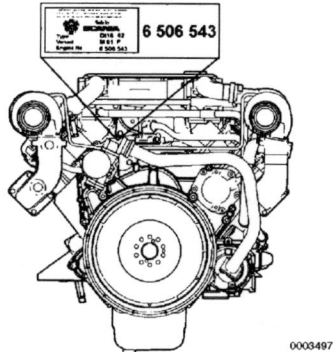

Figure 3-8

8SY Engines

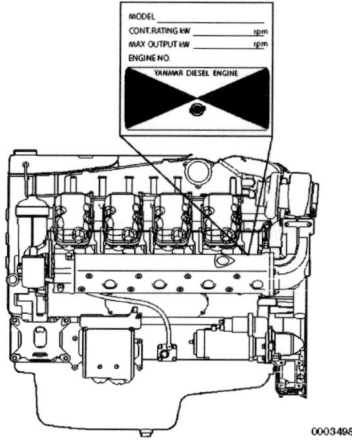

Figure 3-9

The typical location of the engine nameplates is shown for Yanmar 8SY Series marine engines **(Figure 3-8)** and **(Figure 3-9)**.

GENERAL SERVICE INFORMATION

Diesel Fuel

DIESEL FUEL

Diesel Fuel Specifications

Diesel fuel should comply with the following specifications. The table lists several worldwide specifications for diesel fuels.

DIESEL FUEL SPECIFICATION	LOCATION
No. 2-D, No. 1-D, ASTM D975-94	USA
EN590:96	European Union
ISO 8217 DMX	International
BS 2869-A1 or A2	United Kingdom
JIS K2204 Grade No.2	Japan

Additional Technical Fuel Requirements

- The fuel cetane number should be equal to 45 or higher.

- The sulfur content must not exceed 0.5% by volume. Less than 0.05% is preferred.

- Water and sediment in the fuel should not exceed 0.05% by volume.

- Ash content not to exceed 0.01% by volume.

- Carbon residue content not to exceed 0.35% by volume. Less than 0.1% is preferred.

- Total aromatics content should not exceed 35% by volume. Less than 30% is preferred.

- PAH (polycyclic aromatic hydrocarbons) content should be below 10% by volume.

- NEVER mix kerosene, used engine oil, or residual fuels with the diesel fuel.

- Never use Biocide or mix winter and summer fuels.

- Keep the fuel tank and fuel-handling equipment clean at all times.

- Poor-quality fuel can reduce engine performance and / or cause engine damage.

- Fuel additives are not recommended. Some fuel additives may cause poor engine performance.

Diesel Fuel Lines

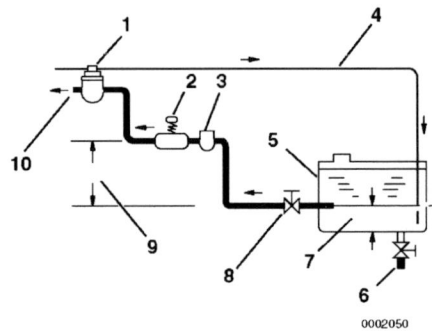

1 – Fuel Filter
2 – Fuel Priming Pump
3 – Fuel Filter / Water Separator
4 – Fuel Return Line
5 – Fuel Tank
6 – Fuel Tank Drain Cock
7 – Approximately 50 mm (1.96 in.)
8 – Fuel Shutoff Valve
9 – Less than 500 mm (19.68 in.)
10 – To Fuel Injection Pump

Figure 3-10

Install the lines between the fuel tank and the fuel injection pump.

Be sure to install a drain cock **(Figure 3-10, (6))** at the bottom of the fuel tank to remove water and contaminants.

Install a fuel filter / water separator **(Figure 3-10, (3))** and a fuel filter **(Figure 3-10, (1))** between the fuel tank and the fuel injection pump.

Diesel Fuel

Filling the Fuel Tank

DANGER! Be sure to place the diesel fuel container on the ground when transferring the diesel fuel from the pump to the container. Hold the hose nozzle firmly against the side of the container while filling it. This prevents static electricity buildup which could cause sparks and ignite fuel vapors. NEVER place diesel fuel or other flammable material such as oil, hay or dried grass close to the engine during engine operation or shortly after shutdown.

CAUTION! Only use diesel fuels recommended by *Yanmar* for the best engine performance, to prevent engine damage and to comply with EPA warranty requirements. Only use clean diesel fuel.

1. Clean the area around the fuel cap. **DANGER!** *Only fill the fuel tank with diesel fuel. Filling the fuel tank with gasoline may result in a fire and will damage the engine. NEVER refuel with the engine running.*
2. Remove the fuel cap from the fuel tank. **WARNING!** *Wipe up all spills immediately. Keep sparks, open flames or any other form of ignition (match, cigarette, static electric source) well away when refueling.*
3. Stop fueling when the gauge shows the fuel tank is full. *NOTICE: NEVER overfill the fuel tank.*
4. Replace the fuel cap and hand-tighten. Over-tightening the fuel cap will damage it. **DANGER!** *Store any containers containing fuel in a well-ventilated area, away from any combustibles or sources of ignition.*

GENERAL SERVICE INFORMATION

Bleeding the Fuel System

The fuel system needs to be bled under the following conditions:

- Before starting the engine for the first time.
- After running out of fuel and fuel has been added to the fuel tank.
- After fuel system maintenance such as changing the fuel filter and draining the fuel filter / water separator, or replacing a fuel system component.

See Bleed the Fuel System on page 6-17 for procedure.

GENERAL SERVICE INFORMATION

ENGINE OIL

Engine Oil Specifications

NOTICE: *Only use the engine oil specified. Other engine oils may affect warranty coverage, cause internal engine components to seize or shorten engine life. NEVER mix different types of engine oil. This may adversely affect the lubricating properties of the engine oil.*

Use an engine oil that meets or exceeds the following guidelines and classifications:

Service Categories

- API Service Categories CD or higher
- ACEA Service Categories E-3, E-4 and E-5
- JASO Service Category DH-1

Definitions

- API Classification (American Petroleum Institute)
- ACEA Classification (Association des Constructeurs Européens d'Automobiles)
- JASO (Japanese Automobile Standards Organization)

Note:

1. Be sure the engine oil, engine oil storage containers, and engine oil filling equipment are free of sediment and water.
2. Change the engine oil after the first 50 hours of operation and then every 250 hours thereafter.
3. Select the oil viscosity based on the ambient temperature where the engine is being operated. See the SAE Service Grade Viscosity Chart **(Figure 3-11)**.
4. Yanmar does not recommend the use of engine oil "additives."

Additional Technical Engine Oil Requirements:

The engine oil must be changed when the Total Base Number (TBN) has been reduced to 2.0. TBN (mgKOH/g) test method; JIS K-201-5.2-2 (HCl), ASTM D4739 (HCl).

Engine Oil Viscosity

Select the appropriate engine oil viscosity based on the ambient temperature shown in the SAE Service Grade Viscosity Chart in **(Figure 3-11)**.

SAE 15W40 is the recommended oil viscosity.

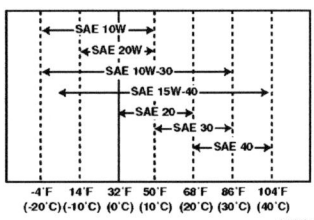

Figure 3-11

Engine Coolant

Maximum Angles of Inclination During Operation

Maximum permissible angles during operation vary depending on the type of oil sump **(Figure 3-12)**.

Note: The specified angle may only occur intermittently.

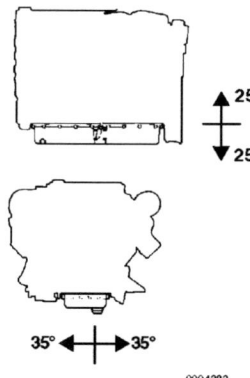

Figure 3-12

Selection of Marine Gear Oil

Refer to the documentation supplied with each marine gear.

GENERAL SERVICE INFORMATION

ENGINE COOLANT

Engine Coolant Specifications

Use a Long Life Coolant (LLC) that meets or exceeds the following guidelines and specifications:
NOTICE: Only use the engine coolant specified. Other engine coolants may affect warranty coverage, cause an internal buildup of rust and scale and / or shorten engine life. NEVER mix different types of engine coolants. This may adversely affect the properties of the engine coolant.

- ASTM D6210, D4985 (US)
- JIS K-2234 (Japan)
- SAE J814C, J1941, J1034 or J2036 (International)

Note: In the U.S., LLC is required for the warranty to be valid.

Coolant (Closed Cooling System)

NOTICE: Always add LLC to soft water - especially when operating in cold weather. Without LLC, cooling performance will decrease due to scale and rust in the cooling system. Water alone may freeze and form ice; it expands approximately 9% in volume.

Use the proper amount of coolant concentrate for the ambient temperature as specified by the LLC manufacturer. LLC concentration should be a minimum of 30% to a maximum of 60%. Too much LLC will decrease the cooling efficiency also.

Do not mix different types or brands of LLC or a harmful sludge may form.

Do not use hard water. Use deionized water. Water should be clean and free from sludge or particles.

GENERAL SERVICE INFORMATION
Engine Coolant

Follow the manufacturer's recommendations. Use a proper LLC which will not have any adverse effects on the materials (cast iron, aluminum, copper, etc.) of the engine's fresh-water cooling system. *See Engine Coolant Specifications on page 3-13.*

Replace engine coolant periodically, according to the maintenance schedule in the *Operation Manual*.

Remove scale from the cooling system periodically by flushing the system.

Note: Yanmar recommends using genuine Yanmar antifreeze / coolant.

Principal Engine Specifications GENERAL SERVICE INFORMATION

PRINCIPAL ENGINE SPECIFICATIONS

Engine Model		6SY-STP2 / 6SY655	8SY-STP
Number of Cylinders		In-line 6	8 (V8, 90°)
Type		Water-cooled, turbocharged	
Combustion System		Direct injection	
Aspiration		Turbocharged with intercooler	
Bore x Stroke		127 mm x 154 mm (5.0 in. x 6.063 in.)	
Displacement		11.7 L (714 cu in.)	15.6 L (952 cu in.)
Firing Order		1-5-3-6-2-4	1-5-4-2-6-3-7-8
Compression Ratio		16:1	
Rated output at crankshaft (fuel 40°C [104°F]) +0% / -5%			
	Continuous output (at 2100 rpm)	405 kW (550 hp)	482 kW (665 hp)
	Maximum output (at 2300 rpm)	6SY-STP2: 530 kW (720 hp) 6SY655: 481 kW (655 hp)	662 kW (900 hp)
	Mean pressure	1.97 MPa (287.2 psi)	1.84 MPa (266.86 psi)
Idle Speed			
	High idle	2400 rpm	
	Low idle	600 rpm	
Rotation Direction		Counterclockwise (viewed from flywheel)	
No. of Valves per Cylinder			
	Intake	2	
	Exhaust	2	
Turbocharger		Single water-cooled	Dual water-cooled
Electrical System		2-pole, 24 V	
Starter		6.7 kW (9.0 hp)	
Charging System		65 A at 24V*	140 A at 24V
Battery Capacity - Recommended		160 Ah	
Injection Timing		Variable (EMS controlled)	
Permissible Value for Exhaust Back Pressure		9.8 kPa (1000 mmAq)	4.9 kPa (500 mmAq)
Cooling System		Closed cooling system with heat exchanger	
	Coolant capacity with coolant recovery tank	40 L (10.5 gal)	75 L (20 gal)
Thermostats			
	Engine type and opening temperature	Dual - 75°C (167°F)	
	Charge air cooler type and opening temperature	Single - 50°C (122°F)	
Seawater Pump		Rubber impeller, gear driven	
	Capacity	315 L/min at 2300 rpm (83 gpm at 2300 engine rpm)	300 L/min at 2300 rpm (79 gpm at 2300 engine rpm)
Gear Oil Cooler Restriction		150 mbar (0.03495 psi)	

GENERAL SERVICE INFORMATION

Principal Engine Specifications

Engine Model		6SY-STP2 / 6SY655	8SY-STP
Lubrication System		Totally enclosed, forced lube system	
	Oil cooler	Closed coolant system	
	Lube oil pressure - Rated speed	300 - 600 kPa (44 - 87 psi)	
	Lube oil pressure - Idling speed	150 kPa (22 psi)	
	Lube system capacity (with filters)	23 - 31 L (6 - 8.2 gal)**	32 - 40 L (8.5 - 10.5 gal)**
Crankcase Ventilation		Closed, with filter	
Engine Size			
	Height	1038 mm (40.9 in.)	1069 mm (42.1 in.)
	Length	Overall - 1559 mm (50.9 in.) Front Bell Housing - 1366 mm (53.8 in.)	Overall - 1295 mm (50.9 in.) Front Bell Housing - 1236 mm (48.6 in.)
	Width	867 mm (34.1 in.)	1250 mm (49.2 in.)
	Weight	1160 kg (2557 lb)	1650 kg (3638 lb)

* *Optional dual 65A alternators available*

** Capacity will vary depending on installation angle

Engine Service Standards GENERAL SERVICE INFORMATION

ENGINE SERVICE STANDARDS

Test and Adjustment Specifications

Inspection Item			Specification		Reference Page
Intake Valve Clearance			0.45 mm (0.018 in.)		See Adjust Valve and Unit Injector Clearances on page 5-18
Exhaust Valve Clearance			0.70 mm (0.028 in.)		
PDE31 Unit Injector Height			66.8 - 67.0 mm (2.63 - 2.64 in.)		See Adjusting Unit Injectors on page 5-19
PDE32 Unit Injector Height			69.8 - 70.0 mm (2.75 - 2.76 in.)		
Fuel Pressure	Minimum at 500 rpm		4.5 bar (65 psi)		See Measure the Fuel Feed Pump Pressure on page 6-7
	Minimum at 1900 rpm		5.5 bar (80 psi)		
Compression Pressure at Cranking	6SY		Not available at time of publication		
	8SY				
Deviation Between Cylinders	All Models		Not available at time of publication		
Oil Pressure Switch Operating Pressure			Not available at time of publication		
Fuel Pressure Relief Valve Pressure	Minimum (Hand Pumping)		4.5 bar (65 psi)		See Test the Fuel Pressure Relief Valve on page 6-8
	Maximum at 1500 rpm		7.5 bar (109 psi)		
Return Line Tubing	6 mm OD		Minimum Internal Diameter of Bend	35 mm (1.38 in.)	See Replace Return Fuel Line on page 6-15
	12 mm OD			95 mm (3.74 in.)	
Cooling System Test Pressure	All		0.4 - 0.5 bar (5.8 - 7.3 psi)		See Pressure Testing Cooling System and Filler Cap on page 7-7
Filler Cap Test Pressure	All		0.4 - 0.6 bar (5.8 - 8.7 psi)		
Thermostat		Marking	Starts Opening	Fully Open	See Testing the Thermostat on page 7-8
	6SY	75°C	73 - 77°C (163 - 171°F)	87°C (189°F)	
	8SY	75°C	73 - 77°C (163 - 171°F)	87°C (189°F)	
Coolant Temperature Switch	All		Not available at time of publication		

GENERAL SERVICE INFORMATION Tightening Torques for Standard Bolts and Nuts

TIGHTENING TORQUES FOR STANDARD BOLTS AND NUTS

Tightening Fasteners

Use the correct amount of torque when tightening the fasteners. Applying excessive torque may damage the fastener or component and not enough torque may cause a leak or component failure.

Flange Bolts and Nuts

Nominal Diameter	Coarse Thread	
Grade	8.8 or 8	10.9 or 10
M5	5.4 N·m (44 in.-lb)	6.7 N·m (55 in.-lb)
M6	8.6 N·m (71 in.-lb)	10.7 N·m (89 in.-lb)
M8'	22 N·m (177 in.-lb)	27 N·m (221 in.-lb)
M10	42 N·m (29 ft-lb)	52 N·m (36 ft-lb)
M12	77 N·m (52 ft-lb)	95 N·m (64 ft-lb)
M14	123 N·m (83 ft-lb)	154 N·m (103 ft-lb)

Unions

Size	Straight	Elbow Union	S-Union Gland Nut
M10 x 1.0	10 N·m (88.5 in.-lb)	8 N·m (70.8 in.-lb)*	-
M12 x 1.5	20 N·m (177 in.-lb)	15 N·m (133 in.-lb)*	30 N·m (22 ft-lb)
M14 x 1.5	25 N·m (221 in.-lb)	20 N·m (177 in.-lb)*	40 N·m (30 ft-lb)
M16 x 1.5	30 N·m (22 ft-lb)	25 N·m (221 in.-lb)*	50 N·m (37 ft-lb)
M18 x 1.5	30 N·m (22 ft-lb)	25 N·m (221 in.-lb)*	60 N·m (44 ft-lb)
M20 x 2.5	45 N·m (33 ft-lb)	40 N·m (30 ft-lb)*	-
M22 x 1.5	45 N·m (33 ft-lb)	40 N·m (30 ft-lb)*	-
M24 x 10	-	-	70 N·m (52 ft-lb)
M26 x 1.5	60 N·m (44 ft-lb)	55 N·m (41 ft-lb)*	-
M30 x 2	-	-	80 N·m (59 ft-lb)

* Continue tightening to the correct position

Hexagon Bolts and Nuts

Nominal Diameter	Coarse Thread		Fine Thread	
Grade	8.8 or 8	10.9 or 10	8.8 or 8	10.9 or 10
M4	2.4 N·m (21.2 in.-lb)	3 N·m (26.5 in.-lb)	-	-
M5	5 N·m (44 in.-lb)	6.2 N·m (55 in.-lb)	-	-
M6	8 N·m (71 in.-lb)	10 N·m (89 in.-lb)	-	-
M8'	20 N·m (177 in.-lb)	25 N·m (221 in.-lb)	21 N·m (186 in.-lb)	27 N·m (239 in.-lb)
M10	39 N·m (29 ft-lb)	49 N·m (36 ft-lb)	42 N·m (31 ft-lb)	52 N·m (38 ft-lb)
M12	70 N·m (52 ft-lb)	87 N·m (64 ft-lb)	77 N·m (57 ft-lb)	96 N·m (71 ft-lb)
M14	112 N·m (83 ft-lb)	140 N·m (103 ft-lb)	120 N·m (89 ft-lb)	150 N·m (111 ft-lb)
M16	180 N·m (133 ft-lb)	220 N·m (162 ft-lb)	190 N·m (140 ft-lb)	240 N·m (177 ft-lb)
M18	240 N·m (177 ft-lb)	300 N·m (221 ft-lb)	270 N·m (199 ft-lb)	340 N·m (251 ft-lb)
M20	350 N·m (258 ft-lb)	440 N·m (325 ft-lb)	390 N·m (288 ft-lb)	490 N·m (361 ft-lb)
M22	490 N·m (361 ft-lb)	610 N·m (450 ft-lb)	530 N·m (391 ft-lb)	670 N·m (494 ft-lb)
M24	600 N·m (443 ft-lb)	760 N·m (561 ft-lb)	700 N·m (516 ft-lb)	870 N·m (642 ft-lb)

ABBREVIATIONS AND SYMBOLS

Abbreviations

A	ampere
AC	alternating current
ACEA	Association des Constructeurs Européens d'Automobilies
Ah	ampere-hour
API	American Petroleum Institute
ARB	Air Resources Board
ATDC	after top dead center
BDC	bottom dead center
BTDC	before top dead center
°C	degree Celsius
CARB	California Air Resources Board
CCA	cold cranking amp
cfm	cubic feet per minute
cm	centimeter
cm^3	cubic centimeter
cm^3/min	cubic centimeter per minute
cu in.	cubic inch
D	diameter
DC	direct current
DI	direct injection
DVA	direct volt adapter
EPA	Environmental Protection Agency
ESG	electronic speed governor
°F	degree Fahrenheit
fl oz	fluid ounce (U.S.)
fl oz/min	fluid ounce (U.S.) per minute
ft	foot
ft-lb	foot pound
ft-lbf/min	foot pound force per minute
g	gram
gal	gallon (U.S.)
gal/hr	gallon (U.S.) per hour
gal/min	gallon (U.S.) per minute
GL	gear lubricant
hp	horsepower (U.S.)
hr	hour
I.D.	inside diameter
ID	identification
IDI	indirect injection
in.	inch
in.Aq	inches Aqueous (water)
in.Hg	inches Mercury
in.-lb	inch pound
J	joule
JASO	Japanese Automobile Standards Organization
K	kelvin
kg	kilogram
kgf/cm^2	kilogram force per square centimeter
kgf/m	kilogram force per meter
km	kilometers
kPa	kilopascal
kW	kilowatt
L	liter
L/hr	liter per hour
lb	pound
lbf	pound force
m	meter
mL	milliliter
mm	millimeter
mmAq	millimeter Aqueous (water)
MPa	megapascal
mV	millivolt
N	newton
N·m	newton meter
No.	number
O.D.	outside diameter
oz	ounce
Pa	pascal
PS	horsepower (metric)
psi	pound per square inch
qt	quart (U.S.)
R	radius
rpm	revolutions per minute
SAE	Society of Automotive Engineers
sec.	second
t	short ton 2000 lb
TBN	total base number
TDC	top dead center
V	volt
VAC	volt alternating current
VDC	volt direct current
W	watt

Symbols

°	degree
+	plus
-	minus
±	plus or minus
Ω	ohm
μ	micro
%	percent

GENERAL SERVICE INFORMATION

UNIT CONVERSIONS

Unit Prefixes

Prefix	Symbol	Power
mega	M	x 1,000,000
kilo	k	x 1,000
centi	c	x 0.01
milli	m	x 0.001
micro	μ	x 0.000001

Units of Length

mile	x	1.6090	= km
ft	x	0.3050	= m
in.	x	2.5400	= cm
in.	x	25.4000	= mm
km	x	0.6210	= mile
m	x	3.2810	= ft
cm	x	0.3940	= in.
mm	x	0.0394	= in.

Units of Volume

gal (U.S.)	x	3.78540	= L
qt (U.S.)	x	0.94635	= L
cu in.	x	0.01639	= L
cu in.	x	16.38700	= mL
fl oz (U.S.)	x	0.02957	= L
fl oz (U.S.)	x	29.57000	= mL
cm³	x	1.00000	= mL
cm³	x	0.03382	= fl oz (U.S.)

Units of Mass

lb	x	0.45360	= kg
oz	x	28.35000	= g
kg	x	2.20500	= lb
g	x	0.03527	= oz

Units of Force

lbf	x	4.4480	= N
lbf	x	0.4536	= kgf
N	x	0.2248	= lbf
N	x	0.1020	= kgf
kgf	x	2.2050	= lbf
kgf	x	9.8070	= N

Units of Torque

ft-lb	x	1.3558	= N·m
ft-lb	x	0.1383	= kgf/m
in.-lb	x	0.1130	= N·m
in.-lb	x	0.0115	= kgf/m
kgf/m	x	7.2330	= ft-lb
kgf/m	x	86.8000	= in.-lb
kgf/m	x	9.8070	= N·m
N·m	x	0.7376	= ft-lb
N·m	x	8.8510	= in.-lb
N·m	x	0.1020	= kgf/m

Units of Pressure

psi	x	0.0689	= bar
psi	x	6.8950	= kPa
psi	x	0.0703	= kg/cm²
bar	x	14.5030	= psi
bar	x	100.0000	= kPa
bar	x	29.5300	= inHg (60°F)
kPa	x	0.1450	= psi
kPa	x	0.0100	= bar
kPa	x	0.0102	= kg/cm²
kg/cm²	x	98.0700	= psi
kg/cm²	x	0.9807	= bar
kg/cm²	x	14.2200	= kPa
in.Hg (60°)	x	0.0333	= bar
in.Hg (60°)	x	3.3770	= kPa
in.Hg (60°)	x	0.0344	= kg/cm²
mmAq	x	0.0394	= in.Aq

Units of Power

hp (metric or PS)	x	0.9863201	= hp SAE
hp (metric or PS)	x	0.7354988	= kW
hp SAE	x	1.0138697	= hp (metric or PS)
hp SAE	x	0.7456999	= kW
kW	x	1.3596216	= hp (metric or PS)
kW	x	1.3410221	= hp SAE

Units of Temperature

°F = (1.8 x °C) + 32
°C = 0.556 x (°F - 32)

Section 4

PERIODIC MAINTENANCE

	Page
Introduction	4-3
The Importance of Periodic Maintenance	4-3
Performing Periodic Maintenance	4-3
Yanmar Replacement Parts	4-3
Required EPA Maintenance - USA Only	4-3
EPA Installation Requirements - USA Only	4-3
Periodic Maintenance Schedule	4-4
Periodic Maintenance Procedures	4-7
After Initial 50 Hours of Operation	4-7
Every 50 Hours of Operation	4-7
Every 250 Hours of Operation	4-8
Every 500 Hours of Operation	4-8
Every 1000 Hours of Operation	4-9
Every 2000 Hours of Operation	4-9
EPA Requirements	4-10
Conditions to Ensure Compliance with EPA Emission Standards	4-10
Inspection and Maintenance	4-10

PERIODIC MAINTENANCE

This Page Intentionally Left Blank

Introduction

INTRODUCTION

This section of the *Service Manual* describes the procedures for proper care and maintenance of the engine.

The Importance of Periodic Maintenance

Engine deterioration and wear occurs in proportion to length of time the engine has been in service and the conditions the engine is subject to during operation. Periodic maintenance prevents unexpected downtime, reduces the number of accidents due to poor machine performance and helps extend the life of the engine.

Performing Periodic Maintenance

Perform periodic maintenance procedures in an open, level area free from traffic. If possible, perform the procedures indoors to prevent environmental conditions such as rain, wind or snow from damaging the engine. **WARNING! NEVER block windows, vents or other means of ventilation if the engine is operating in an enclosed area. All internal combustion engines create carbon monoxide gas during operation. Accumulation of this gas within an enclosure could cause illness or even death.**

Yanmar Replacement Parts

Yanmar recommends that you use genuine Yanmar parts when replacement parts are needed. Genuine replacement parts help ensure long engine life.

Required EPA Maintenance - USA Only

To maintain optimum engine performance and compliance with the Environmental Protection Agency (EPA) Regulations, it is essential that you follow the *Periodic Maintenance Schedule on page 4-4* and *Periodic Maintenance Procedures on page 4-7*.

PERIODIC MAINTENANCE

EPA Installation Requirements - USA Only

The following are the installation requirements for the EPA. Unless these requirements are met, the exhaust gas emissions will not be within the limits specified by the EPA.

See *Conditions to Ensure Compliance with EPA Emission Standards on page 4-10* for operating conditions.

PERIODIC MAINTENANCE

PERIODIC MAINTENANCE SCHEDULE

Daily and periodic maintenance is important to keep the engine in good operating condition. The following is a summary of maintenance items by periodic maintenance intervals. Periodic maintenance intervals vary depending on engine application, loads, diesel fuel and engine oil used and are hard to establish definitively. The following should be treated only as a general guideline.

O: Check or Clean ◇: Replace

System	Item	Daily	Every 50 hours or one month whichever comes first	Every 250 hours or one year whichever comes first	Every 500 hours or 2 years whichever comes first	Every 1000 hours or 4 years whichever comes first	Every 2000 hours or 8 years whichever comes first
Whole	Visual inspection of engine exterior	O					
Fuel System	Check the fuel level and refill	O					
	Drain the fuel tank				O		
	Drain the fuel filter and the fuel / water separator		O (Initial 50)				
	Replace the fuel filter element		◇ (Initial 50)	◇			
	Check and adjust unit injector / rocker arms			O* (Initial 250)		O*	
	Overhaul and check fuel feed pump						O
	Replace rubber fuel hoses	Replace every 2 years or every 2000 hours, whichever comes first.					
Lubricating System	Check the engine oil level	O					
	Change the engine oil		◇ (Initial 50)	◇			
	Replace the engine oil filter element		◇ (Initial 50)	◇			
	Replace the closed crankcase ventilation filter			◇			
	Clean the centrifugal engine oil cleaner		O (Initial 50)	O			
	Clean engine oil cooler						O
Air Intake and Exhaust System	Clean or replace the air intake filter element			O			
	Clean the exhaust / water mixing elbow			O			
	Clean the turbocharger			O*			
	Clean the charge air cooler			O			

Periodic Maintenance Schedule

PERIODIC MAINTENANCE

O: Check or Clean ◇: Replace

System	Item	Periodic Maintenance Interval					
		Daily	Every 50 hours or one month whichever comes first	Every 250 hours or one year whichever comes first	Every 500 hours or 2 years whichever comes first	Every 1000 hours or 4 years whichever comes first	Every 2000 hours or 8 years whichever comes first
Cooling System	Check the seawater outlet	O During Operation					
	Check the coolant level	O					
	Check or replace seawater pump impeller				O	◇	
	Change the engine coolant	Every year. When Long Life Coolant is used, replace every two years. *See Drain, Flush and Fill the Engine with Engine Coolant on page 7-8.*					
	Clean and check the seawater passages					O	
	Clean the seawater and engine closed cooling system						O
	Check or replace the anodes			◇			
	Clean the closed cooling system (Internal)			O			
Electrical System	Check the alarm indicators	O					
	Check the battery charge	O					
	Clean the battery	O					
	Check the battery electrolyte level		O				
	Adjust the tension of the alternator belt or replace belt		O (Initial 50)		O	◇	
	Check the wiring connectors			O			O
Engine Cylinder Head and Block	Check for leakage of fuel, engine oil and engine coolant	O After starting					
	Tighten all major nuts and bolts			O			
	Adjust intake / exhaust valve clearance			O (Initial 250)		O	
Miscellaneous Items	Check the electronic control system (EMS) operation	O	O (Initial 50)				
	Adjust the propeller shaft alignment		O (Initial 50)		O		
	Check / replace flexible engine mounts			O		◇	

* *Required to conform to US EPA regulations. See EPA Requirements on page 4-10.*

Note: The above procedures are considered normal maintenance and are performed at the owner's expense.

PERIODIC MAINTENANCE

Inspection and Maintenance of EPA Emission-Related Parts

Parts	Interval
Clean fuel injection nozzle	1500 hours
Check fuel injection nozzle adjustment	3000 hours
Check fuel injection pump adjustment	
Check turbocharger adjustment	
Check electronic engine control unit (ECU) and its associated sensors and actuators	

Periodic Maintenance Procedures

PERIODIC MAINTENANCE

PERIODIC MAINTENANCE PROCEDURES

After Initial 50 Hours of Operation

Perform the following maintenance after the initial 50 hours of operation.

- Drain the Fuel Filter and Fuel / Water Separator
- Replace the Fuel Filter Element
- Change the Engine Oil and Replace the Engine Oil Filter
- Clean the Centrifugal Oil Cleaner
- Check and Adjust Alternator Belt
- Check Electronic Management System (EMS) Operation
- Adjust Propeller Shaft Alignment

Every 50 Hours of Operation

After you complete the initial 50 hour maintenance procedures, perform the following procedures every 50 hours thereafter.

- Check Battery Electrolyte Level

PERIODIC MAINTENANCE

Periodic Maintenance Procedures

Every 250 Hours of Operation

Perform the following maintenance every 250 hours of operation or 1 year, whichever comes first.

- **Adjust Intake / Exhaust Valve Clearance (Initial 250)**
- **Adjust Unit Injectors (Initial 250)**
- **Drain the Fuel Tank**
- **Replace the Fuel Filter Element**
- **Change the Engine Oil**
- **Replace the Engine Oil Filter Element**
- **Replace the Closed Crankcase Ventilation Filter**
- **Clean the Centrifugal Engine Oil Cleaner**
- **Check the Seawater Pump Impeller**
- **Replace the Anodes**
- **Clean the Closed Cooling System (Internal)**
- **Clean the Air Intake Filter Element**
- **Clean the Exhaust / Water Mixing Elbow**
- **Clean the Turbocharger**
- **Flush the Charge Air Cooler**
- **Check the Wiring Connectors**
- **Tighten All Major Nuts and Bolts**
- **Check or Replace the Flexible Engine Mounts**
- **Drain, Flush and Refill the Engine Coolant**

Every 500 Hours of Operation

Perform the following maintenance every 500 hours of operation or 2 years, whichever comes first.

- **Replace Seawater Pump Impeller**
- **Check Alternator Belt Tension**
- **Adjust the Propeller Shaft Alignment**

Periodic Maintenance Procedures

PERIODIC MAINTENANCE

Every 1000 Hours of Operation

Perform the following maintenance every 1000 hours of operation or 4 years, whichever comes first.

- Adjust Unit Injectors / Rocker Arms
- Clean and Check the Seawater Passages
- Replace Alternator Belt
- Adjust Intake / Exhaust Valve Clearance
- Replace the Flexible Engine Mounts

Every 2000 Hours of Operation

Perform the following maintenance every 2000 hours of operation or 8 years, whichever comes first.

- Overhaul and Check Fuel Feed Pump
- Replace Rubber Fuel Hoses
- Clean Engine Oil Cooler
- Clean Seawater and Engine Coolant System
- Check the Wiring Connectors

PERIODIC MAINTENANCE

EPA REQUIREMENTS

The EPA emission regulation is applicable only in USA.

Conditions to Ensure Compliance with EPA Emission Standards

This product is an EPA-approved engine.

The following are the conditions that must be met in order to ensure that the emissions during operation meet the EPA standards. Be sure to follow these:

The operating conditions should be as follows:

- Ambient temperature: -20 to 40°C (-4 to 104°F)
- Relative humidity: 80% or lower
- Permissible value for intake negative pressure: 3.9 kPa (400 mmAq) or lower
- Permissible value for exhaust back pressure:
  6SY: 9.8 kPa (1000 mmAq) or lower
  8SY: 4.9 kPa (500 mmAq) or lower

The fuel and lubricating oil used should be as follows:

- Diesel fuel oil: ASTM D975 No. 1-D or No. 2-D, or equivalent (minimum of cetane No. 45)
- Lubricating Oil: ACEA Class E3, E4 or E5; Type API, Class CH-4, CI-4

Be sure to perform inspections as outlined in *Periodic Maintenance Procedures on page 4-7* and keep a record of the results.

Pay particular attention to these important points:

- Replacing the engine oil
- Replacing the lube oil filter
- Replacing the fuel filter
- Cleaning the intake silencer (air cleaner)

Note: Inspections are divided into two sections in accordance with who is responsible for performing the inspection: the user or the maker.

Inspection and Maintenance

See Inspection and Maintenance of EPA Emission-Related Parts on page 4-6 for the EPA emission-related parts. Inspection and maintenance procedures not shown in the *Inspection and Maintenance of EPA Emission-Related Parts* section are covered in *Periodic Maintenance Schedule on page 4-4.*

This maintenance must be performed to keep the emission values of your engine in the standard values during the warranty period. The warranty period is determined by the age of the engine or the number of hours of operation.

Section 5

ENGINE

	Page
Safety Precautions	5-3
Introduction	5-4
Principal Engine Specifications	5-4
Adjustment Specifications	5-4
Cylinder Head Specifications	5-5
Camshaft and Timing Gear Train Specifications	5-6
Crankshaft and Pistons Specifications	5-7
Special Torque Chart	5-9
Special Service Tools	5-11
Measuring Instruments	5-16
Tests and Adjustments	5-18
Adjust Valve and Unit Injector Clearances	5-18
Repair	5-21
Cylinder Head	5-22
Cylinder Head Components	5-22
General Guidelines	5-23
Remove and Install Rocker Covers	5-23
Remove the Cylinder Head	5-26
Disassemble the Cylinder Head	5-27
Clean the Cylinder Head Components	5-27
Inspect the Cylinder Head Components	5-27
Replace the Valve Stem Seals	5-29
Replace the Valve Seat	5-29
Machine the Valves	5-30
Machine the Valve Seat Inserts	5-30
Replace the Valve Guides	5-33
Replace the Unit Injector Sleeves	5-33
Reassemble the Cylinder Head	5-34
Install the Cylinder Head	5-34

ENGINE

Pistons and Cylinder Liners 5-36
    Remove and Disassemble Piston and Connecting Rod............ 5-37
    Inspect the Connecting Rods 5-38
    Replace the Wrist Pin Bushing 5-40
    Inspect the Pistons and Piston Rings... 5-41
    Assemble the Piston and Connecting Rod................................ 5-41
    Remove the Cylinder Liners 5-42
    Measure the Cylinder Liner Height... 5-44
    Install the Cylinder Liners 5-44
    Install the Piston and Connecting Rod 5-45
Flywheel and Flywheel Housing 5-48
    Flywheel Housing Components - 6SY Engines......................... 5-48
    Flywheel Housing Components - 8SY Engines......................... 5-50
    Remove the Flywheel.. 5-51
    Flywheel Inspection and Repair 5-52
    Replace the Rear Crankshaft Seal 5-52
    Remove the Flywheel Housing 5-53
    Install the Flywheel Housing... 5-53
    Install the Flywheel.. 5-54
Timing Gear Train 5-56
    6SY Components 5-56
    8SY Components 5-58
    Check the Camshaft Timing 5-60
    Remove the Front Gear Housing - 8SY 5-60
    Install the Front Gear Housing - 8SY 5-62
    Intermediate Gear 5-62
    Camshaft Gear 5-67
    Crankshaft Gear 5-69
    Remove the Camshaft... 5-70
    Replace the Camshaft Bearings - 6SY....................................... 5-71
    Replace the Camshaft Bearings - 8SY....................................... 5-75
    Install the Camshaft.. 5-78
Cylinder Block and Crankshaft... 5-82
    Remove the Crankshaft... 5-84
    Measure the Oil Clearance.. 5-85
    Inspect the Crankshaft 5-86
    Recondition the Crankshaft 5-87
    Inspect the Cylinder Block 5-87
    Install Crankshaft... 5-88
    Replace the Front Crankshaft Seal 5-90
Exhaust Manifold.. 5-91
    Replacing Gaskets 5-91
Lifting the Engine 5-92
Attaching Engine to Repair Stand 5-93

SAFETY PRECAUTIONS

⚠ WARNING

Avoid serious injury or death. ALWAYS ensure that all connections are tightened to specifications after repair is made to the exhaust system. All internal combustion engines create carbon monoxide gas during operation and special precautions are required to avoid carbon monoxide poisoning.

NOTICE

NEVER attempt to adjust the low or high idle speed limit screw. This may impair the safety and performance of the engine and shorten its life. If adjustment is ever required, see your authorized Yanmar marine dealer or distributor.

ENGINE

INTRODUCTION

This section of the *Service Manual* describes the disassembly, inspection, and reassembly of the 6SY and 8SY engines.

Principal Engine Specifications

See *Principal Engine Specifications on page 3-15*.

Adjustment Specifications

Adjustments

Inspection Item	Specification
Intake Valve Clearance	0.45 mm (0.018 in.)
Exhaust Valve Clearance	0.70 mm (0.028 in.)
PDE31 Unit Injector Spring Height	66.8 - 67.0 mm (2.63 - 2.64 in.)
PDE32 Unit Injector Spring Height	69.8 -70.0 mm (2.75 - 2.76 in.)

Introduction

ENGINE

Cylinder Head Specifications

Cylinder Head and Valves

Inspection Item			Standard	Oversize	Reference Page
Valve Recession		Intake	0.75 - 1.8 mm (0.030 - 0.071 in.)		See Valve Recession on page 5-27.
		Exhaust	0.66 - 1.8 mm (0.026 - 0.071 in.)		
Valve Face Angle		Intake	19.5°		See Inspection of Intake and Exhaust Valves on page 5-27.
		Exhaust	44.5°		
Valve Margin (Minimum)		Intake	2.6 mm (0.102 in.)		
		Exhaust	1.8 mm (0.071 in.)		
Valve Seat	Seat Angle	Intake	20.0 - 20.5°		
		Exhaust	45.0 - 45.5°		
	Seat Undercut Angle	Intake	60°		
		Exhaust	60°		
	Seat Overcut Angle	Intake	60°		
		Exhaust	NA		
	Seat Contact Width	Intake	1.9 - 2.6 mm (0.075 - 0.102 in.)		
		Exhaust	1.8 - 2.6 mm (0.071 - 0.102 in.)		
	Cutting Tool Setting - Diameter	Intake	39.3 - 40.3 mm (1.547 - 1.587 in.)		
		Exhaust	37.3 - 38.3 mm (1.472 - 1.512 in.)		
Replacement Valve Seat Insert	Outside Diameter	Intake	46.054 - 46.065 mm (1.8131 - 1.8136 in.)	46.254 - 46.265 mm (1.8210 - 1.8215 in.)	
		Exhaust	44.081 - 44.092 mm (1.7355 - 1.7359 in.)	44.281 - 44.292 mm (1.7433 - 1.7438 in.)	
	Bore Diameter in Cylinder Head	Intake	46.000 - 46.016 mm (1.8110 - 1.8116 in.)	46.200 - 46.216 mm (1.8189 - 1.8195 in.)	
		Exhaust	44.000 - 44.016 mm (1.7323 - 1.7329 in.)	44.200 - 44.216 mm (1.7402 - 1.7408 in.)	
	Bore Depth	Intake	11.25 - 11.35 mm (0.443 - 0.447 in.)		
		Exhaust			

ENGINE Introduction

Camshaft and Timing Gear Train Specifications

Camshaft

Inspection Item		Standard		Reference Page
End Play		0.10 - 0.25 mm (0.004 - 0.010 in.)		See Remove the Camshaft on page 5-70.
Timing - 6SY		Intake	Exhaust	See Check the Camshaft Timing on page 5-60
		0.37 - 1.47 mm 0.015 - 0.058 in	0.16 - 1.16 mm 0.006 - 0.046 in	

Intermediate Gear and Bushing

Inspection Item	Standard	Limit	Reference Page
End Play	-	0.238 mm (0.009 in.)	See Intermediate Gear on page 5-62

Timing Gear Backlash

Inspection Item	6SY	8SY	Reference Page
Camshaft-to-Intermediate Gear	0.03 - 0.15 mm (0.002 - 0.006 in.)	*	-

* *Not available at time of publication*

Introduction

ENGINE

Crankshaft and Pistons Specifications

Crankshaft

Inspection Item		6SY 8SY	Reference Page
Connecting Rod Journals	Standard Diameter	86.978 - 87.000 mm (3.4247 - 3.4252 in.)	See Inspect the Crankshaft on page 5-86
	Undersize 1 Diameter	86.728 - 86.750 mm (3.4247- 3.4153 in.)	
	Undersize 2 Diameter	86.478 - 86.500 mm (3.4046 - 3.4055 in.)	
	Undersize 3 Diameter	86.228 - 86.250 mm (3.3948 - 3.3957 in.)	
	Undersize 4 Diameter	85.978 - 86.000 mm (3.3850 - 3.3858 in.)	
	Hole Recess Radius	4.8 - 5.2 mm (0.189 - 0.205 in.)	
	Surface Quality	0.25 Ra	
	Width, Max.	56.05 mm (2.207 in.)	
	Oil Clearance	0.051 - 0.114 mm (0.0020 - 0.0045 in.)	
Main Bearing Journals	Standard Diameter	107.978 - 108.000 mm (4.2511 - 4.2520 in.)	
	Undersize 1 Diameter	107.728 - 107.750 mm (4.2412 - 4.2421 in.)	
	Undersize 2 Diameter	107.428 - 107.450 mm (4.2294 - 4.2303 in.)	
	Undersize 3 Diameter	107.228 - 107.250 mm (4.2216 - 4.2224 in.)	
	Undersize 4 Diameter	106.978 - 107.000 mm (4.2117 - 4.2126 in.)	
	Oil Hole Radius	4.75 - 4.85 mm (0.187 - 0.191 in.)	
	Surface Quality	0.25 Ra	
Main Bearing Bore	Standard Diameter	112.200 - 112.222 mm (4.4173 - 4.4182 in.)	See Inspect the Cylinder Block on page 5-87
	Out-of-Round (Max.)	0.016 mm (0.0006 in.)	

Thrust Bearing

Inspection Item		6SY	8SY	Reference Page
Thrust Bearing	Standard Thickness	3.37 - 3.43 mm (0.133 - 0.135 in.)		See Inspect the Crankshaft on page 5-86
	Oversize 1 Thickness	3.45 - 3.51 mm (0.136 - 0.138 in.)		
	Oversize 2 Thickness	3.50 - 3.56 mm (0.138 - 0.140 in.)		
	Oversize 3 Thickness	3.63 - 3.69 mm (0.143 - 0.145 in.)		
	Oversize 4 Thickness	3.88 - 3.94 mm (0.153 - 0.155 in.)		
	End Play	0.138 - 0.380 mm (0.0054 - 0.0149 in.)		

ENGINE

Introduction

Cylinder Liner

Inspection Item	Standard	Limit	Reference Page
Cylinder Liner Protrusion	0.15 - 0.30 mm (0.006 - 0.012 in.)		See Measure the Cylinder Liner Height on page 5-44
Protrusion Variation on One Liner (Max.)		0.02 mm (0.0008 in.)	
Available Shims	0.20, 0.25, 0.30, 0.40, 0.50, 0.75 mm		

Connecting Rod

Inspection Item	Standard	Limit	Reference Page
Wrist Pin Bushing ID	54.030 - 54.043 mm (2.1272 - 2.1277 in.)	-	See Inspect the Pistons and Piston Rings on page 5-41
Twist - 6SY	-	0.10 mm (0.004 in.)	
Bend - 6SY	-		
Twist - 8SY		0.05 mm (0.002 in.)	
Bend - 8SY			
Bend - "S" Shape - 6SY		0.60 mm (0.024 in.)	
Bend - "S" Shape - 8SY		4.5 mm (0.177 in.)	

Piston Ring

Inspection Item		Standard	Limit	Reference Page
Top Ring	End Gap	0.35 - 0.60 mm (0.014 - 0.024 in.)	-	See Inspect the Pistons and Piston Rings on page 5-41
Second Ring	Side Clearance	-	0.25 mm (0.010 in.)	
	End Gap	0.45 - 0.65 mm (0.018 - 0.026 in.)	-	
Oil Ring	Side Clearance	-	0.25 mm (0.010 in.)	
	End Gap	0.40 - 0.65 mm (0.016 - 0.026 in.)	-	

SPECIAL TORQUE CHART

Component		Torque	Lubricating Oil Application (Thread Portion and Seat Surface)	Reference Page
Rocker Arm Adjusting Screw Lock Nut		39 N·m (29 ft-lb)	-	See Adjust Valve and Unit Injector Clearances on page 5-18
Rocker Arm Shaft Support Bracket Bolt		105 N·m (77 ft-lb)	Not Applied	See Install the Cylinder Head on page 5-34
Rocker Arm Shaft Bolt		105 N·m (77 ft-lb)	Not Applied	
Cylinder Head Bolt	First tightening	60 N·m (44 ft-lb)	Applied	
	Second tightening	150 N·m (110 ft-lb)		
	Third tightening	250 N·m (184 ft-lb)		
	Fourth tightening	Plus 90°		
Unit Injector Fork Clamp Bolt (torque-turn)		20 N·m (133 in.-lb) plus 75°	Not Applied	
Injector Electrical Terminal Screw		2 N·m (283 in.-oz)	Not Applied	
Rocker Cover Bolt (Upper and Lower Cover)		26 N·m (230 in.-lb)	Not Applied	
Exhaust Manifold Bolt	6SY	59 N·m (44 ft-lb)	Not Applied	
	8SY	63 N·m (46 ft-lb)	Not Applied	
Turbocharger Bolt	6SY	50 N·m (37 ft-lb)	Not Applied	
	8SY	63 N·m (46 ft-lb)	Not Applied	
Lower Intake Manifold		26 N·m (230 in.-lb)	Not Applied	
Charge Air Cooler Bolt		26 N·m (230 in.-lb)	Not Applied	
Upper Intake Manifold	6SY	26 N·m (230 in.-lb)		
	8SY	50 N·m (37 ft-lb)	Not Applied	
Fuel Delivery Union Nut		20 N·m (133 in.-lb)	Not Applied	
Fuel Manifold Mounting Bolt		26 N·m (230 in.-lb)	Not Applied	
Fuel Return Banjo Bolt		11 N·m (97 in.-lb)	Not Applied	
Flywheel Mounting Bolt (torque-turn)		130 N·m (96 ft-lb) plus 90°	Not Applied	See Install the Flywheel on page 5-54
Flywheel Housing Bolt	M10	50 N·m (37 ft-lb)	Not Applied	See Install the Flywheel Housing on page 5-53
	M12	90 N·m (66 ft-lb)	Not Applied	
Timing Gear Plate Bolt - 6SY		63 N·m (46 ft-lb)	Not Applied	See Install the Camshaft on page 5-78
Tappet Mounting Bolt		32 N·m (24 ft-lb)	Not Applied	
Intermediate Gear Bolt (torque-turn)		50 N·m (37 ft-lb) plus 60°	Not Applied	
Camshaft Gear Bolt		63 N·m (46 ft-lb)	Not Applied	

ENGINE

Special Torque Chart

Component		Torque	Lubricating Oil Application (Thread Portion and Seat Surface)	Reference Page
Oil Sump Bolt		30 N·m (22 ft-lb)	Not Applied	*See Install Crankshaft on page 5-88*
Oil Pump Mounting Bolt		26 N·m (19 ft-lb)	Applied	
Piston Cooling Nozzle Bolt		23 N·m (17 ft-lb)	Applied	
Connecting Rod Bolt (torque-turn)	6SY	20 N·m (177 in.-lb) plus 90°	Applied	
	8SY	50 N·m (37 ft-lb) plus 90°	Applied	
Main Bearing Cap Bolt (torque-turn)	6SY	50 N·m (37 ft-lb) plus 90°	Applied	
	8SY	90 N·m (66 ft-lb) plus 90°		
Main Bearing Side Bolts	8SY	180 N·m (133 ft-lb)		
Crankshaft Driver Bolt		135 N·m (100 ft-lb)	Not Applied	
Crankshaft Damper Bolt	6SY	110 N·m (81 ft-lb)	Not Applied	
	8SY	135 N·m (100 ft-lb)	Not Applied	
Belt Pulley Bolt	6SY	110 N·m (81 ft-lb)	Not Applied	
	8SY	92 N·m (67 ft-lb)	Not Applied	

Special Service Tools

ENGINE

SPECIAL SERVICE TOOLS

Note: The tool numbers used in this section are either Yanmar or Scania part numbers. Yanmar part numbers are referred to as **Yanmar Part No.** Scania part numbers are referred to as **OEM Part No.** Tools not having part numbers must be obtained locally.

No.	Tool Name	Applicable Model and Tool Size	Illustration
1	Valve Guide Tool (For Removing Valve Guides)	OEM Part No. 99 383	0002668
2	Valve Guide Tool (For Installing Valve Guides)	OEM Part No. 99 382	0002669
3	Guide (For Removal and Installation of Injector Sleeves. Use with 588 221 Pilot Tap)	OEM Part No. 99 394	0002670
4	Drift (For Installing Valve Seats)	OEM Part No. 99 384	0002664
5	Driver (For Use with 99 384 Drift)	OEM Part No. 99 385	0002665
6	Pilot Tap (For Removing Injector Sleeves)	OEM Part No. 588 221	0002667

ENGINE

Special Service Tools

No.	Tool Name	Applicable Model and Tool Size	Illustration
7	Flywheel Turning Tool	OEM Part No. 99 309	0002660
8	Slide Hammer	OEM Part No. 87 596	0002655
9	Valve Spring Compressor	OEM Part No. 99 322	0002662
10	Valve Stem Seal Installer	OEM Part No. 99 323	0002663
11	Valve Seat Cutter	OEM Part No. 587 277	0002671
12	Unit Injector Adjustment Tool	OEM Part No. 99 414 - PDE31 OEM Part No. 99 442 - PDE32	0002672

Special Service Tools

ENGINE

No.	Tool Name	Applicable Model and Tool Size	Illustration
13	Hydraulic Cylinder (For Removing and Installing Camshaft Bearings)	OEM Part No. 99 003	
14	Air-Operated Hydraulic Pump (For Removing and Installing Camshaft Bearings)	OEM Part No. 99 004	
15	Camshaft Bearing Replacement Tool (For Removing and Installing Camshaft Bearings - 6SY)	OEM Part No. 99 373	
16	Bearing Drift (For Removing and Installing Camshaft Bearings - 8SY)	OEM Part No. 99 516	
17	Socket (For Removing and Installing Camshaft Bearings - 8SY)	OEM Part No. 99 517	
18	Bar (For Removing and Installing Camshaft Bearings - 8SY)	OEM Part No. 99 518	
19	Spacer (For Removing and Installing Camshaft Bearings - 8SY)	OEM Part No. 99 519	

ENGINE

Special Service Tools

No.	Tool Name	Applicable Model and Tool Size	Illustration
20	Flex-Hone (For Preparing Cylinder Walls)	Obtain Locally	
21	Piston Ring Compressor (For Installing Piston)	Obtain Locally	
22	Piston Ring Tool (For Removing/ Installing Piston Rings)	Obtain Locally	
23	Lifting Eyes (Used to Lift Engine)	OEM Part No. 99 398	
24	Lifting Eyes (Used to Lift Engine)	OEM Part No. 1 360 442	
25	Lifting Eyes (Used to Lift Engine)	OEM Part No. 1 512 730	
26	Lifting Chain (Used to Lift Engine)	OEM Part No. 98 094	

Special Service Tools

ENGINE

No.	Tool Name	Applicable Model and Tool Size	Illustration
27	Lever Block (Used to Lift Engine)	OEM Part No. 587 308	

ENGINE

Measuring Instruments

MEASURING INSTRUMENTS

No.	Instrument Name	Application	Illustration
1	Dial Indicator	Measure shaft bend and end play	0000831
2	Test Indicator	Measurements of narrow or deep portions that cannot be measured by dial indicator	0000832
3	Magnetic Stand	For holding the dial indicator when measuring	0000833
4	Micrometer	For measuring the outside diameters of crankshaft, pistons, piston pins, etc.	0000834
5	Cylinder Bore Gauge	For measuring the inside diameters of cylinder liners, bearing bores, etc.	0000835
6	Calipers	For measuring outside diameters, depth, thickness and width	0000836
7	Depth Micrometer	For measuring valve recession	0000837

Measuring Instruments　　　　　　　　　　　　　　　　　　　　　　　　　ENGINE

No.	Instrument Name	Application	Illustration
8	Square	For measuring valve spring inclination and straightness of parts	
9	Torque Wrench	For tightening nuts and bolts to the specified torque	
10	Feeler Gauge	For measuring piston ring gaps, piston ring clearance, fuel injector adjustment clearance, and valve adjustment clearance	

ENGINE

Tests and Adjustments

TESTS AND ADJUSTMENTS

Adjust Valve and Unit Injector Clearances

Note: Check and adjust the valve clearance and unit injector adjustment at the same time with the engine cold.

Order of Adjustment - 6SY

Adjustment Item	Adjust Cylinder Number					
Intake and Exhaust Valves	1	5	3	6	2	4
Injector Rocker Arm	5	3	6	2	4	1

Order of Adjustment - 8SY

Mark on Flywheel (Degrees)	Valve Overlap on Cylinder	Adjust Injector Rocker Arm on Cylinder	Adjust Intake Valve on Cylinder	Adjust Exhaust Valve on Cylinder
TDC Down (0°)	6	4 and 5	7 and 8	4 and 5
TDC Up (180°)	7	2 and 6	1 and 5	2 and 6
TDC Down (360°)	1	3 and 7	2 and 4	3 and 7
TDC Up (540°)	4	1 and 8	3 and 6	1 and 8

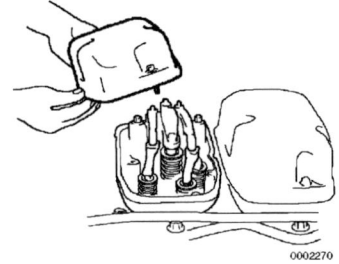

Figure 5-1

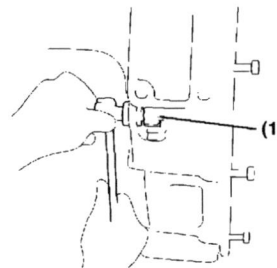

Figure 5-2

1. Clean the rocker covers and surrounding area.
2. Remove the upper rocker covers **(Figure 5-1)**.
3. Turn the flywheel using the flywheel turning tool (OEM Part No. 99 309) **(Figure 5-2, (1))** until No. 1 piston is at TDC of the compression stroke. The rocker arms for No. 1 cylinder will be loose and the valves for No. 6 cylinder will be in overlap (both rocker arms under tension).
4. Refer to the appropriate chart for the order of adjustment. *See Order of Adjustment - 6SY on page 5-18* or *Order of Adjustment - 8SY on page 5-18.*
5. Identify the model of unit injector to be adjusted. *See Identifying Unit Injector on page 5-19.*

Tests and Adjustments
ENGINE

6. Check and adjust the clearance of the appropriate valves using a feeler gauge.

Note: The intake valves are actuated by the short rocker arms and the exhaust valves by the long rocker arms. Make sure the valve bridge is resting correctly against the valves.

7. Check and adjust unit injector of the appropriate cylinder before rotating the crankshaft. Unit injectors can be adjusted using a special tool or a digital sliding caliper. *See Adjusting Unit Injectors on page 5-19.*
   CAUTION! *Use care when adjusting the unit injector if the dimension is outside the specification. The spring is under considerable tension and may cause personal injury if it is unexpectedly released.*

8. Mark the rocker arms with a permanent marker to identify the rocker arms that have been adjusted.

9. Rotate the flywheel and adjust the valves and unit injector for the next cylinder(s).

- **6SY:** Rotate the flywheel 120° (1/3 turn) and adjust the next cylinder.

- **8SY:** Rotate the flywheel 180° (1/2 turn) and adjust the next cylinders.

   Repeat for the remaining cylinders per the order of adjustment tables. *See Order of Adjustment - 6SY on page 5-18* or *Order of Adjustment - 8SY on page 5-18.*

10. Install the upper rocker covers. Ensure the gasket is in good condition and in place. Tighten bolts to 26 N·m (230 in.-lb).

Specifications

Inspection Item	Intake	Exhaust
Valve Clearance	0.45 mm (0.018 in.)	0.70 mm (0.028 in.)

Adjusting Unit Injectors

Note: The PDE31 unit injector is adjusted using the setting tool (OEM Part No. 99 414) or a digital sliding caliper. The PDE32 unit injector is adjusted using the setting tool (OEM Part No. 99 442) or a digital sliding caliper.

Identifying Unit Injector

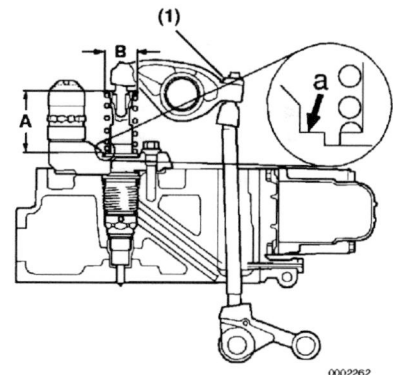

Figure 5-3

Measure spring diameter **(Figure 5-3, (B))** to identify the injector.

Unit Injector Identification

Inspection Item	PDE31	PDE32
Injector Spring Diameter **(B)**	36.5 mm (1.44 in.)	38.8 mm (1.53 in.)

ENGINE

Tests and Adjustments

Digital Caliper Method:

Note: Use this method if the appropriate setting tool is not available.

1. Loosen the adjusting screw locknut. **CAUTION! *Use care when adjusting the unit injector if the dimension is outside the specification. The spring is under considerable tension and may cause personal injury if it is released unexpectedly.***
2. Carefully turn the adjusting screw (**Figure 5-3, (1)**) while measuring the spring height (**Figure 5-3, (A)**) between plane (**Figure 5-3, (a)**) and the top of the valve spring retainer using a digital sliding caliper.
3. Tighten the locknut to specification.

Specifications

Inspection Item	PDE31	PDE32
Spring Height (A)	66.8 - 67 mm (2.63 - 2.64 in.)	69.8 - 70 mm (2.75 - 2.76 in.)
Adjustment Screw Locknut Torque	39 N·m (29 ft-lb)	

Special Tool Method:

NOTICE: Adjust the spring roughly using a sliding caliper (see Digital Caliper Method: on page 5-20), then perform fine adjustment using the special tool. Failure to do so may result in the unit injector assuming an incorrect position, which will result in poor performance and possible breakdown.

1. Select the correct setting tool for the unit injector being adjusted. Use OEM Part No. 99 414 to adjust PDE31 or OEM Part No. 99 442 to adjust PDE32.

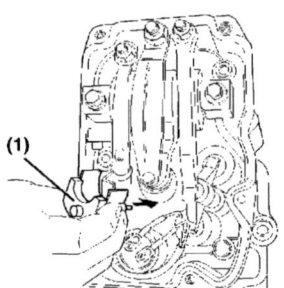

Figure 5-4

2. Position the appropriate setting tool (**Figure 5-4, (1)**) with the metal plate around the injector spring.

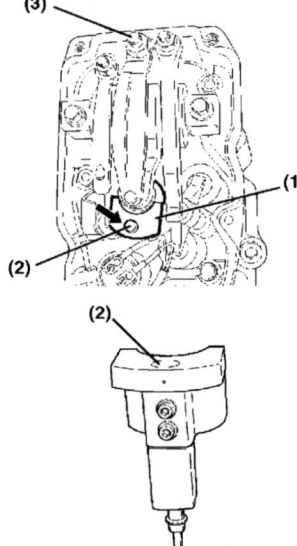

Figure 5-5

Repair

ENGINE

3. Carefully turn the adjusting screw **(Figure 5-5, (3))** while simultaneously using a finger to sense the position of the small piston **(Figure 5-5, (2))**. Adjustment is correct when the piston is flush with the flat upper surface **(Figure 5-5, (1))** of the tool.
4. Tighten the adjusting screw locknut to 39 N·m (29 ft-lb).

REPAIR

If the engine is to be completely disassembled, perform the following preliminary steps:

1. Disconnect battery cables at the battery. Always disconnect negative (-) battery cable first.
2. Close all valves in the fuel supply system.
3. Remove throttle cable, electrical connections, intake and exhaust system connections, and fuel supply lines from engine. Cap or plug all open fuel connections.
4. Drain engine coolant from cylinder block.
5. Remove engine from boat. *See Lifting the Engine on page 5-92*. Mount engine to a suitable engine repair stand having adequate weight capacity. **DANGER!** *NEVER stand under a hoisted engine. If the hoist mechanism fails, the engine will fall on you, causing death or serious injury.*
6. Cap or plug all openings to prevent contamination.
7. Remove starter motor and alternator.
8. Clean engine by washing with solvent, air or steam cleaning. Carefully operate cleaning equipment so as to prevent any foreign matter or fluids from entering engine or any fuel system or electrical components remaining on the engine.
9. Remove cooling system components from engine.
10. Drain engine oil into a suitable container. Remove oil filter.

ENGINE

Cylinder Head

CYLINDER HEAD

Cylinder Head Components

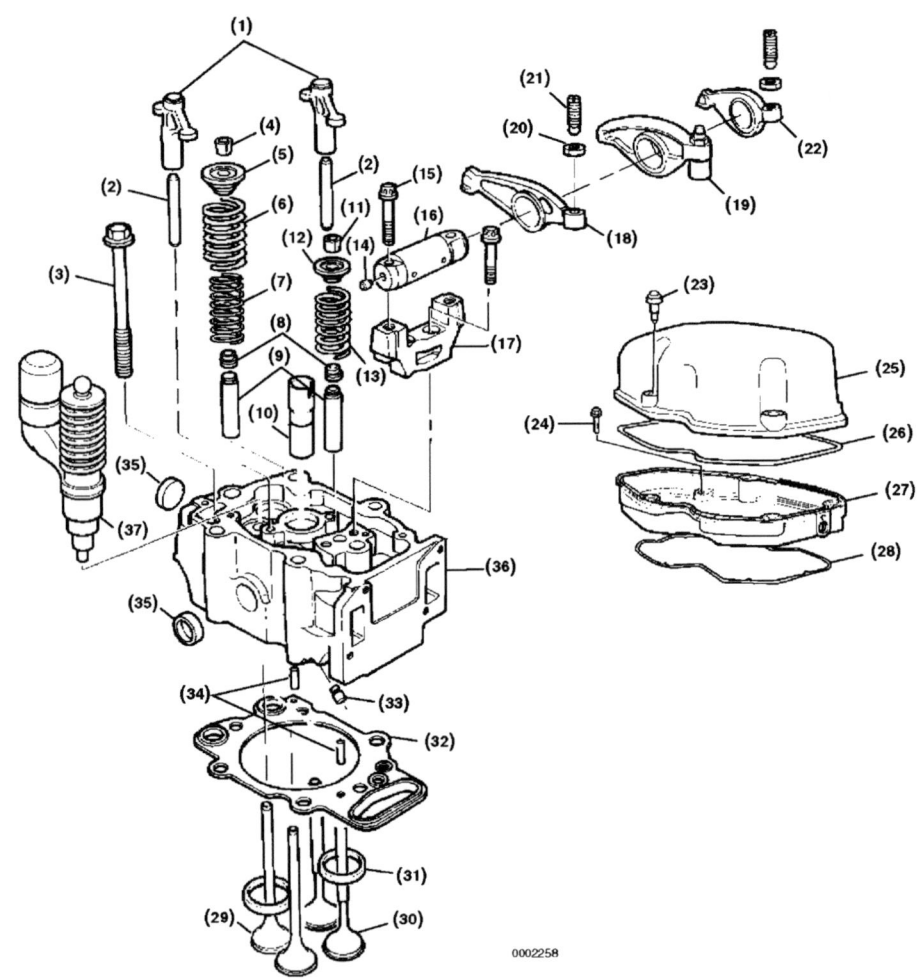

Cylinder Head

ENGINE

1 – Valve Bridge
2 – Pin
3 – Bolt
4 – Valve Keeper
5 – Valve Spring Collar
6 – Exhaust Valve Spring
7 – Exhaust Valve Spring
8 – Valve Stem Seal
9 – Valve Guide
10 – Socket
11 – Valve Keeper
12 – Valve Spring Collar
13 – Intake Valve Spring
14 – Rivet Plug
15 – Tight-Fit Screw
16 – Rocker Arm Shaft
17 – Bearing Bracket
18 – Exhaust Valve Rocker Arm
19 – Unit Injector Rocker Arm
20 – Jam Nut
21 – Adjusting Screw
22 – Intake Valve Rocker Arm
23 – Flange Bolt
24 – Flange Bolt
25 – Rocker Cover, Upper Section
26 – Rocker Cover Gasket
27 – Rocker Cover, Lower Section
28 – Rocker Cover Gasket
29 – Exhaust Valve
30 – Intake Valve
31 – Valve Seat Insert
32 – Gasket
33 – Rivet Plug
34 – Alignment Pin
35 – Core Plug
36 – Cylinder Head
37 – Unit Injector

Figure 5-6

General Guidelines

NOTICE: *Identify all parts and their location using an appropriate method. It is important that all parts are returned to the same position during the reassembly process.*

Note: Record all measurements taken during disassembly and inspection.

Remove and Install Rocker Covers

Upper Rocker Cover

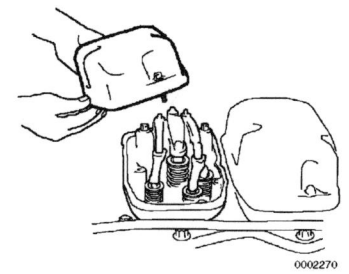

Figure 5-7

1. Clean the rocker cover and the surrounding area.
2. Remove the upper rocker cover.
3. Clean all old gasket material and sealant from the upper and lower rocker covers.
4. Install the upper rocker cover using a new gasket.
5. Tighten bolts to 26 N·m (230 in.-lb).

ENGINE

Cylinder Head

Lower Rocker Cover

1. Remove upper rocker cover. *See Upper Rocker Cover on page 5-23*.

Note: If the spring comes loose from the unit injector, the unit injector must be replaced.

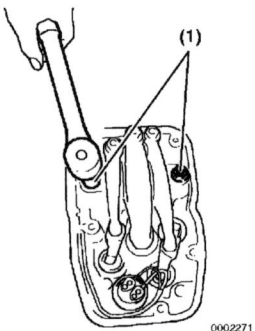

Figure 5-8

2. Remove bolts **(Figure 5-8, (1))** retaining the rocker arm shaft. Alternately loosen each bolt until valve tension is relieved. **CAUTION!** *Never lean over the engine when removing the rocker arm shaft. The unit injector spring is under considerable tension and can unexpectedly come loose and cause personal injury.*

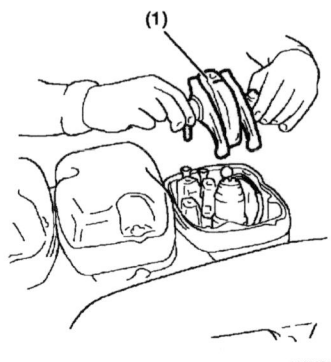

Figure 5-9

3. Remove the rocker arm shaft assembly **(Figure 5-9, (1))**.

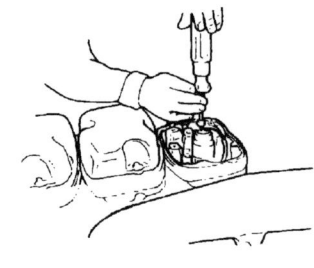

Figure 5-10

4. Disconnect the electrical wires from the unit injector. The screws cannot be removed **(Figure 5-10)**.

Cylinder Head   ENGINE

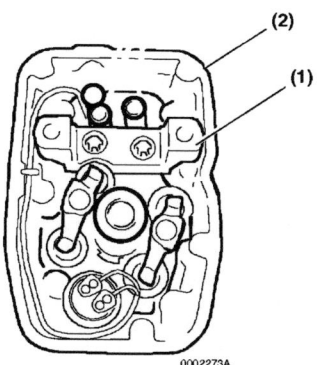

Figure 5-11

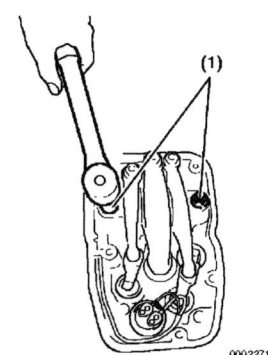

Figure 5-12

5. Remove the rocker arm shaft bracket **(Figure 5-11, (1))**.
6. Remove the lower rocker cover **(Figure 5-11, (2))**.
7. Clean all old gasket material and sealant from the upper and lower rocker covers and the cylinder head.
8. Install the lower rocker cover using a new gasket.
9. Tighten bolts to 26 N·m (230 in.-lb).
10. Install the rocker arm shaft bracket. Tighten the bolts to 105 N·m (77 ft-lb).
11. Install the rocker arm shaft and rockers. Tighten the bolts **(Figure 5-12, (1))** to 105 N·m (77 ft-lb).
12. Check and adjust valve and injector clearance when all cylinder heads have been installed. *See Adjust Valve and Unit Injector Clearances on page 5-18.*
13. Install the upper rocker cover and tighten the bolts to 26 N·m (230 in.-lb). *See Upper Rocker Cover on page 5-23.*

ENGINE

Cylinder Head

Remove the Cylinder Head

1. Drain the coolant from the engine.

6SY Engines

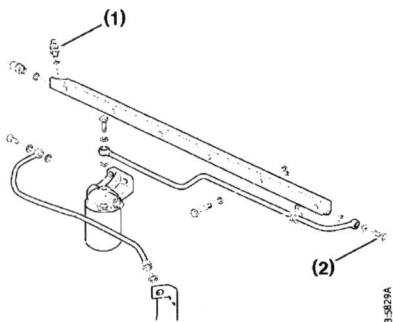

Figure 5-13

8SY Engines

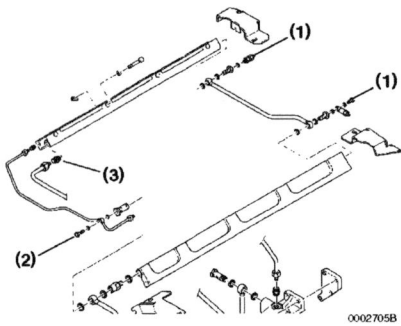

Figure 5-14

2. Open bleeder valve(s) **(Figure 5-13 and Figure 5-14 (1))** and drain fuel system by loosening banjo bolt **(Figure 5-13 and Figure 5-14 (2))** on opposite end of fuel manifold. On 8SY engines, also loosen union **(Figure 5-14 (3))**.

3. 8SY Engines:
   (a) Remove the connection pipe between upper intake manifold housings.
   (b) Remove coolant recovery tank and catwalk.
4. Remove connection pipe(s) between charge air cooler and turbocharger.
5. Remove the upper intake manifold. Remove the intake air cooling element.
6. Remove bolts retaining intake manifold and fuel manifold to cylinder head(s) to be removed.

Note: If all cylinder heads on the left-hand side (cylinder numbers 5-8) are to be removed, remove intake manifold and fuel manifold.

If all cylinder heads on the right-hand side (cylinder numbers 1-4) are to be removed, remove charge air sensor, intake manifold and fuel manifold.

7. Remove cooling system ventilation pipe(s).
8. Clean rocker cover and the surrounding area.
9. Remove upper rocker cover, rocker arm shaft assembly, pushrods and lower rocker cover. *See Remove and Install Rocker Covers on page 5-23.*
10. Remove unit injector. *See Remove the Unit Injector on page 6-8.*
11. Remove intake manifold, fuel manifold and exhaust manifold.
12. Remove cylinder head bolts and remove cylinder head. Mark cylinder heads if removing more than one at a time.
13. Remove the cylinder head gasket.

ENGINE

Cylinder Head

Disassemble the Cylinder Head

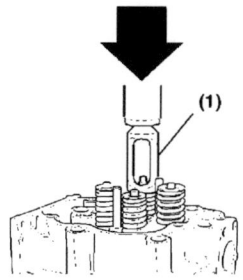

Figure 5-15

1. Use OEM Part No. 99 322 **(Figure 5-15, (1))** in a press, or an appropriate valve spring compressor, to compress the valve springs. Remove valve keepers, valve spring retainers, springs and valves.
2. Mark and place the valves in a rack so that they can be installed in the same position in the cylinder head.
3. Identify the cylinder heads if removing more than one at a time.

Clean the Cylinder Head Components

Thoroughly clean all components using a non-metallic brush and an appropriate solvent. Each part must be free of carbon, metal filings and other debris. **WARNING!** *Always read and follow safety-related precautions found on containers of hazardous substances like parts cleaners, primers, sealants and sealant removers.*

Inspect the Cylinder Head Components

Clean all gasket material, sealant and carbon from components. Use a suitable solvent and a soft bristle brush to clean parts.

Visually inspect parts. Replace any parts that are obviously discolored, heavily pitted or otherwise damaged. Discard any part that does not meet its specified limit. *NOTICE: Any part which is found defective as a result of inspection or any part whose measured value does not satisfy the standard or limit must be replaced.*

NOTICE: Mark all valve train components so they can be installed in their original locations.

Note: Record all measurements taken during inspection.

Inspection of Intake and Exhaust Valves

Visually inspect intake and exhaust valves. Replace any valves that are obviously discolored, heavily pitted or otherwise damaged.

Valve Recession

Note: Valve guides must be installed and in good condition to perform this check.

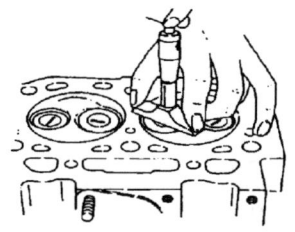

Figure 5-16

ENGINE

Cylinder Head

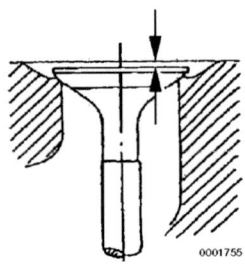

Figure 5-17

Insert valves into their original locations and press down until they are fully seated. Use a depth micrometer **(Figure 5-16)** to measure the distance between the cylinder head gasket surface and the combustion surface of each exhaust and intake valve **(Figure 5-17)**.

Specifications

Inspection Item		Standard
Valve Recession	Intake	0.75 - 1.8 mm (0.030 - 0.071 in.)
	Exhaust	0.66 - 1.8 mm (0.026 - 0.071 in.)

Valve Face and Valve Seat

Always check the clearance between the valve and valve guide before grinding or lapping the valve seats. If the clearance exceeds the limit, replace the valve and / or valve guide to bring the clearance within the limit.

Roughness or burrs will cause poor seating of a valve. Visually inspect the seating surfaces of each valve and valve seat to determine if lapping or grinding is needed.

Visually inspect all valves faces and valve seats for pitting, distortion, cracking or evidence of overheating. Usually the valves and valve seats can be lapped or ground to return them to serviceable condition. Severely worn or damaged components will require replacement.

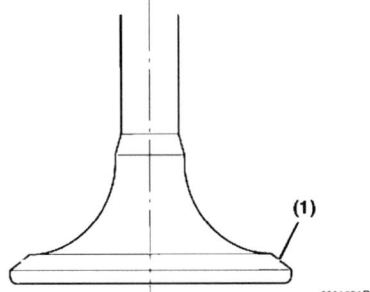

Figure 5-18

Coat the valve seat with a thin coat of bluing compound. Install valve and rotate to distribute bluing onto the valve face. The contact pattern should be approximately centered on the valve face **(Figure 5-18, (1))** and even in width.

Also visually inspect the valve seat for even contact.

Light cutting can be performed by the use of a hand-operated cutter.

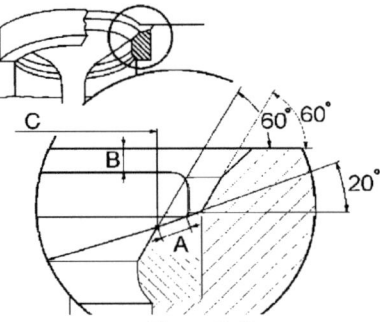

Figure 5-19

Note: Intake valve shown; exhaust valve is similar.

Cylinder Head

ENGINE

Valve seat diameter **(Figure 5-19, (C))** can be adjusted by bottom-grinding using a 60° stone to make the seat diameter larger. Once the seat location has been corrected, grind and lap the seat angle to specification. *See Machine the Valve Seat Inserts on page 5-30* for specifications.

Grinding is needed if the valve and the valve seat do not contact correctly. Grind the valve face and / or valve seat only enough to return them to serviceable condition. Check valve recession after grinding.

If the valve or seat require grinding, lap the valve after grinding. Lap the valve face to the valve seat using a mixture of valve lapping compound and engine oil.

Be sure to thoroughly wash all parts to remove all grinding powder or compound.

Replace the Valve Stem Seals

1. Remove the valve.

Figure 5-20

2. Remove valve stem seal with a pair of pliers **(Figure 5-20)**.
3. Install the valve.

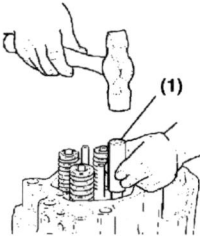

Figure 5-21

4. Carefully install new valve stem seal using an installer (OEM Part No. 99 323) **(Figure 5-21, (1))** and a hammer. **WARNING!** *Avoid personal injury. ALWAYS wear safety glasses when servicing the engine.*

Replace the Valve Seat

Note: Oversize valve seat inserts are available if the valve seat bore has been damaged. See the parts catalog for available replacement parts.

Removal

1. Use a discarded valve that has been ground so that the diameter of the disc is slightly smaller than the inside diameter of the seat.

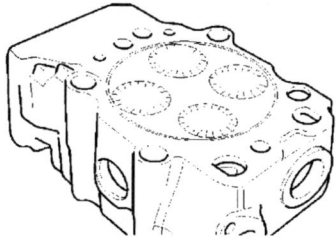

Figure 5-22

2. Install a valve and weld it to the valve seat **(Figure 5-22)**. Cool with water.

ENGINE

Cylinder Head

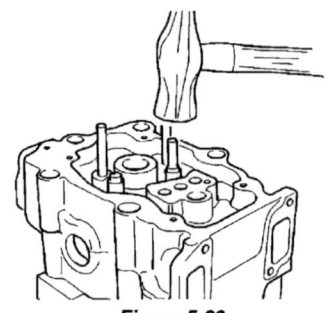

Figure 5-23

3. Turn cylinder head over and drive valve and seat out of cylinder head **(Figure 5-23)**.

4. Cool the drift and valve seat to approximately -112°F (-80°C) in dry ice or using liquid air.
   WARNING! *Use thermal gloves when handling super-cooled components. Failure to comply could result in moderate to severe frost injuries.* Pressing must be carried out rapidly.

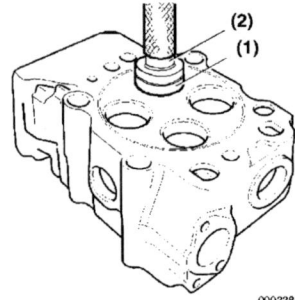

Figure 5-24

5. Press in new valve seat inserts using drift (OEM Part No. 99 384) **(Figure 5-24, (1))** and driver (OEM Part No. 99 385) **(Figure 5-24, (2))**.

Machine the Valves

Reface the valves using a valve face grinder. Remove only enough material to return the valve to serviceable condition.

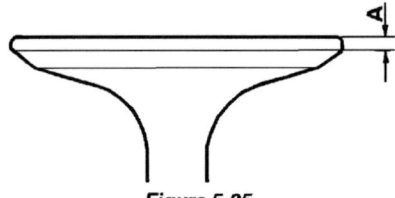

Figure 5-25

Check valve margin **(Figure 5-25, (A))** after grinding is complete.

Machine the Valve Seat Inserts

Specifications

Intake Valve

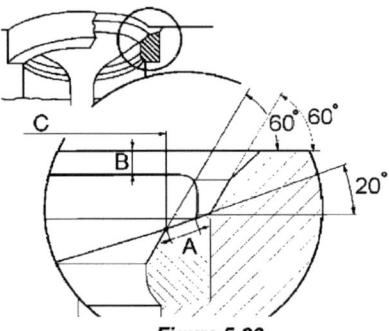

Figure 5-26

Cylinder Head — ENGINE

Exhaust Valve

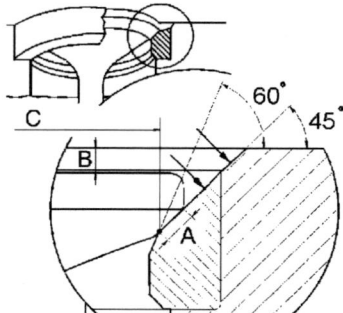

Figure 5-27

Item	Intake Valve	Exhaust Valve
Seat Contact Width (A)	1.9 - 2.6 mm (0.075 - 0.102 in.)	1.8 - 2.6 mm (0.071 - 0.102 in.)
Valve Recession (B)	0.75 - 1.8 mm (0.030 - 0.071 in.)	0.66 - 1.8 mm (0.026 - 0.102 in.)
Cutting Tool Setting - Diameter (C)	39.3 - 40.3 mm (1.547 - 1.587 in.)	37.3 - 38.3 mm (1.472 - 1.512 in.)
Seat Angle	20.0 - 20.5°	45.0 - 45.5°
Undercut Angle	60°	60°
Overcut Angle	60°	-

Procedure

The following description applies to using a valve seat cutter (OEM Part No. 587 277).

1. Check that cylinder head surface and the magnetic base are smooth and clean. Clean the valve guides using a wire brush and solvent.

ENGINE

Cylinder Head

Figure 5-28

2. Select the largest spindle that slides easily into the valve guide. Insert the spindle and turn the feed screw to its uppermost position (**Figure 5-28**).

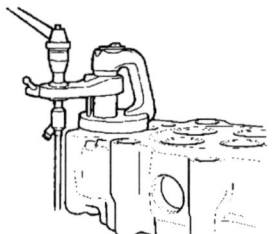

Figure 5-29

3. Select and install the cutter (**Figure 5-29**).

Figure 5-30

4. Release the quick-action lock and move the pivot plate to the upper position with the adjusting screw (**Figure 5-30**).

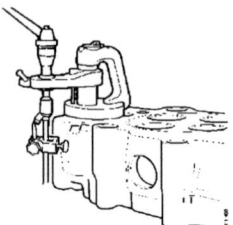

Figure 5-31

5. Set the dial on the cutter adjuster using a valve (**Figure 5-31**).
6. Adjust the cutter diameter to the dimension Seat Diameter (C) as listed the chart in *Machine the Valve Seat Inserts on page 5-30*.
7. Disconnect the magnetic base. Insert the guide spindle into the valve bushing. Adjust the pivot plate so that the distance between the cutter and the valve seat is approximately 1 mm (0.039 in.). Center the tool precisely.

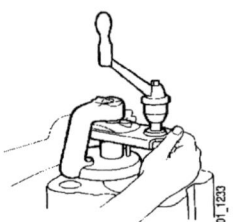

Figure 5-32

8. Connect the magnetic base (**Figure 5-32**).
9. Apply the quick-action lock. Make sure the crank can be turned easily. If not, redo the centering.

Cylinder Head

ENGINE

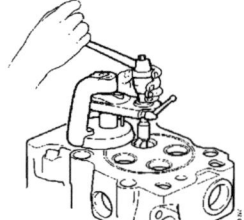

Figure 5-33

10. Machine the valve seat by cranking clockwise while turning the feed screw. Never crank counterclockwise, as this could damage the cutter. Lubricate with cutting oil during the procedure **(Figure 5-33)**.

11. When the machining of the valve seat is completed, reduce the cutting pressure by turning the crank 2-3 turns without feeding. Continue to turn the crank while turning the feed screw counterclockwise. The valve seat cutter is now ready for the next valve seat.

Replace the Valve Guides

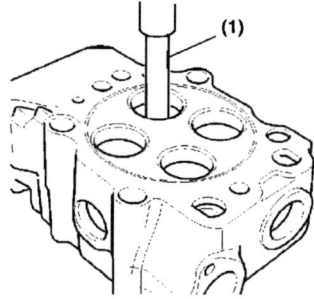

Figure 5-34

1. Press out valve guide using a removal drift (OEM Part No. 99 383) **(Figure 5-34, (1))**.

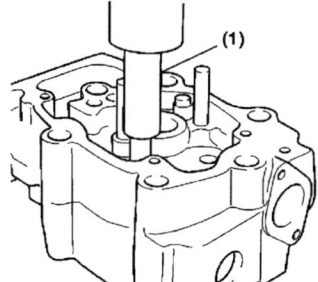

Figure 5-35

2. Press in new valve guides using installation drift (OEM Part No. 99 382) **(Figure 5-35, (1))**. Press guide down until tool contacts valve spring seat.

Replace the Unit Injector Sleeves

- The cylinder head must be removed when replacing the injector sleeve.

- The valves do not need to be removed. For clarity, the illustrations show the cylinder head with valves removed.

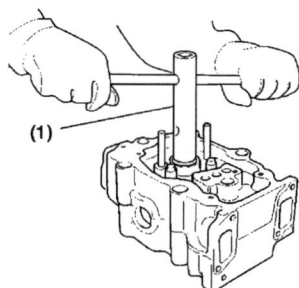

Figure 5-36

1. Use pilot tap and guide **(Figure 5-36, (1))** to thread the bottom part of the sleeve.

ENGINE   Cylinder Head

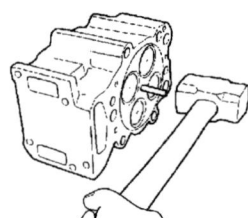

Figure 5-37

2. Use a 9 mm diameter metal rod, 100 mm long, to drive out the pilot tap and sleeve from the combustion side **(Figure 5-37)**.
3. Degrease and check the contact surfaces of the sleeve and cylinder head. Remove any burrs and irregularities that may score the new sleeve.
4. Remove all grease from the new injector sleeve and apply a thin film of sealing agent (OEM Part No. 561 200) on the sleeve and cylinder head contact surfaces.

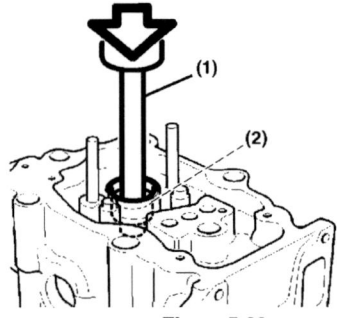

Figure 5-38

5. Press in the sleeve using drift **(Figure 5-38, (1))** and guide **(Figure 5-38, (2))**.

Reassemble the Cylinder Head

1. Liberally lubricate all moving parts with clean engine oil during reassembly.
2. Install new valve stem seals.
3. Place the valve springs and valve spring retainers on the cylinder head.

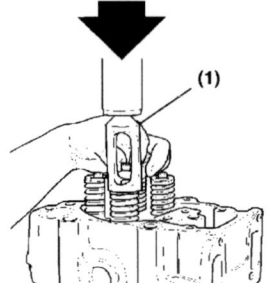

Figure 5-39

4. Compress the springs using a press and tool **(Figure 5-39, (1))**, or a suitable valve spring compressor (OEM Part No. 99 322). Install the valve keepers, making sure they are seated inside the grooves in the valve stems.
5. Allow the valve spring to expand against the keepers. Repeat with remaining valves.

Install the Cylinder Head

1. Check liner height. *See Measure the Cylinder Liner Height on page 5-44.*
2. Ensure the gasket surfaces of the cylinder head and cylinder block are clean and dry.
3. Install a new cylinder head gasket.
4. Install the cylinder head and ensure that the guide pins fit correctly. *NOTICE: The cylinder head bolts can be reused up to three times. Therefore, make sure the bolts have no more than two punch marks on top of the bolt head. If any bolt has three marks, it must be replaced with a new one.*
5. Lightly lubricate the threads on the cylinder head bolts and bolt holes.

Cylinder Head ENGINE

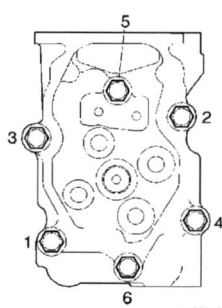

Figure 5-40

6. Tighten the bolts in the order shown in **Figure 5-40** and in four stages as follows:
   (a) Tighten all bolts to 60 N·m (44 ft-lb).
   (b) Tighten all bolts to 150 N·m (110 ft-lb).
   (c) Tighten all bolts to 250 N·m (184 ft-lb).
   (d) Tighten all bolts an additional 90°.
7. Make a mark with a center punch on the head of the bolt.
8. Install the unit injector. *See Install the Unit Injector on page 6-11.*
9. Install lower rocker cover, valve bridges, rocker shaft assembly, pushrods, and upper rocker covers. *See Remove and Install Rocker Covers on page 5-23.*
10. Check and adjust valve and injector clearance after all cylinder heads have been installed. *See Adjust Valve and Unit Injector Clearances on page 5-18.*
11. Install exhaust manifold. Tighten nuts and bolts to:
    - **6SY:** 59 N·m (44 ft-lb)
    - **8SY:** 63 N·m (46 ft-lb)
12. Install turbocharger(s) (if equipped) and tighten to:
    - **6SY:** 50 N·m (37 ft-lb)
    - **8SY:** 63 N·m (46 ft-lb)
13. Connect turbocharger oil and water lines. Install heat shields.
14. Install cooling system ventilation pipe(s) from the cylinder head(s).
15. Install fuel manifold(s). Tighten bolts to 26 N·m (230 in.-lb).
16. Connect fuel lines to fuel manifold(s). Tighten union nuts to 20 N·m (133 in.-lb). Tighten return line banjo bolts to 11 N·m (97 in.-lb). Install fuel delivery pipe clamps.
17. Install lower intake manifold(s) using a new gasket. Tighten bolts to 26 N·m (230 in.-lb).
18. Install charge air cooler(s) using a new gasket. Tighten bolts to 20 N·m (177 in.-lb).
19. Install upper intake manifold(s). Tighten bolts to:
    - **6SY:** 26 N·m (230 in.-lb)
    - **8SY:** 50 N·m (37 ft-lb)
20. **8SY:** Install connection pipe between intake manifolds.
21. Connect coolant hoses to charge air coolers.
22. Install and connect charge air sensor.
23. Install and secure all remaining air inlet pipes and hoses. Tighten V-clamps to:
    - M6 Screw: 8 N·m (71 in.-lb)
    - M8 Screw: 20 N·m (177 in.-lb)
24. **8SY:** Install closed crankcase ventilation filter.
25. Install and secure exhaust system connections.
26. **8SY:** Install coolant recovery tank and catwalk.
27. Fill engine with coolant.
28. Connect negative (-) battery cable.
29. Bleed fuel system. *See Bleed the Fuel System on page 6-17.*
30. Start the engine and check for leaks.

ENGINE

Pistons and Cylinder Liners

PISTONS AND CYLINDER LINERS

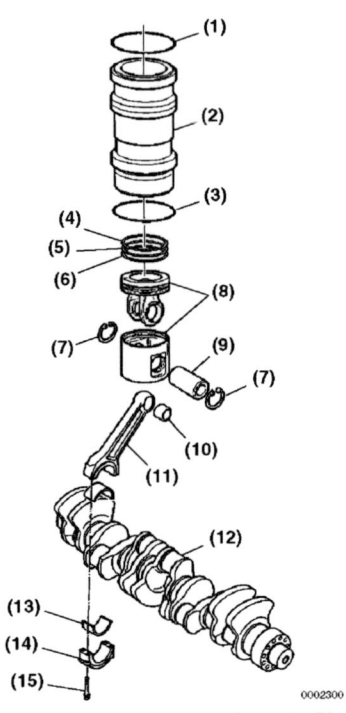

1 – O-Ring
2 – Cylinder Liner
3 – O-Ring
4 – Compression Ring
5 – Compression Ring
6 – Oil Scraper Ring
7 – Circlip (2 used)
8 – Piston
9 – Wrist Pin
10 – Wrist Pin Bushing
11 – Connecting Rod
12 – Crankshaft
13 – Connecting Rod Bearing Insert
14 – Connecting Rod Cap
15 – Rod Cap Bolt

Figure 5-41

Note: 6SY components shown. 8SY is similar.

Pistons and Cylinder Liners

ENGINE

Remove and Disassemble Piston and Connecting Rod

1. Remove the cylinder heads. *See Remove the Cylinder Head on page 5-26.*
2. Remove oil sump.
3. Remove the piston cooling nozzles from the cylinder block. *NOTICE: Use care not to damage the piston cooling nozzles. The oil spray must hit the piston precisely. If it does not, the piston will become too warm, resulting in engine breakdown. Do not straighten damaged nozzles. They must be replaced.*
4. Remove the ridge at the top of the cylinder if necessary. *NOTICE: Engines with high operating hours may have a ridge near the top of the cylinders that will catch the piston rings and make it impossible to remove the pistons. Use a suitable ridge reamer to remove ridges and carbon prior to removing pistons.*

Note: Pistons can fall from the cylinder block if the engine is inverted. Use care when removing the connecting rod caps.

5. Remove the connecting rod cap and bearing inserts.
6. Mark each piston and connecting rod before removing them. They must be installed in the same location and orientation as they were removed. *NOTICE: Keep the piston pin parts, piston assemblies, and connecting rod assemblies together to be returned to the same position during the reassembly process. Label the parts using an appropriate method.*
7. Check the bearing oil clearance as each piston and rod assembly is removed to help determine extent of wear. *See Measure the Oil Clearance on page 5-85.*
8. Push the piston and connecting rod out of the cylinder. Use a wooden dowel against the connecting rod, if necessary. *NOTICE: Do not allow the connecting rod to bump the crankshaft journal during piston removal. Damage to the bearing journal may result.*
9. Wrap tape with the adhesive side out around the crankshaft journal to protect it

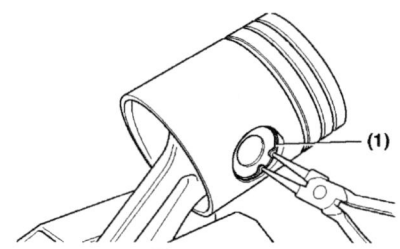

Figure 5-42

10. Place the connecting rod in a vise with soft jaws. Remove the wrist pin retaining rings **(Figure 5-42, (1))**.

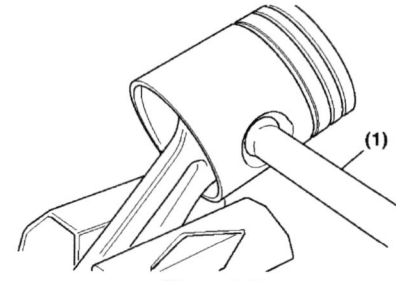

Figure 5-43

11. Push out the wrist pin using a drift **(Figure 5-43, (1))**.

ENGINE

Pistons and Cylinder Liners

12. Separate piston crown from skirt.

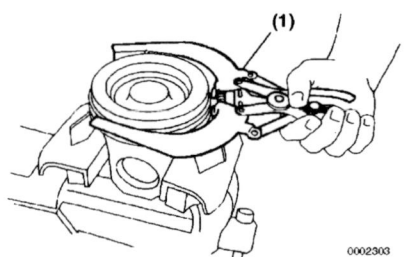

Figure 5-44

13. Use a piston ring expander **(Figure 5-44, (1))** to remove the piston rings, taking care not to scratch the surface of the piston.

Note: When cleaning graphite-coated pistons in a machine, the graphite coating may disappear. Used pistons are not affected by this condition. However, new pistons should be cleaned carefully using an appropriate parts cleaning solvent only, and not cleaned by machine.

Inspect the Connecting Rods

NOTICE: Always inspect the connecting rod in cylinders which have seized, been filled with water or where a valve has broken. Bent connecting rods must not be straightened.

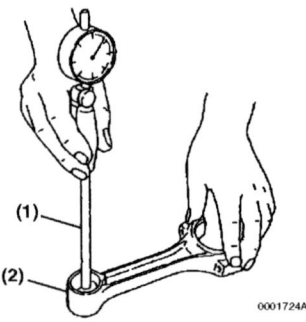

Figure 5-45

1. Measure the wrist pin bushing bore **(Figure 5-45, (2))** using a bore gauge **(Figure 5-45, (1))**. Replace the bushing if not within specifications.

Specifications

Inspection Item	Measurement
Wrist Pin Bushing ID	54.030 - 54.043 mm (2.1272 - 1.1277 in.)

2. Place the connecting rod bearing inserts into the connecting rod and connecting rod cap. Install the rod cap and tighten the bolts to the specified torque.

Torque Specifications

Engine	Connecting Rod Bolt Torque
6SY	20 N·m (177 in.-lb) plus 90°
8SY	50 N·m (37 ft-lb) plus 90°

3. Assemble the connecting rod to the alignment tool. Install the wrist pin.

Note: The distance between the gauge studs is 75 mm (2.953 in.).

Pistons and Cylinder Liners

ENGINE

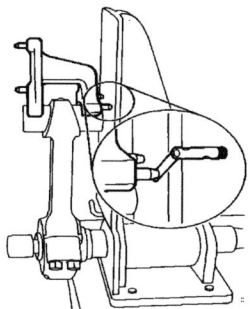

Figure 5-46

4. Place the gauge as shown in **Figure 5-46**. Use a feeler gauge to measure clearance between one gauge pin and the gauge surface to check connecting rod twist.

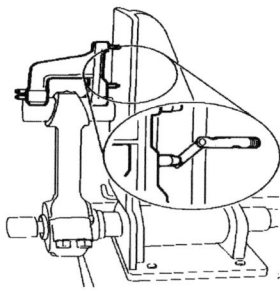

Figure 5-47

5. Place the gauge as shown in **Figure 5-47**. Use a feeler gauge to measure clearance between one gauge pin and the gauge surface to check connecting rod bend.

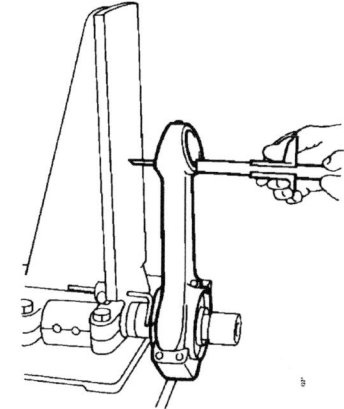

Figure 5-48

6. Check if the connecting rod is bent into an "S" shape. Measure the distance from the outside of the rod and the surface of the tool. Turn the connecting rod 180° and measure again **(Figure 5-48)**.

Connecting Rod Specifications

Inspection Item	6SY	8SY
Twist (Limit)	0.10 mm (0.004 in.)	0.05 mm (0.002 in.)
Bend (Limit)		
Bend - "S" Shape (Limit)	0.60 mm (0.024 in.)	4.5 mm (0.177 in.)

ENGINE

Pistons and Cylinder Liners

Replace the Wrist Pin Bushing

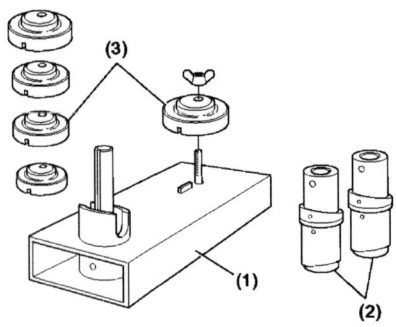

1 – Press Plate with Guide Pin
2 – Press Drift
3 – Supports

Figure 5-49

There are different supports, depending on the engine type **(Figure 5-49)**.

The support marked with a "D" should be used for the 6SY engine. The support marked with an "E" should be used for the 8SY engine.

NOTICE: Check the connecting rod for bend before replacing the wrist pin bushing. See Inspect the Connecting Rods on page 5-38.

1. Install the correct support on the press plate and place the connecting rod so that the wide end of the connecting rod is resting against the support. Place the press drift with the smaller diameter against the bushing and press it out **(Figure 5-50)**.

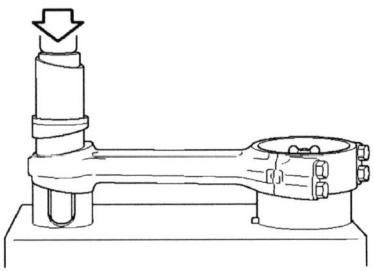

Figure 5-50

2. Turn over the drift and mount a new bushing onto it. Press in the bushing **(Figure 5-50)**.

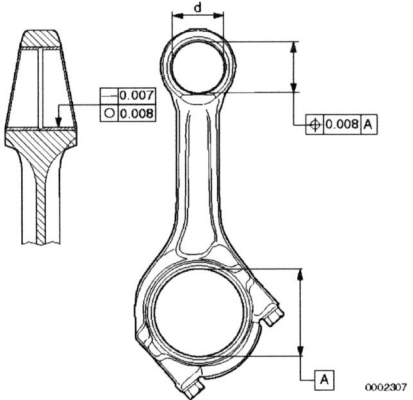

Figure 5-51

3. After pressing in new bushing, it must be finish-turned. This requires special equipment. Refer to illustration for the dimensions required **(Figure 5-51)**.

Specifications

Item	Specification
Diameter (d)	54.030 - 54.043 mm (2.1272 - 2.1277 in.)
Surface Quality	0.6 Ra (roughness average)

Inspect the Pistons and Piston Rings

1. Clean piston ring grooves using a piston ring groove cleaning tool. Follow manufacturer's instructions for correct operation.
2. Wash pistons in an appropriate solvent using a soft brush.
3. Visually inspect each piston for cracks. Pay particular attention to the ring lands between the piston ring grooves.

Note: The top piston ring is tapered and cannot be checked for side clearance.

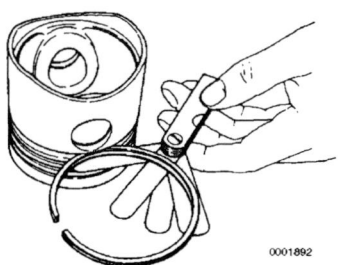

Figure 5-52

4. Place a new piston ring in the oil groove as shown (Figure 5-52). Use a feeler gauge to measure the gap between the ring and the piston. Replace the piston if not within specification. Repeat with the second ring.

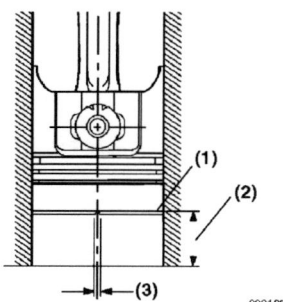

Figure 5-53

5. Insert each piston ring (Figure 5-53, (1)), one at a time, into the cylinder. Use a piston with the piston rings removed to slide the ring into the cylinder bore until it is approximately 1.18 in. (30 mm) (Figure 5-53, (2)) from the bottom of the bore. Measure the end gap (Figure 5-53, (3)) of each piston ring.

Specifications

Inspection Item		Standard	Limit
Top Ring	Side Clearance	-	-
	End Gap	0.35 - 0.60 mm (0.014 - 0.024 in.)	
Second Ring	Side Clearance	-	0.25 mm (0.010 in.)
	End Gap	0.45 - 0.65 mm (0.018 - 0.026 in.)	-
Oil Ring	Side Clearance	-	0.25 mm (0.010 in.)
	End Gap	0.40 - 0.65 mm (0.016 - 0.026 in.)	-

6. Repeat the above steps for each of the cylinders and the piston rings for that specific cylinder.

Assemble the Piston and Connecting Rod

1. Clean the piston and rings thoroughly without scratching the sides of the ring grooves. The oil holes in the piston should be cleaned using a suitable drill.
2. Oil all the bushings, wrist pin bore and wrist pin before assembling.
3. Place one of the retaining rings in the piston crown. Assemble the crown and skirt.

ENGINE

Pistons and Cylinder Liners

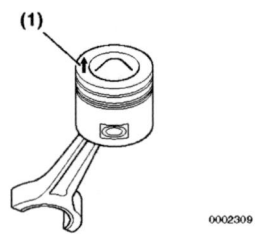

Figure 5-54

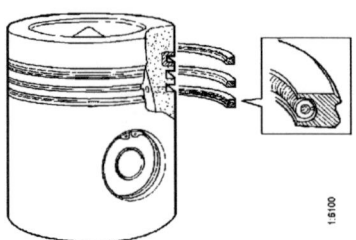

Figure 5-56

4. Orient the piston and connecting rod **(Figure 5-54)**. The arrow **(Figure 5-54, (1))** on top of the piston must be on the same side as the cap side of the connecting rod big end.

6. Install the piston rings using a piston ring tool. The oil scraper ring has an expander underneath it **(Figure 5-56)**. Put the expander end gap and oil ring end gap 180° apart. Stagger all exposed ring gaps 120° from each other.

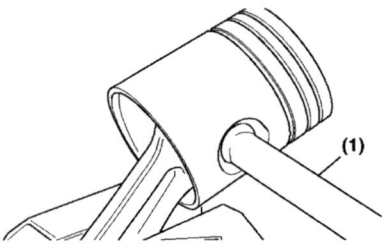

Figure 5-55

Remove the Cylinder Liners

6SY Engines

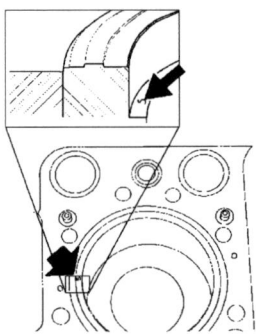

Figure 5-57

5. Insert the wrist pin using a tool **(Figure 5-55, (1))**, if necessary. Install the second retaining ring.

Note: Piston rings marked with TOP must be installed with TOP facing up.

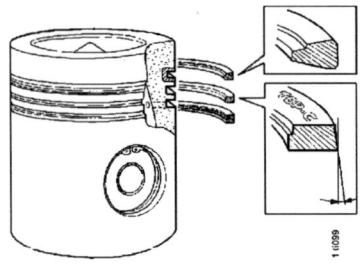

Pistons and Cylinder Liners — ENGINE

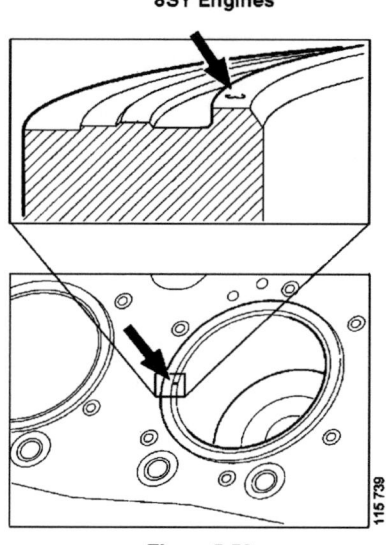

Figure 5-58

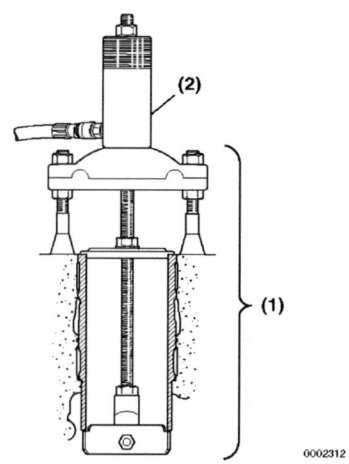

Figure 5-59

1. Mark each liner with the appropriate cylinder number **(Figure 5-57)** or **(Figure 5-58)**.
   *NOTICE: The mark must be made only on the surface indicated in **Figure 5-57**. Other surfaces are used for sealing.*

2. Remove the cylinder liner using a puller **(Figure 5-59, (1))** and hydraulic cylinder **(Figure 5-59, (2))**. Install spacers under the support lugs to avoid damaging the gasket surface of the block.

3. Remove the sealing ring in the cylinder block.

ENGINE

Pistons and Cylinder Liners

Measure the Cylinder Liner Height

1. Thoroughly clean the cylinder block liner flange, the sealing face around the cylinder, the cylinder liner flange and the upper face of the cylinder liner.
2. Install the cylinder liner without O-rings and twist down by hand into position.

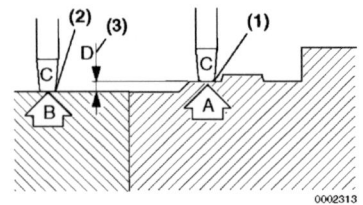

Figure 5-60

3. Place a dial indicator on the liner at position "A" **(Figure 5-60, (1))** and zero the dial indicator. Slide the tip of the dial indicator over to the cylinder block (position "B") **(Figure 5-60, (2))** and read the dial indicator. Measurement (D) **(Figure 5-60, (3))** is the reading on the dial indicator. Record each measurement taken.
4. Measure each liner at two diametrically opposite points 180° apart.

   The cylinder liner must be above the face of the cylinder block per the specification. Add or remove shims from under liner to achieve correct protrusion.

Specifications

Inspection Item	Specification
Dimension D	0.15 - 0.30 mm (0.006 - 0.012 in.)
Protrusion Variation on One Liner (Maximum)	0.02 mm (0.0008 in.)

Install the Cylinder Liners

1. Check cylinder liner height. *See Measure the Cylinder Liner Height on page 5-44.* Choose the appropriate shims as necessary. *See Cylinder Liner on page 5-8 for available sizes.*
2. Make sure the liner bore of the cylinder block is clean. Clean the O-ring surfaces.
3. Check that the coolant passages going to the cylinder head and cylinder liner are not clogged.
4. Carefully check the cylinder liners, both new and used, for cracks which might have occurred during transport or careless handling.
   - Tap the liner carefully with a metal object. If intact, it should give a clear metallic ring. If not, replace liner.

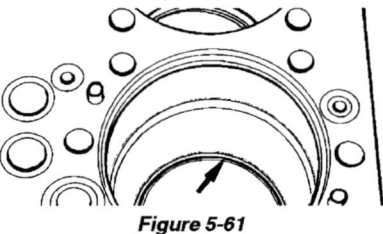

Figure 5-61

5. Lubricate the sealing surfaces with engine oil **(Figure 5-61)**.
6. Install O-rings on the liner and lubricate with engine oil.

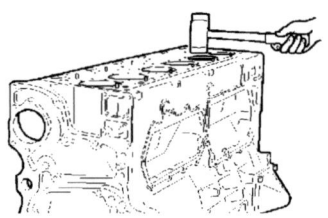

Figure 5-62

7. Install the liner with the stamped cylinder number facing forward and carefully tap it down with a non-metallic mallet **(Figure 5-62)**.

Pistons and Cylinder Liners

ENGINE

Install the Piston and Connecting Rod

1. Lubricate the piston, piston rings, cylinder liner, and piston ring compressor with clean engine oil.

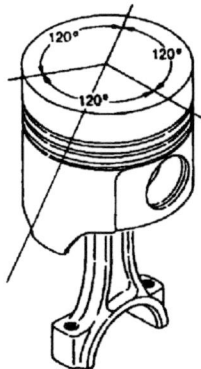

Figure 5-63

2. Turn the piston rings so that the ring gaps are distributed evenly around the piston **(Figure 5-63)**. *NOTICE: Ensure the bearing inserts, and connecting rod and cap mounting surfaces are absolutely clean.*
3. Install the connecting rod bearing inserts in the connecting rod and cap.
4. Apply a light coat of clean engine oil to the bearing insert.
5. Rotate the crankshaft so the journal for the piston being installed is near BDC.
6. Remove the protection on the connecting rod journal and apply a light coat of clean engine oil.

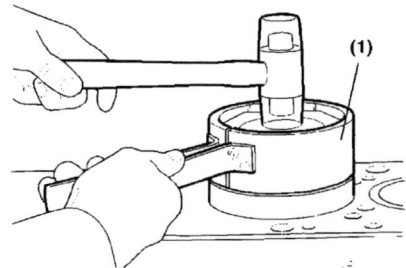

Figure 5-64

7. Using a piston ring compressor **(Figure 5-64, (1))**, carefully install the connecting rod and piston so that the arrow mark on the piston points toward the coolant pump end of the engine.

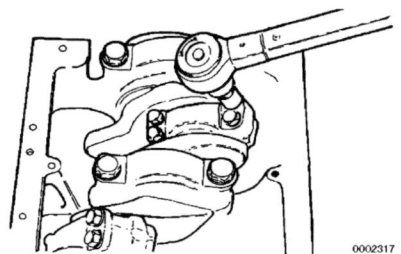

Figure 5-65

8. Install the connecting rod cap. Ensure the connecting rod and cap have the same marking number and that the marks are on the same side.
9. Lubricate the bolts and install **(Figure 5-65)**. Tighten to specification.

Specifications

Item	6SY	8SY
Connecting Rod Cap Torque	20 N·m (177 in.-lb) plus 90°	50 N·m (37 ft-lb) plus 90°

ENGINE   **Pistons and Cylinder Liners**

10. Install the piston cooling nozzles and tighten the banjo bolts to 23 N·m (17 ft-lb). *NOTICE: Use care not to damage the piston cooling nozzles. The oil spray must hit the piston precisely. If it does not, the piston will become too warm, resulting in engine breakdown. Do not straighten damaged nozzles. They must be replaced.* Check that the piston cooling nozzles are in perfect condition and fully open. If necessary, clean with compressed air.
CAUTION! ***ALWAYS wear eye protection when servicing the engine and when using compressed air or high-pressure water. Dust, flying debris, compressed air, pressurized water or steam may injure your eyes.***

11. Install the oil sump and tighten the bolts to 30 N·m (22 ft-lb).

12. Install the cylinder head. *See Install the Cylinder Head on page 5-34.*

This Page Intentionally Left Blank

ENGINE

Flywheel and Flywheel Housing

FLYWHEEL AND FLYWHEEL HOUSING

Flywheel Housing Components - 6SY Engines

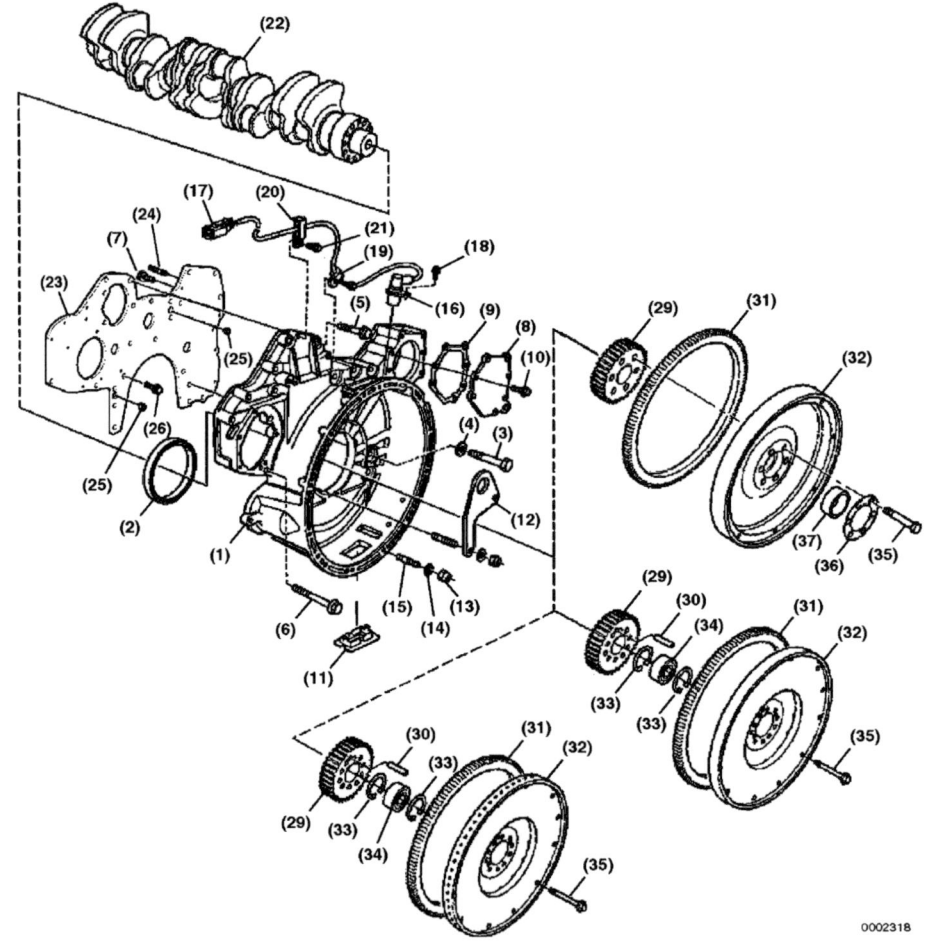

Flywheel and Flywheel Housing   **ENGINE**

1 – Flywheel Housing
2 – Seal
3 – Bolt
4 – Washer
5 – Flange Bolt
6 – Flange Bolt
7 – Flange Bolt
8 – Cover
9 – Gasket
10 – Flange Bolt
11 – Timing Window Cover
12 – Lifting Eye
13 – Hexagon Nut
14 – Washer
15 – Stud
16 – Engine Speed Sensor
17 – Wire Connector
18 – Flange Bolt
19 – Clamp
20 – Clamp
21 – Bolt
22 – Crankshaft
23 – Timing Gear Plate
24 – Stud
25 – Pin
26 – Flange Bolt
27 – Cover
28 – O-Ring
29 – Crankshaft Gear
30 – Pin
31 – Ring Gear
32 – Flywheel
33 – Circlip
34 – Ball Bearing
35 – Bolt
36 – Washer
37 – Guide Sleeve

Figure 5-66

ENGINE

Flywheel and Flywheel Housing

Flywheel Housing Components - 8SY Engines

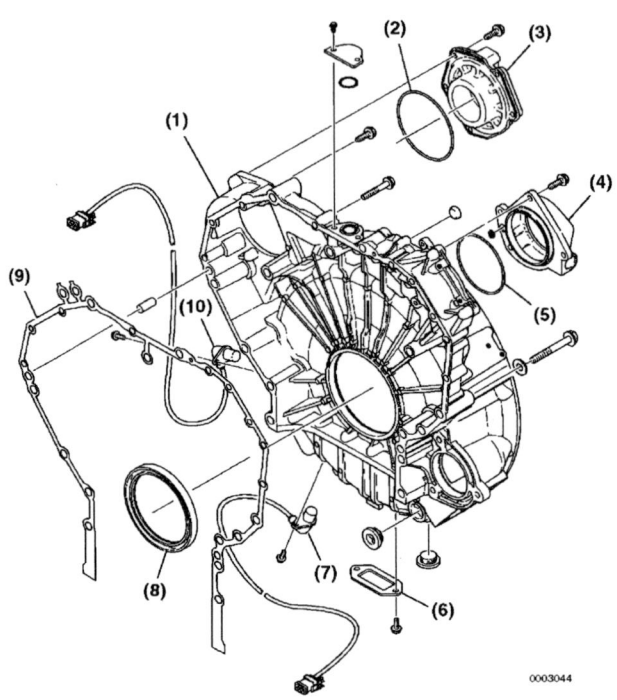

1 – Flywheel Housing
2 – O-Ring
3 – Housing
4 – Flange
5 – O-Ring

6 – Timing Window Cover
7 – Engine Speed Sensor
8 – Rear Crankshaft Seal
9 – Gasket
10 – Engine Speed Sensor

Figure 5-67

Flywheel and Flywheel Housing **ENGINE**

Remove the Flywheel

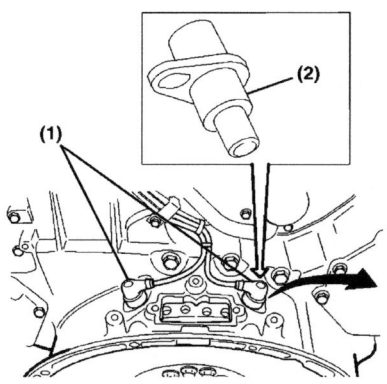

Figure 5-68

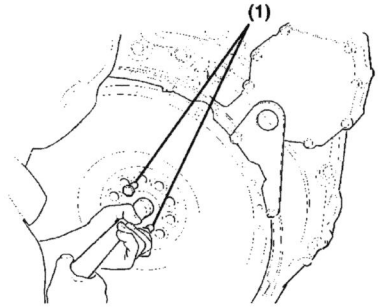

Figure 5-70

5. Use jack bolts **(Figure 5-70, (1))** to remove the flywheel from the crankshaft.

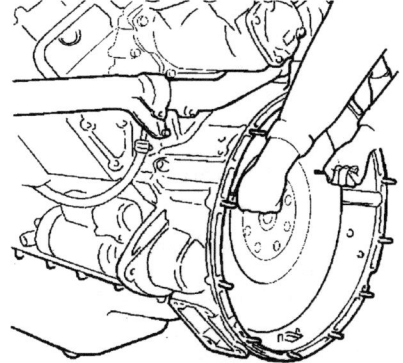

Figure 5-71

Note: 6SY engine shown. 8SY engine is similar.

1. Remove the engine speed sensor(s) **(Figure 5-68, (1))** from the flywheel housing.
2. Install a flywheel holder **(Figure 5-68, (2))**.
3. Remove the bolts retaining the flywheel.
   CAUTION! *The flywheel is heavy and may fall unexpectedly. Always use guide pins and wear gloves when removing or installing the flywheel.*

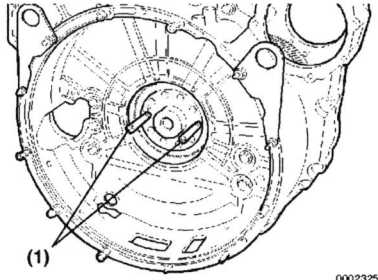

Figure 5-69

4. Install two guide pins **(Figure 5-69, (1))**.

Note: The flywheel can be lifted using two M10 x 100 bolts threaded into the flywheel **(Figure 5-71)**.

ENGINE

Flywheel Inspection and Repair

Support Bearing Replacement

1. Remove retaining rings from both sides of support bearing.

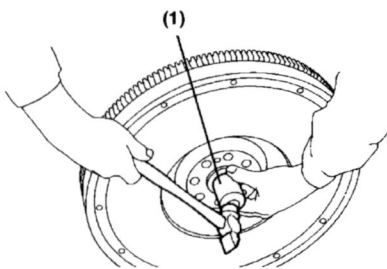

Figure 5-72

2. Drive out support bearing from flywheel using a driver **(Figure 5-72, (1))**.
3. Install inner retaining ring. Drive in new support bearing using drift. Drive only against outer race of bearing.
4. Install the outer retaining ring.

Remove the Ring Gear

Replace flywheel ring gear if gear teeth are chipped, broken, or have become so worn that starter motor pinion will not engage properly.

1. Grind a groove as deep as possible in ring gear and crack it open with a chisel. **CAUTION!** *ALWAYS wear safety glasses while servicing the engine.*
2. Remove ring gear from flywheel.
3. Clean the contact surfaces on flywheel with a wire brush.
4. Heat new ring gear evenly around its circumference to 100 - 150°C (212 - 302°F). **CAUTION!** *Handle hot components with heat-resistant gloves.*

Flywheel and Flywheel Housing

5. Place heated ring gear on flywheel so that the marking with the part number is facing the engine when the flywheel is installed. Make sure ring gear is securely against flywheel. Ensure ring gear is fully seated by tapping with non-metallic hammer.
6. The ring gear must not be cooled rapidly but be left to cool in the open air.

Replace the Rear Crankshaft Seal

1. Remove flywheel. *See Remove the Flywheel on page 5-51.*
2. Remove crankshaft seal using a screwdriver. Take care not to scratch the sealing surfaces on the crankshaft and the flywheel housing.

Note: The crankshaft seal must be installed dry and must not be lubricated. The sleeve in the seal should be left in place until the seal is installed. The crankshaft should be degreased before the new seal is installed.

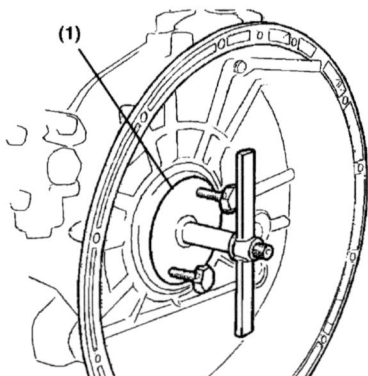

Figure 5-73

3. Place crankshaft seal on tool and fasten tool to the crankshaft **(Figure 5-73, (1))**.
4. Turn tool clockwise until it stops. The seal will be at the correct installed position.
5. Remove tool.

Flywheel and Flywheel Housing ENGINE

6. Install flywheel. *See Install the Flywheel on page 5-54.*

Remove the Flywheel Housing

1. Remove flywheel. *See Remove the Flywheel on page 5-51.*
2. Remove starter motor. *See Remove and Install Starter Motor on page 10-7.*
3. Remove PTO cover or hydraulic pump (if equipped). Place to one side.
4. Remove closed crankcase ventilation filter.
5. Remove turbocharger oil lines.
6. Remove seawater pump and connecting pipes.
7. **8SY:** Remove oil sump.
8. Remove flywheel housing.

Install the Flywheel Housing

1. Remove all old gasket material and sealing compound from the sealing surfaces of the flywheel housing and mounting surfaces of the engine. Clean off any oil and grease using an alcohol-based cleaning agent.

Note: The sealing surfaces must be absolutely clean and free from grease. Do not touch the surfaces after degreasing.

2. *NOTICE: Assembly must be completed within 25 minutes of starting to apply the sealing agent.*

   6SY: Install flywheel housing as follows:

   (a) Apply sealing agent (OEM Part No. 816 064) on timing gear plate side of flywheel housing. The width of the bead should be 0.8 - 1.2 mm (0.031 - 0.047 in.). Apply sealing agent around bolt holes. *NOTICE: Ensure that sealing agent is applied inside the bolt holes, but without allowing sealing agent into the crankcase. Excess sealing agent may block channels and nozzles, particularly around oil passages.*

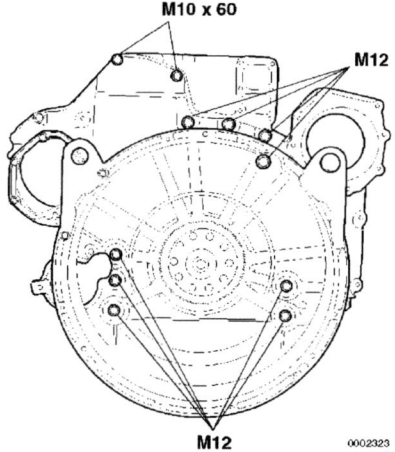

Figure 5-74

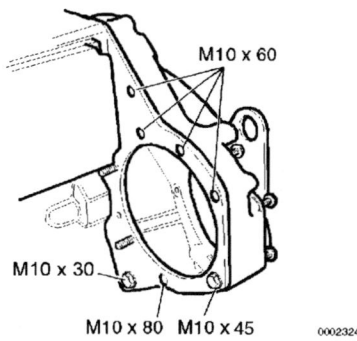

Figure 5-75

Note: The bolts are of various sizes and lengths. Ensure that they are installed in the correct places.

   (b) Install bolts. Tighten M12 bolts to 90 N·m (66 ft-lb) and M10 bolts to 50 N·m (37 ft-lb) **(Figure 5-75)**.

ENGINE

Flywheel and Flywheel Housing

3. **8SY:** Install flywheel housing as follows:

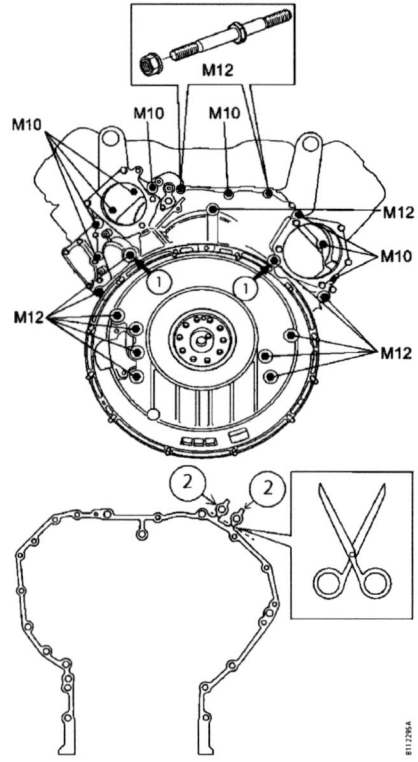

Figure 5-76

(a) Cut portions **(2)** from new gasket and place in locations **(1)** on engine block. Hold in place with a small amount of sealant.

(b) Install flywheel housing using remainder of new gasket.

(c) Install bolts. Tighten M12 bolts and studs to 90 N·m (66 ft-lb) and M10 bolts to 50 N·m (37 ft-lb) **(Figure 5-76)**.

4. **8SY:** Install oil sump using a new gasket. Tighten bolts to 32 N·m (24 ft-lb).

5. Install PTO cover or hydraulic pump (if equipped).
6. Install seawater pump and connect lines.
7. Install turbocharger oil lines.
8. Install closed crankcase ventilation filter and connect lines.
9. Install starter motor. *See Remove and Install Starter Motor on page 10-7.*
10. Install flywheel. *See Install the Flywheel on page 5-54.*

Install the Flywheel

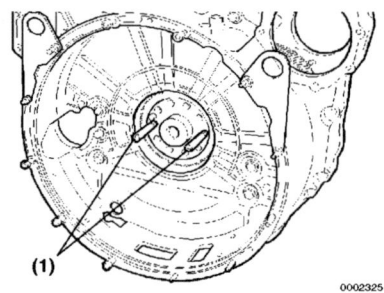

Figure 5-77

Note: 6SY engine shown. 8SY engine is similar.

1. Install two guide pins **(Figure 5-77, (1))** in the crankshaft flange. *NOTICE: Never reuse flywheel bolts. Always install new flywheel bolts.*

Flywheel and Flywheel Housing   ENGINE

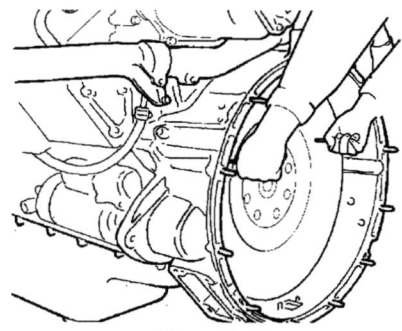

Figure 5-78

5. Remove the flywheel holder and install the engine speed sensor(s).

Note: The flywheel can be lifted using two M10 x 100 bolts threaded into the flywheel **(Figure 5-78)**.

2. Install the flywheel on the crankshaft. Install bolts. If equipped with a 14-in. flywheel, install washers.

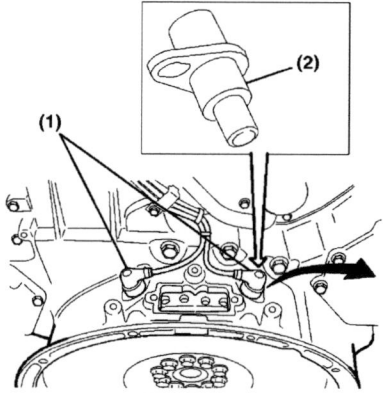

Figure 5-79

3. Install a flywheel holder **(Figure 5-79, (2))** in one of the sensor **(Figure 5-79, (1))** holes.
4. Tighten the flywheel bolts alternately to 130 N·m (96 ft-lb) and then a further 90°.

ENGINE

Timing Gear Train

TIMING GEAR TRAIN

6SY Components

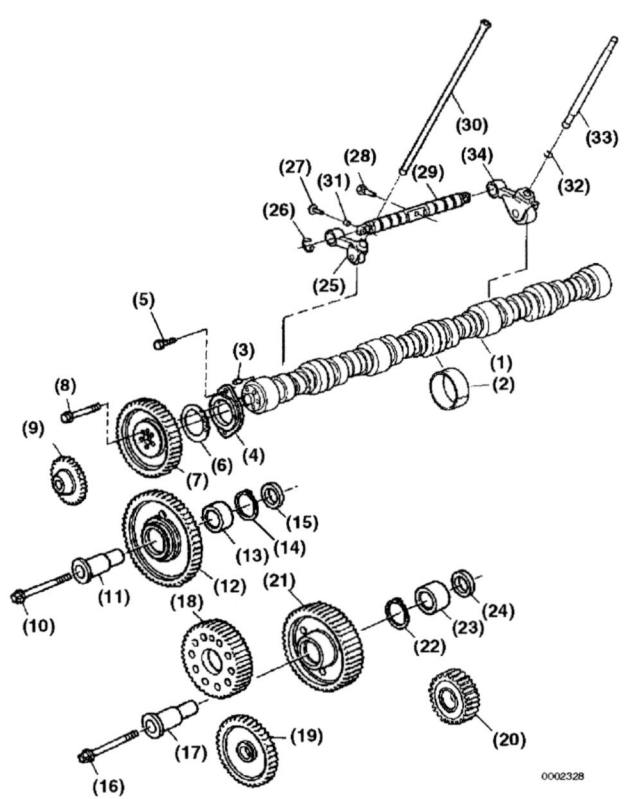

Timing Gear Train   **ENGINE**

1 – Camshaft
2 – Camshaft Bearing
3 – Pin
4 – Guide Flange
5 – Flange Bolt
6 – Thrust Washer
7 – Camshaft Gear
8 – Flange Bolt
9 – Hydraulic Pump Wheel
10 – Flange Bolt
11 – Shaft
12 – Intermediate Gear
13 – Ball Bearing
14 – Snap Ring
15 – Spacing Sleeve
16 – Bolt
17 – Shaft
18 – Crankshaft Gear
19 – Oil Pump Gear
20 – Compressor Gear
21 – Intermediate Gear
22 – Snap Ring
23 – Shaft
24 – Spacing Sleeve
25 – Roller Tappet
26 – Circlip
27 – Flange Bolt
28 – Banjo Bolt
29 – Tappet Shaft
30 – Pushrod
31 – Guide Sleeve
32 – Snap Ring
33 – Pushrod
34 – Roller Tappet

Figure 5-80

ENGINE

Timing Gear Train

8SY Components

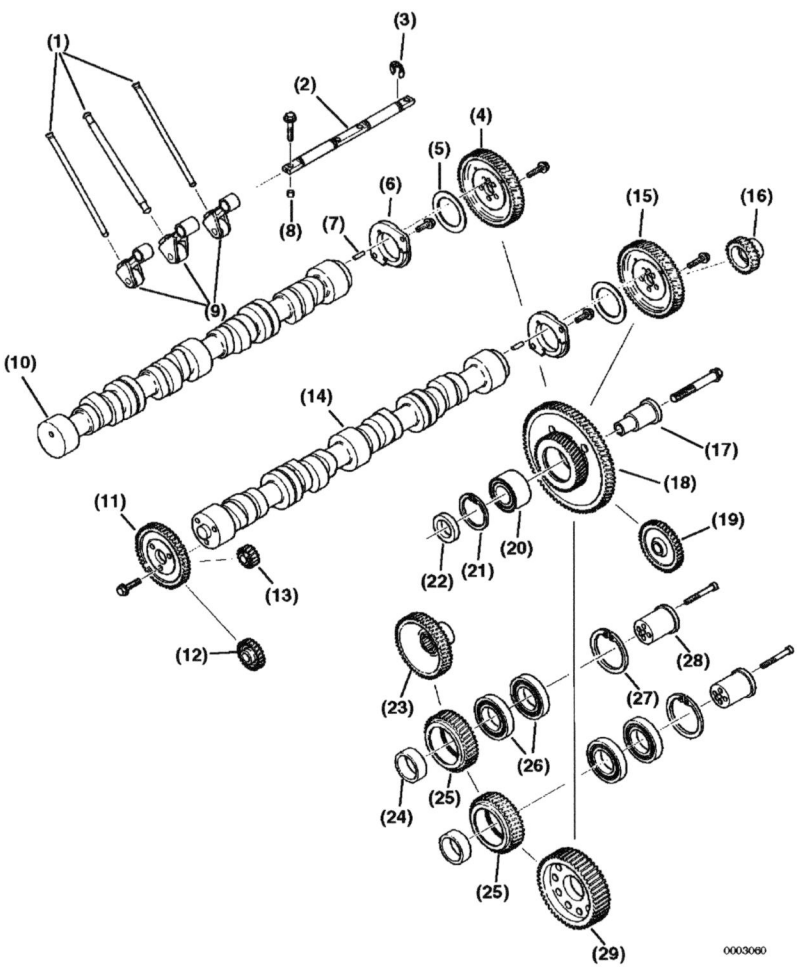

Timing Gear Train — ENGINE

1 – Pushrod
2 – Tappet Shaft
3 – Circlip (4 used)
4 – Camshaft Gear, Right
5 – Thrust Washer
6 – Guide Flange
7 – Alignment Pin
8 – Guide Sleeve (2 used)
9 – Roller Tappet
10 – Camshaft, Right
11 – Front Camshaft Gear (left side only)
12 – Fuel Feed Pump Drive Gear
13 – Hydraulic Pump Drive Gear (if equipped)
14 – Camshaft, Left
15 – Camshaft Gear, Left
16 – Seawater Pump Gear
17 – Intermediate Gear Shaft
18 – Intermediate Timing Gear
19 – Oil Pump Gear
20 – Ball Bearing
21 – Snap Ring
22 – Spacer
23 – Gear, Optional Power Take-Off
24 – Spacer
25 – Intermediate Gear (2 used)
26 – Ball Bearing (4 used)
27 – Snap Ring (2 used)
28 – Shaft (2 used)
29 – Crankshaft Gear

Figure 5-81

ENGINE

Timing Gear Train

Check the Camshaft Timing

6SY Engines

1. Set crankshaft to TDC of compression stroke on cylinder No. 1.
2. Set two dial indicators against the valve spring retainers of an intake and exhaust valve on No. 1 cylinder.
3. Adjust rocker arms so that both valves are open 0.1 mm (0.004 in.).
4. Zero both dial indicators.
5. Turn crankshaft one revolution in direction of rotation until TDC position is again achieved.
6. Read both dial indicators and compare with specifications:

Specifications

Valve	Measurement
Intake	0.37-1.47 mm (0.015-0.058 in.)
Exhaust	0.16-1.16 mm (0.006-0.046 in.)

7. Adjust valves to correct clearance. *See Adjust Valve and Unit Injector Clearances on page 5-18.*

8SY Engines

Right Camshaft

1. Adjust unit injector on No. 1 cylinder. *See Adjust the Unit Injectors on page 6-7.* The crankshaft position will be such that "TDC Up (540°)" is visible in the timing window of the flywheel housing.
2. Zero dial indicator against the spring collar on the unit injector.
3. Turn flywheel 180° in the direction of rotation so that "TDC Down (0°)" is visible in the timing window of flywheel housing.
4. Compare reading on dial indicator with specifications.

Left Camshaft

1. Adjust unit injector on No. 6 cylinder. *See Adjust the Unit Injectors on page 6-7.* The engine position will be such that "TDC Up (180°)" is visible in timing window of the flywheel.
2. Zero dial indicator against the spring collar on the unit injector.
3. Turn flywheel 180° in the direction of rotation so that "TDC Down (360°)" is visible in timing window of flywheel housing.
4. Compare reading on dial indicator with specifications.

Camshaft Timing Specifications

Inspection Item	Specification
Dial Indicator Reading at Given Crankshaft Position	4.5 - 5.1 mm (0.177 - 0.201 in.)

Remove the Front Gear Housing - 8SY

1. Drain engine coolant.
2. Remove belt guard and poly V-belt.

Timing Gear Train   ENGINE

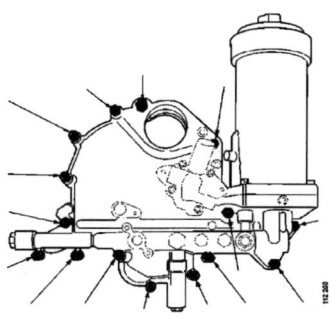

Figure 5-83

7. Remove 15 bolts and remove front gear housing **(Figure 5-83)**.

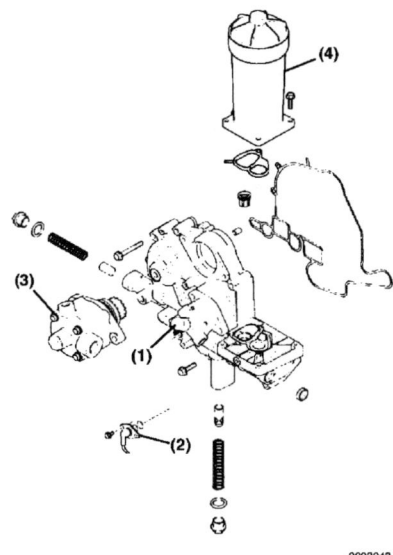

Figure 5-82

3. Disconnect fuel line connections from fuel feed pump **(Figure 5-82, (1))**.
4. Remove coolant temperature sensor and oil pressure sender **(Figure 5-82, (2))**.
5. Remove hydraulic pump (if equipped) **(Figure 5-82, (3))** and swing to one side.
6. Remove oil filter housing **(Figure 5-82, (4))** from gear housing.

ENGINE

Timing Gear Train

Install the Front Gear Housing - 8SY

Intermediate Gear

Remove

- The 6SY timing gear train has two intermediate gears. One drives the camshaft and one drives the seawater pump. Both gears should be removed in the same manner.

- The 8SY timing gear train has three intermediate gears. One drives the camshafts, the other two drive an optional PTO gear.

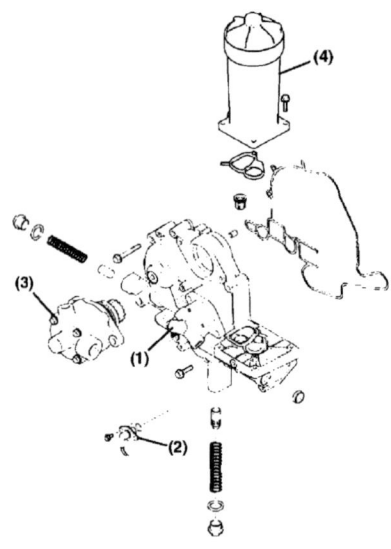

Figure 5-84

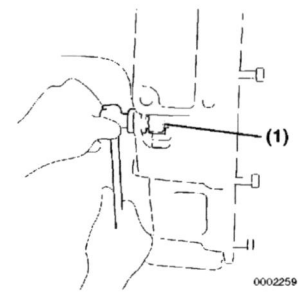

Figure 5-85

1. Install front gear housing **(Figure 5-84)** using new gasket.
2. Install oil filter housing.
3. Connect fuel line connections to fuel feed pump **(Figure 5-84, (1))**.
4. Install hydraulic pump (if equipped) **(Figure 5-84, (3))**.
5. Install coolant temperature sensor and oil pressure sender **(Figure 5-84, (2))**.
6. Install poly V-belt and belt guard.
7. Fill engine with coolant.

1. Use a flywheel turning tool **(Figure 5-85, (1))** to turn the crankshaft so that No. 1 cylinder is approximately at TDC on the compression stroke (both valve rocker arms loose). "Down TDC (0°)" will be visible in the lower timing window of the flywheel housing.
2. Remove flywheel. *See Remove the Flywheel on page 5-51.*
3. Remove flywheel housing. *See Remove the Flywheel Housing on page 5-53.*

Timing Gear Train — ENGINE

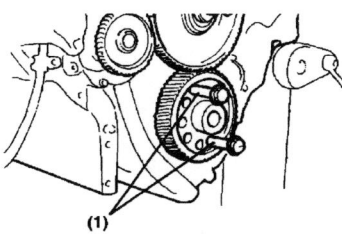

Figure 5-86

4. **8SY:** Temporarily secure crankshaft gear using flywheel bolts with 50 mm (2 in.) spacers **(Figure 5-86, (1))**.

6SY Engines

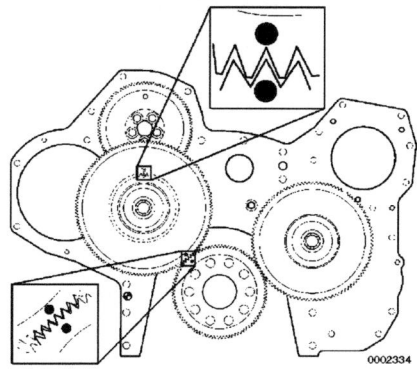

Figure 5-87

8SY Engines

(figure of 8SY timing gears)

Figure 5-88

5. Ensure all timing marks are aligned **(Figure 5-87)** or **(Figure 5-88)**.

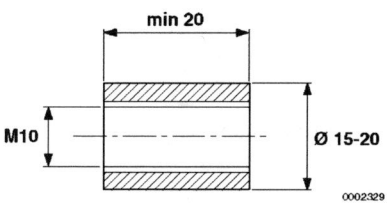

Figure 5-89

6. **6SY:** Fabricate a thread block according to the sketch **(Figure 5-89)**. (Measurements are in millimeters.)
7. Check intermediate gear end play using a dial indicator. If not within specification, replace bearings after removal. *See Bearing Replacement - 6SY on page 5-64 or Bearing Replacement - 8SY on page 5-65.*

Specifications

Inspection Item	Limit
Timing Gear End Play	0.238 mm (0.009 in.)

ENGINE

Timing Gear Train

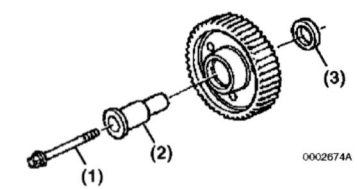

Figure 5-90

8. Remove bolt **(Figure 5-90, (1))** retaining intermediate gear.

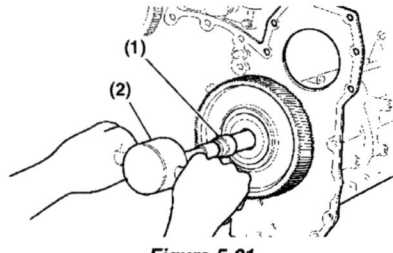

Figure 5-91

9. **6SY:** The shaft on which the gear is located has a groove. Install puller **(Figure 5-91, (1))**, slide hammer **(Figure 5-91, (2))** and the shop-made thread block.

   - **6SY:** Remove the gear, shaft **(Figure 5-90, (2))** and spacer **(Figure 5-90, (3))**.
   - Repeat steps on remaining intermediate gear.

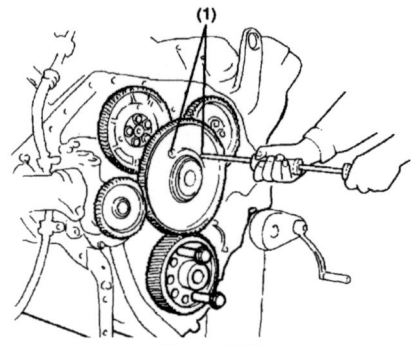

Figure 5-92

10. **8SY:** Remove gear, shaft and spacer using a slide hammer. Pull alternately from the two timing holes **(Figure 5-92, (1))**. *NOTICE: Do not allow the crankshaft to turn while the timing gear train is disassembled.*

Bearing Replacement - 6SY

Intermediate Gear for Seawater Pump

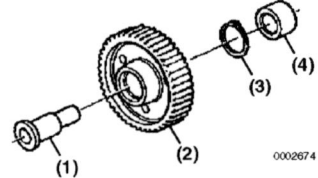

Figure 5-93

1. Remove snap ring **(Figure 5-93, (3))**.
2. Press bearing **(Figure 5-93, (4))** out of gear **(Figure 5-93, (2))**.
3. Press shaft **(Figure 5-93, (1))** out of bearing. *NOTICE: Do not press on the outer race.*
4. Press shaft into a new bearing.
5. Press ring on shaft journal.
6. Press bearing packet into intermediate gear.
7. Install snap ring.

Timing Gear Train — ENGINE

Intermediate Gear for Camshaft

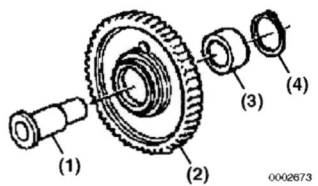

Figure 5-94

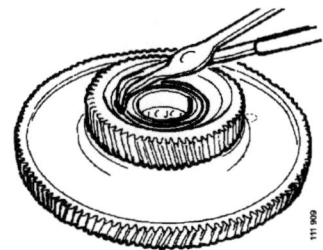

Figure 5-96

1. Press shaft (**Figure 5-94, (1)**) out of bearing (**Figure 5-94, (3)**).
2. Press bearing inner race shell from shaft and remove retaining ring (**Figure 5-94, (4)**).
3. Place removed bearing inner race in bearing and press out bearing (**Figure 5-93, (3)**).
4. Press a new bearing onto shaft journal.
   NOTICE: *Do not press on the outer bearing race.*
5. Press bearing and shaft journal into intermediate gear.
6. Install snap ring.
7. Support end of shaft on press table and press spacing ring onto shaft journal.

2. Remove spacing sleeve and snap ring (**Figure 5-96**).

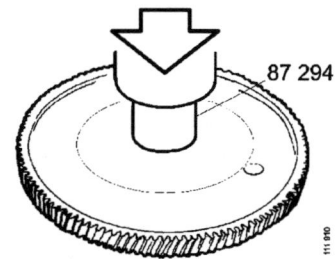

Figure 5-97

3. Turn gear over. Press bearing and shaft from gear (**Figure 5-97**).
4. Press bearing off of shaft.

Bearing Replacement - 8SY

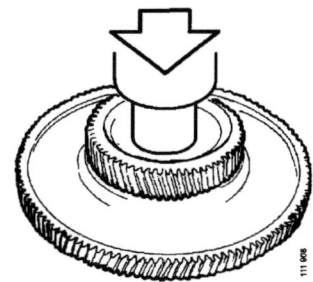

Figure 5-95

1. Press shaft until it is flush with face of small gear (**Figure 5-95**).

ENGINE Timing Gear Train

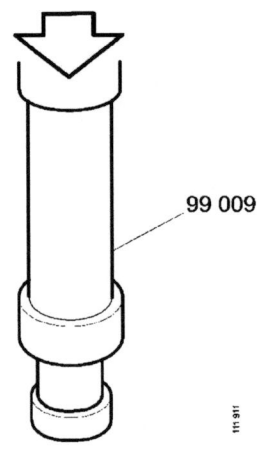

Figure 5-98

5. Press a new bearing onto shaft **(Figure 5-98)**.

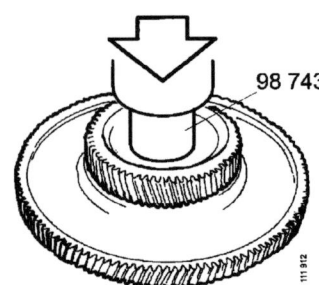

Figure 5-99

6. Press bearing and shaft into gear until it stops. Use care to press only on the outer bearing race using the tube section of tool **(Figure 5-99)**.
7. Install retaining ring.
8. Support end of shaft on press table and press spacer ring until it seats against bearing.

Intermediate Gear Installation

6SY Engines

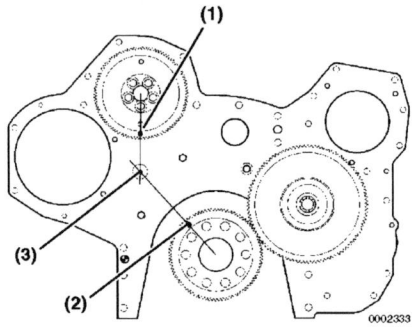

Figure 5-100

8SY Engines

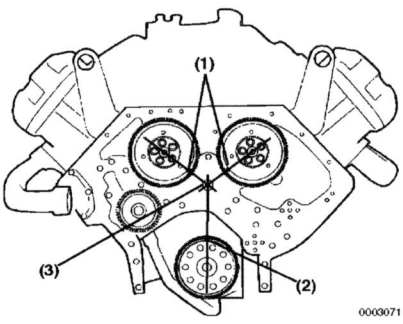

Figure 5-101

1. Check that cylinder No. 1 is at TDC (both valve rocker arms loose). "Down TDC (0°)" will be visible in the lower timing window of the flywheel housing.
2. The timing marks on the camshaft gear **(Figure 5-100 (1)) and Figure 5-101 (1))** and crankshaft gear **(Figure 5-100 (2)) and Figure 5-101 (2))** must point toward the center of the intermediate gear mounting hole **(Figure 5-100 (3)) and Figure 5-101 (3))**.

Timing Gear Train

ENGINE

3. Lubricate bearing surfaces.

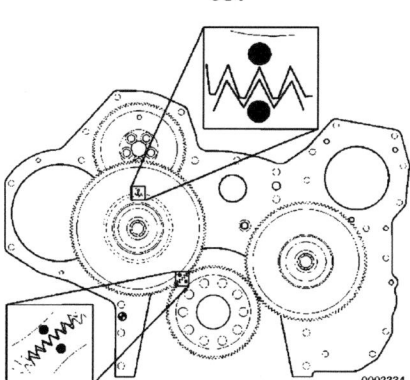

Figure 5-102

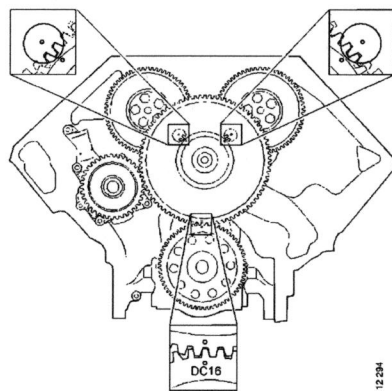

Figure 5-103

4. Install camshaft intermediate gear and shaft assembly. Ensure timing marks **(Figure 5-102** and **Figure 5-103)** are aligned.
5. Install bolt. Torque-turn tighten to 50 N·m (37 ft-lb) plus 60°.

Note: **6SY:** The installation procedure for the seawater pump intermediate gear is the same except there are no timing marks to align.

6. **6SY:** Repeat steps for seawater pump intermediate gear.
7. Install flywheel housing. See Install the Flywheel Housing on page 5-53.
8. Install flywheel. See Install the Flywheel on page 5-54.
9. Check valve timing to verify installation. See Check the Camshaft Timing on page 5-60.

Camshaft Gear

Remove

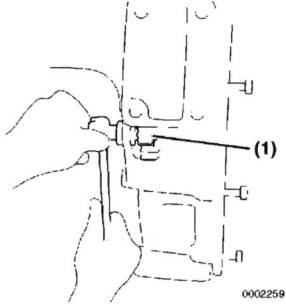

Figure 5-104

1. Use a flywheel turning tool **(Figure 5-104, (1))** to turn the crankshaft so that No. 1 cylinder is approximately at TDC on the compression stroke (both valve rocker arms loose). "Down TDC (0°)" will be visible in the lower timing window of the flywheel housing.
2. Remove flywheel. See Remove the Flywheel on page 5-51.
3. Remove flywheel housing. See Remove the Flywheel Housing on page 5-53.
4. Remove camshaft intermediate gear. See Intermediate Gear on page 5-62. NOTICE: Do not allow the crankshaft to turn while the timing gear train is disassembled.

ENGINE

Timing Gear Train

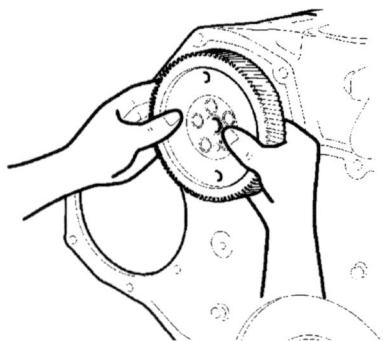

Figure 5-105

5. Remove camshaft gear and thrust washer **(Figure 5-105)**.

Install

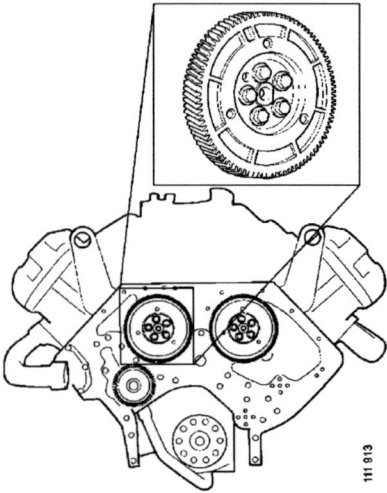

Figure 5-106

8SY Engines: The camshaft gears differ between the left and right sides. The left camshaft gear can be identified by having raised bosses as shown in **Figure 5-106** and is used for engine speed indication.

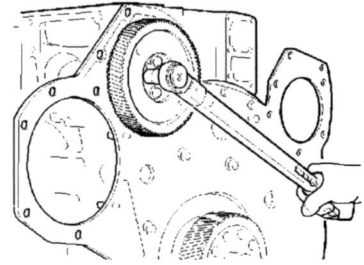

Figure 5-107

6. Install camshaft gear and tighten bolts to 63 N·m (46 ft-lb) **(Figure 5-107)**.
7. Install intermediate gear. *See Intermediate Gear on page 5-62.*
8. Install flywheel housing. *See Install the Flywheel Housing on page 5-53.*
9. Install flywheel. *See Install the Flywheel on page 5-54.*
10. Check valve timing to verify installation. *See Check the Camshaft Timing on page 5-60.*

Timing Gear Train

ENGINE

Crankshaft Gear

Remove

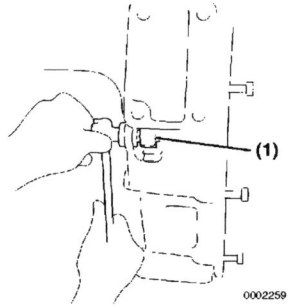

Figure 5-108

1. Use a flywheel turning tool **(Figure 5-108, (1))** to turn the crankshaft so that No. 1 cylinder is approximately at TDC on the compression stroke (both valve rocker arms loose). "Down TDC (0°)" will be visible in the lower timing window of the flywheel housing.
2. Remove the flywheel. *See Remove the Flywheel on page 5-51.*
3. Remove the flywheel housing. *See Remove the Flywheel Housing on page 5-53.*
4. Remove the intermediate gear(s). *See Intermediate Gear on page 5-62.* NOTICE: Do not allow the crankshaft to turn while the timing gear train is disassembled.

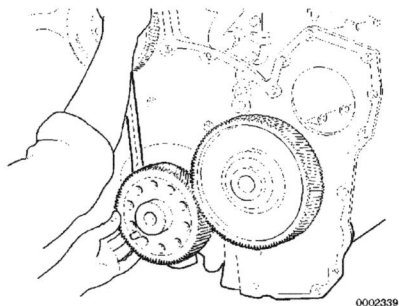

Figure 5-109

5. Remove the crankshaft gear. Use a puller or pry bar to remove the gear if necessary **(Figure 5-109)**.

Install

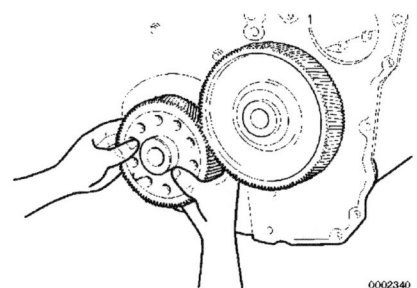

Figure 5-110

1. Install the crankshaft gear and guide pin **(Figure 5-110)**.
2. Install the intermediate gears. *See Intermediate Gear on page 5-62.*
3. Install the flywheel housing. *See Install the Flywheel Housing on page 5-53.*
4. Install the flywheel. *See Install the Flywheel on page 5-54.*
5. Check valve timing to verify installation. *See Check the Camshaft Timing on page 5-60.*

ENGINE

Remove the Camshaft

1. Drain cooling system. Use a suitable container of sufficient volume.

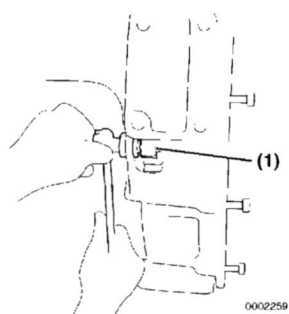

Figure 5-111

2. Use a flywheel turning tool **(Figure 5-111, (1))** to turn the crankshaft so that No. 1 cylinder is approximately at TDC on the compression stroke (both valve rocker arms loose). "Down TDC (0°)" will be visible in the lower timing window of the flywheel housing.

3. Clean the rocker cover and the surrounding area. *NOTICE: Identify all parts and their location using an appropriate method. It is important that all parts are returned to the same position during the reassembly process.*

6SY Engines

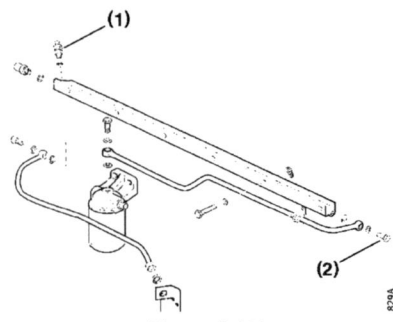

Figure 5-112

Timing Gear Train

8SY Engines

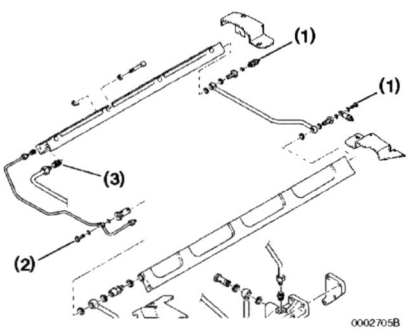

Figure 5-113

4. Open bleeder valve(s) **(Figure 5-112, (1) or (Figure 5-113, (1))** and drain fuel system by loosening banjo bolt **(Figure 5-112, (2) or (Figure 5-113, (2))** on the opposite end of the fuel manifold. On 8SY engines, also loosen union **(Figure 5-112, (3) or (Figure 5-113, (3))**. *DANGER! When you remove any fuel system component to perform maintenance put an approved container under the opening to catch the fuel. NEVER use a shop rag to catch the fuel. Vapors from the rag are flammable and explosive. Wipe up any spills immediately. Wear eye protection. The fuel system is under pressure and fuel could spray out when you remove any fuel system component.*

5. **8SY Engines:**
   (a) Remove connection pipe between charge air coolers.
   (b) Remove coolant recovery tank and catwalk.

6. Remove connection pipe(s) between charge air cooler and turbocharger.

7. Remove centrifugal oil cleaner and oil cooler.

8. Remove cooling system ventilation pipe(s). *NOTICE: Mark all valve train components so they can be installed in their original locations.*

Timing Gear Train

ENGINE

9. Remove upper rocker covers, rocker arm shaft assemblies, pushrods and lower rocker covers from all cylinder heads. *See Remove and Install Rocker Covers on page 5-23.*
10. Remove flywheel. *See Remove the Flywheel on page 5-51.*
11. Remove flywheel housing. *See Remove the Flywheel Housing on page 5-53.* NOTICE: Do not allow the crankshaft to turn while the timing gear train is disassembled.
12. Remove the intermediate gear(s). *See Intermediate Gear on page 5-62.*
13. Check camshaft end play.

Specifications

Inspection Item	Measurement
Camshaft End Play	0.10 - 0.25 mm (0.004 - 0.010 in.)

14. Remove camshaft gear. *See Camshaft Gear on page 5-67.*
15. **8SY Engines:** Remove front gear housing. *See Remove the Front Gear Housing - 8SY on page 5-60.* Remove front camshaft gear from left camshaft.
16. **6SY Engines:** Remove timing gear plate.
17. Remove guide flanges.

6SY Engine Shown

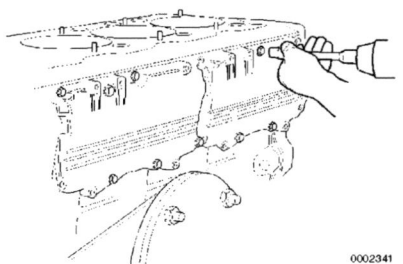

Figure 5-114

18. Remove tappet covers (**Figure 5-114**).

6SY Engine Shown

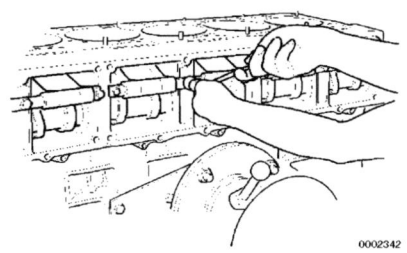

Figure 5-115

19. Remove roller tappets (**Figure 5-115**).
20. Remove camshaft from cylinder block. Take care not to damage the lobes or bearings.

Replace the Camshaft Bearings - 6SY

1. Remove the camshaft. *See Remove the Camshaft on page 5-70.*
2. **6SY:** Remove camshaft cover at front end of the engine.
3. Wipe all residue from the bearing bores and the edges of the old bearings. NOTICE: The new bearings are used to remove the old bearings. Any debris along the edge of the bearing can cause damage to the new bearing during installation. Be sure the old bearing and bearing bore are clean.

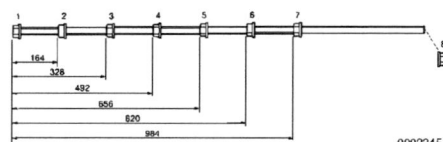

Figure 5-116

Note: All dimensions are metric.

ENGINE

Timing Gear Train

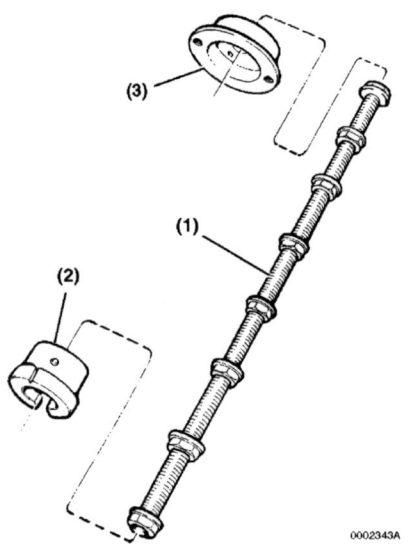

1 – Threaded Rod with Eight Flange Nuts
2 – Press Drift
3 – Flange

Figure 5-117

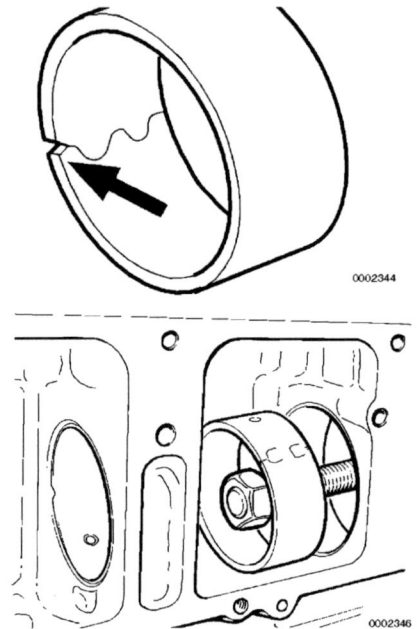

Figure 5-118

4. Assemble the installation tool as shown in **Figure 5-117**. Position nuts as shown in **Figure 5-116**.

5. Place new bearings in the spaces between the camshaft bearing seats **(Figure 5-118)**.
   NOTICE: The notch in the bearing joint must be turned toward the front of the engine.

6. Insert the threaded stem through the camshaft bore from the rear of the engine until the end flange nut protrudes from the front of the engine.

Timing Gear Train ENGINE

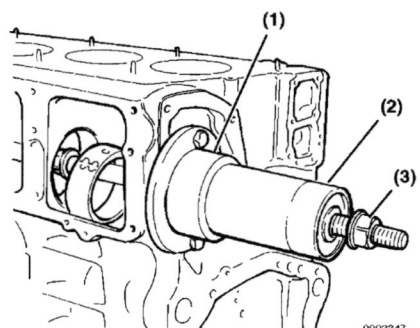

Figure 5-119

7. Attach flange **(Figure 5-119, (1))** securely to hydraulic cylinder **(Figure 5-119, (2))** with two M6 x 12 bolts. Be sure the cylinder is fully retracted.
8. Attach flange and cylinder securely to rear of engine with two M10 x 25 bolts.
9. Install flange nut **(Figure 5-119, (3))**.

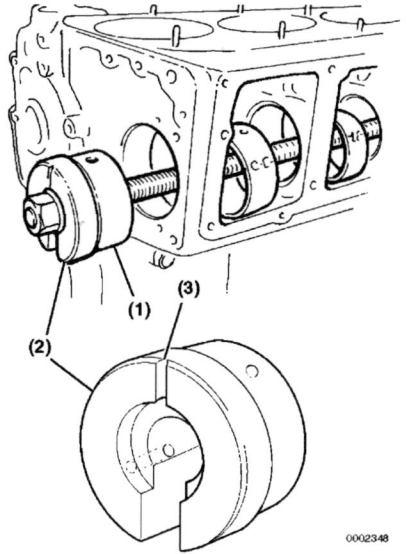

Figure 5-120

10. Place a new bearing **(Figure 5-120, (1))** on the stem at the front of the engine.
11. Place press drift **(Figure 5-120, (2))** on the threaded rod and place the bearing on the drift. The notch in the bearing joint must be against the flange on the drift. Secure the bearing on the drift by placing the spring-loaded ball in an oil hole. The bearing is correctly located on the drift when the ball and a marking hole are centered on the bearing oil hole.

    Note: Camshaft bearings No. 2, 4 and 6 have two oil ports. The others only have the lower port.

12. Ensure the edges of the old and new bearings are clean. The V-groove **(Figure 5-120, (3))** on the drift must be up and vertical to correctly align the oil holes in the bearing with the oil passages in the cylinder block.

ENGINE

Timing Gear Train

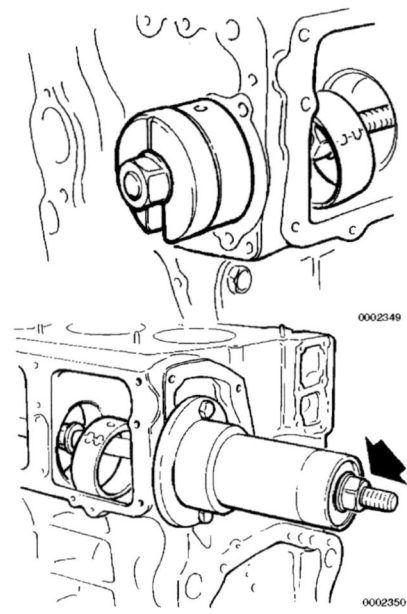

Figure 5-121

13. Hold the drift with the new bearing against the old. Tighten the flange nut against the cylinder **(Figure 5-121)**.

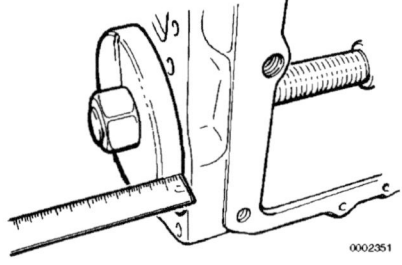

Figure 5-122

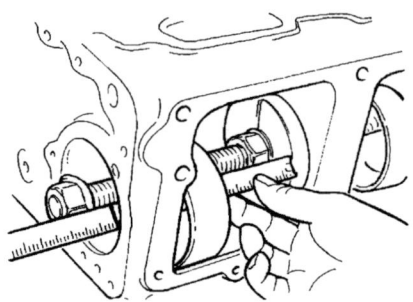

Figure 5-123

14. Press in the new bearing while pressing out the old bearing. The bearing is correctly installed when the dimension from the front of the cylinder block to the drift is within the installed distance specification. *See Camshaft Bearing Installed Specifications - 6SY Engines on page 5-74.*

Camshaft Bearing Installed Specifications - 6SY Engines

Camshaft Bearing No.	Installed Distance
1	Protruding 12 - 14 mm
2	150 - 152 mm
3	314 - 316 mm
4	478 - 480 mm
5	642 - 644 mm
6	806 - 808 mm
7	970 - 972 mm

Note: The new bearing will reach the correct position before the old bearing is completely released. The drift will protrude out of the block when installing No. 1 bearing as shown in **Figure 5-122**.

Timing Gear Train

ENGINE

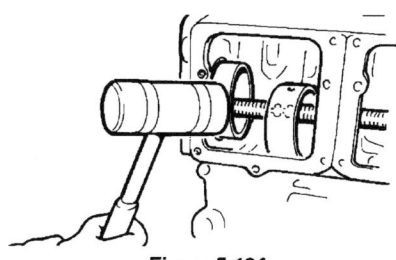

Figure 5-124

15. Carefully tap the old bearing with a plastic hammer to release it **(Figure 5-124)**.
16. Retract the cylinder.
17. Remove the press drift.
18. Check that the bearing oil holes are aligned with the cylinder block oil ports.

Note: The bores for camshaft bearings No. 2, 4 and 6 have two oil ports. The others only have the lower port.

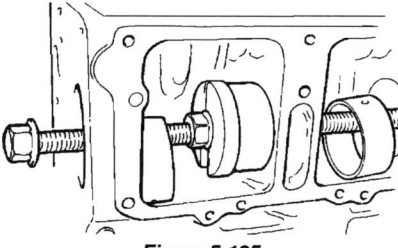

Figure 5-125

19. Repeat the procedure for the remaining bearings **(Figure 5-125)**.
20. Remove all old gasket material from front camshaft cover and the associated area on the cylinder block. *NOTICE: The sealing surfaces must be absolutely clean and free from grease. Do not touch the surfaces after degreasing.*
21. **6SY Engines:** Install camshaft cover on front of cylinder block using new gasket.
22. Install camshaft. *See Install the Camshaft on page 5-78.*

Replace the Camshaft Bearings - 8SY

1. Remove camshafts. *See Remove the Camshaft on page 5-70.*
2. Wipe all residue from the bearing bores and the edges of the old bearings.

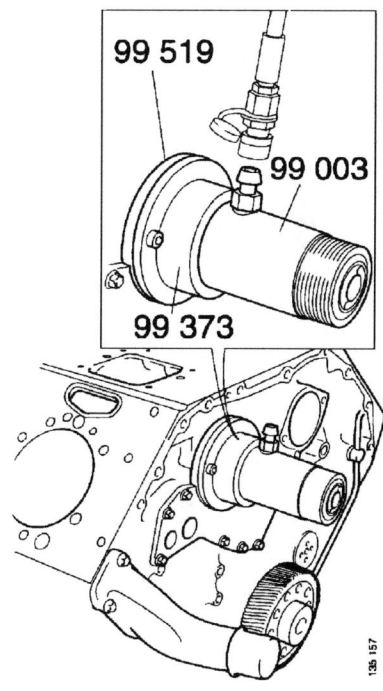

Figure 5-126

3. Attach flange (OEM Part No. 99 373) to hydraulic cylinder (OEM Part No. 99 003) **(Figure 5-126)**.
4. Align spacer (OEM Part No. 99 519) and attach flange and cylinder to cylinder block with bolts.
5. Insert bar through hydraulic cylinder until the outer hole in bar is behind the bearing to be removed.

ENGINE

Timing Gear Train

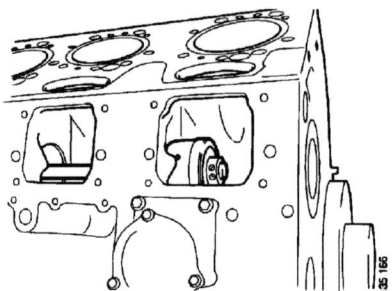

Figure 5-127

6. Secure drift (OEM Part No. 99 516) in the outer hole on the bar using a 12.9 M8 screw **(Figure 5-127)**.

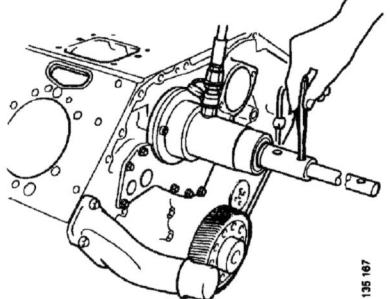

Figure 5-128

7. Pull the bar until the drift is locked in the bearing. Attach the socket next to the hydraulic cylinder using an 8 mm (3/16 in.) pin punch **(Figure 5-128)**.

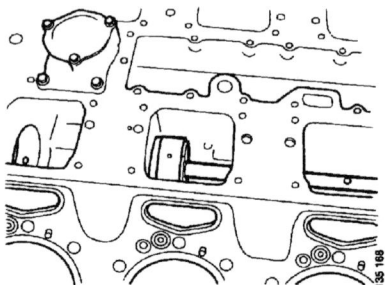

Figure 5-129

8. Connect the hydraulic cylinder to the hydraulic pump. Run the hydraulic pump until the bearing has become completely removed from the bore **(Figure 5-129)**.

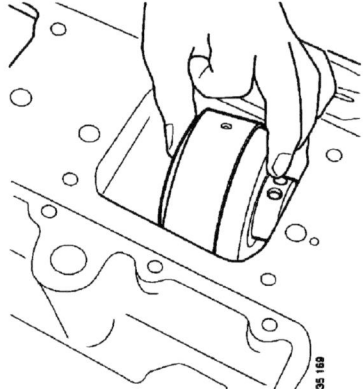

Figure 5-130

9. Remove the drift from the bar **(Figure 5-130)**. Remove the bearing.

Timing Gear Train

ENGINE

10. Ensure the bearing bore is clean. Release the hydraulic cylinder and push the bar back through the bearing bore. *NOTICE: The bearing must be installed in the correct direction. The right camshaft must have the notch in the bearing facing the direction of the water pump. The left camshaft must have the notch in the bearing facing the direction of the flywheel.*

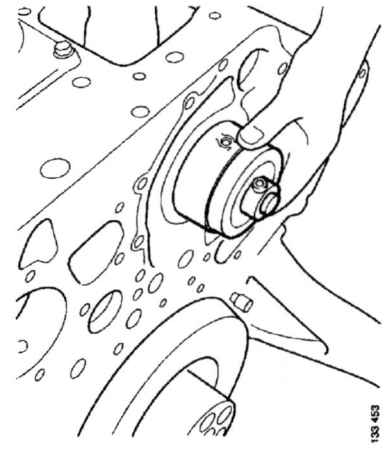

Figure 5-132

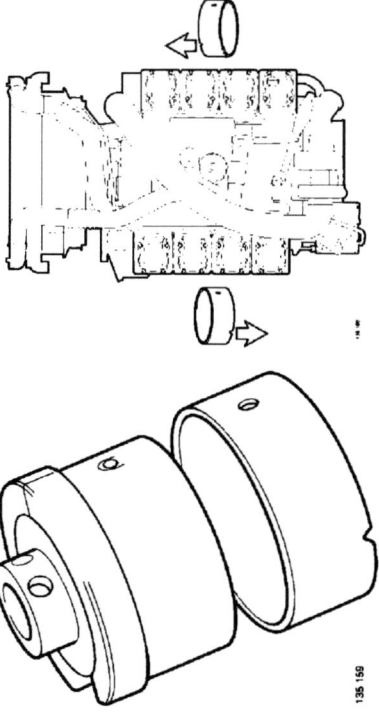

Figure 5-131

11. Put a new bearing on drift (OEM Part No. 99 516). Ensure that the ball on drift engages the round bearing lubrication hole correctly **(Figure 5-131)**. Lubricate the bearing externally.

12. Attach drift (OEM Part No. 99 516) to the outer hole on the bar with a 12.9 M8 bolt. Ensure the lubrication hole faces upwards **(Figure 5-132)**. *NOTICE: Ensure the notch in the bearing is facing the correct direction and the lubrication hole is up.*

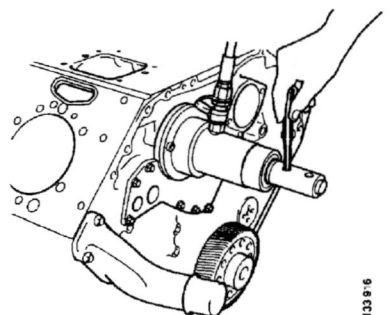

Figure 5-133

ENGINE
Timing Gear Train

13. Pull the bar through the hydraulic cylinder until socket (OEM Part No. 99 517) can be locked onto it using an 8 mm (3/16 in.) pin punch. The pin punch must point vertically so that the lubrication hole is correctly located **(Figure 5-133)**.
14. Pull the bearing into position until the distance from the front face of the cylinder block and the front edge of the drift is at the specified distance. Check that the drift is still vertical when the bearing is in position.

Note: The drift will protrude out of the block when installing No. 1 bearing.

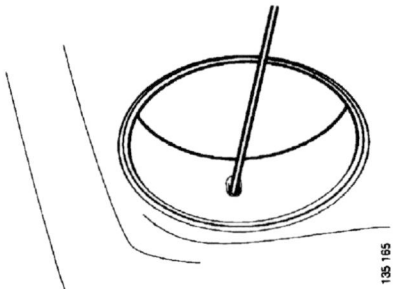

Figure 5-134

15. Check that the lubrication hole is open by looking or by probing with something such as a spray lubricant straw or wire **(Figure 5-134)**.

Camshaft Bearing Installed Specifications - 8SY Engines

Camshaft Bearing No.	Installed Distance
1	Protruding 13 mm
2	196 mm
3	400 mm
4	603 mm
5	811 mm

16. Replace the remaining bearings in the same way.

Install the Camshaft

*NOTICE: **8SY engines**: The left camshaft has provisions for mounting a gear to each end. The end having five M10 threaded holes must be installed toward the rear of the engine.*

1. Remove all old gasket material and sealing compound from camshaft covers, front camshaft cover, timing gear plate, flywheel housing and all associated areas on the cylinder block.
2. Lubricate all camshaft bearings, journals and lobes with clean engine oil.
3. Carefully install camshaft taking care not to damage the lobes or bearings.
4. Install guide flanges.

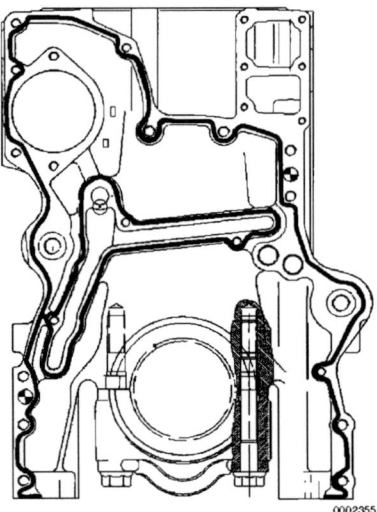

Figure 5-135

Timing Gear Train — ENGINE

5. **6SY Engines:** Apply sealing agent (OEM Part No. 816 064 or equivalent) to cylinder block in the pattern shown **(Figure 5-135)**. The bead width should be 0.8 - 1.2 mm (0.032 - 0.047 in.). *NOTICE: Ensure that sealing agent is applied inside the bolt holes, but without allowing sealing agent into the crankcase. Excess sealing agent may block channels and nozzles, particularly around oil passages. Assembly must be completed within 25 minutes of the beginning of sealant application.*

9. Install camshaft gear(s). *See Camshaft Gear on page 5-67.*
10. Install intermediate gear(s). *See Intermediate Gear on page 5-62.*
11. Install flywheel housing. *See Install the Flywheel Housing on page 5-53.*
12. Install flywheel. *See Install the Flywheel on page 5-54.*

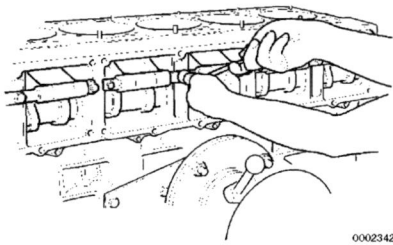

Figure 5-138

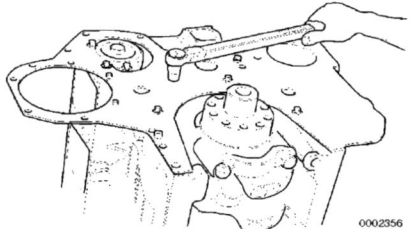

Figure 5-136

6. **6SY Engines:** Install timing gear plate on engine block. Tighten the bolts to 63 N·m (46 ft-lb).

13. Lubricate valve tappets with clean engine oil and install in original locations. Tighten banjo bolts to 32 N·m (24 ft-lb) **(Figure 5-138)**. *NOTICE: The sealing surfaces must be absolutely clean and free from grease. Do not touch the surfaces after degreasing.*
14. Install camshaft covers using new gaskets.
15. **8SY Engines:**
    (a) Install the fuel manifolds. Tighten bolts to 26 N·m (230 in.-lb).
    (b) Install the coolant recovery tank and catwalk.
    (c) Install the connection pipe(s) between the charge air cooler and turbocharger.
    (d) Install the connection pipe between the charge air coolers.
16. Install the centrifugal oil cleaner assembly.
17. Install lower rocker covers, valve bridges, push rods and rocker shaft assemblies. *See Remove and Install Rocker Covers on page 5-23.*
18. Check valve timing to verify installation. *See Check the Camshaft Timing on page 5-60.*

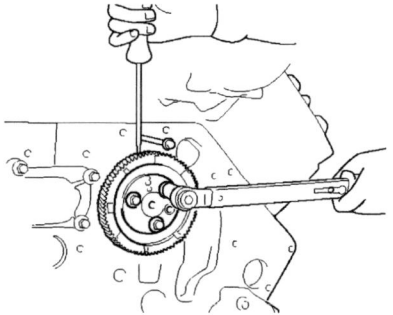

Figure 5-137

7. **8SY Engines:** Install front camshaft gear. Tighten bolts to 63 N·m (46 ft-lb).
8. **8SY Engines:** Install front gear housing. *See Install the Front Gear Housing - 8SY on page 5-62.*

ENGINE

Timing Gear Train

19. Check and adjust valve and unit injector clearances. *See Adjust Valve and Unit Injector Clearances on page 5-18.*
20. Install upper rocker covers. *See Remove and Install Rocker Covers on page 5-23.*

Timing Gear Train **ENGINE**

This Page Intentionally Left Blank

ENGINE

Cylinder Block and Crankshaft

CYLINDER BLOCK AND CRANKSHAFT

8SY Engine Shown

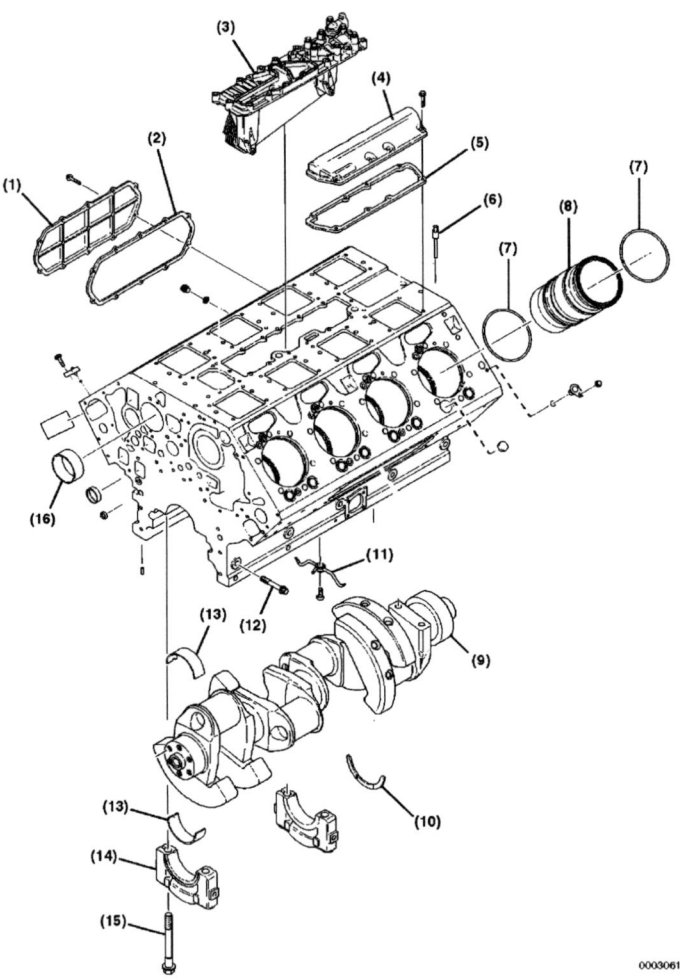

Cylinder Block and Crankshaft   ENGINE

1 – Side Cover (1 each side)
2 – Gasket
3 – Oil Cooler Assembly
4 – Tappet Cover (4 used)
5 – Gasket
6 – Plug
7 – O-Ring
8 – Cylinder Liner
9 – Crankshaft
10 – Thrust Bearing (4 used)
11 – Piston Cooling Nozzle (4 used)
12 – Main Bearing Cap Side Bolt
13 – Main Bearing Insert
14 – Main Bearing Cap
15 – Main Bearing Bolt
16 – Camshaft Bearing

Figure 5-139

Note: Service procedures for 6SY and 8SY engines are similar, therefore graphics shown will be representative and might not match the engine being serviced.

ENGINE

Remove the Crankshaft

1. Remove front crankshaft seal housing.
2. Remove spacer sleeve and crankshaft damper from crankshaft.
3. Remove flywheel. *See Remove the Flywheel on page 5-51.*
4. Remove flywheel housing. *See Remove the Flywheel Housing on page 5-53.*
5. Remove crankshaft gear. *See Crankshaft Gear on page 5-69.*
6. Remove cylinder heads. *See Remove the Cylinder Head on page 5-26.*
7. Remove oil sump, oil suction pipe and strainer and the oil pump. *See Oil Pump on page 8-14.*
8. Remove piston cooling nozzles.
9. Remove pistons and connecting rods. *See Remove and Disassemble Piston and Connecting Rod on page 5-37.*
10. Before removing main bearing caps, measure crankshaft end play.

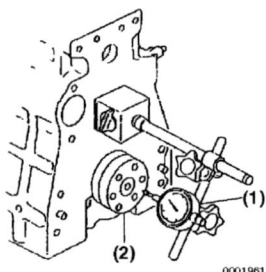

Figure 5-140

- Mount a dial indicator **(Figure 5-140, (1))** on the cylinder block. Move the crankshaft **(Figure 5-140, (2))** in and out to measure end play.

Cylinder Block and Crankshaft

Specifications

Inspection Item	Engine	Specification
Crankshaft End Play	6SY	0.18 - 0.37 mm (0.007 - 0.015 in.)
	8SY	0.138 - 0.380 mm (0.0054 - 0.0150 in.)

11. Measure bearing oil clearance to help determine extent of wear. *See Measure the Oil Clearance on page 5-85.*

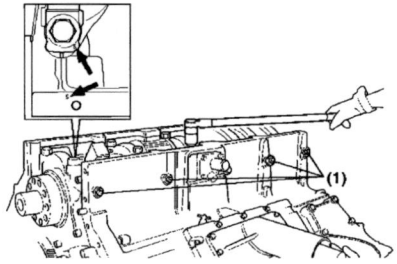

Figure 5-141

Note: The main bearing caps **(Figure 5-141, (1))** are marked and must be installed in their original locations.

Main bearing caps on 8SY engines are bolted through both the bottom and side of the engine block.

12. Remove the crankshaft bearing caps and main bearing inserts.

Cylinder Block and Crankshaft

ENGINE

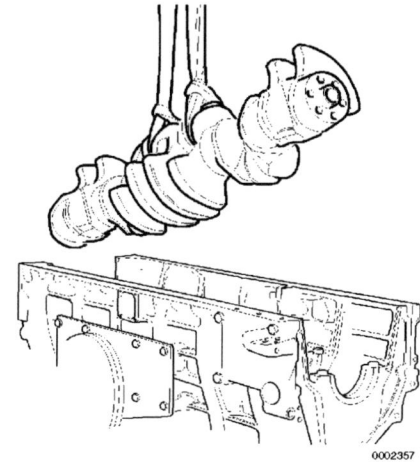

0002357

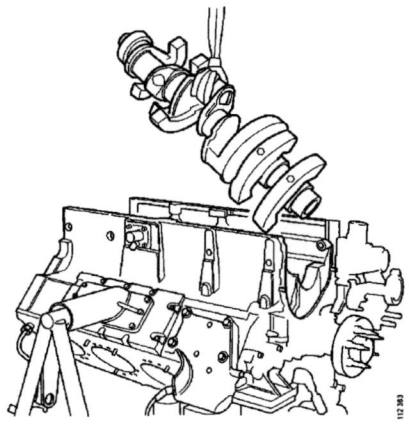

Figure 5-142

13. Lift out the crankshaft **(Figure 5-142)**.

Measure the Oil Clearance

Oil clearance should be checked during disassembly to determine the extent of wear and during reassembly to ensure long engine life. The same procedure is done for both connecting rods and main bearings.

1. Remove the bearing cap. Do not remove the bearing inserts at this time.
2. Wipe oil from the bearing insert and crankshaft journal surfaces.

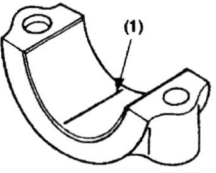

Figure 5-143

3. Place a piece of PLASTIGAGE® **(Figure 5-143, (1))** along the full width of the bearing insert.

Note: Do not rotate crankshaft when using PLASTIGAGE. A false reading may result.

4. Install the bearing cap and tighten to specification. *See Special Torque Chart on page 5-9.*
5. Remove the bearing cap.

ENGINE

Cylinder Block and Crankshaft

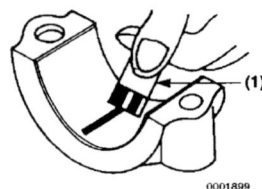

Figure 5-144

6. Compare the width of the flattened PLASTIGAGE to the graduation marks on the package **(Figure 5-144, (1))**. The mark that most closely matches the width of the flattened PLASTIGAGE will indicate the bearing oil clearance.

7. Repeat with the remaining bearings.

Inspect the Crankshaft

1. Use the color check method or Magnaflux to inspect the crankshaft for cracks. Replace the crankshaft if evidence of fractures are found.

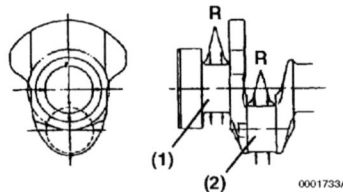

Figure 5-145

2. Measure the outside diameter of each crankpin **(Figure 5-145, (2))** and main bearing journal **(Figure 5-145, (1))**. Take measurements at several places around each bearing surface. If not within specification, grind the journals and install undersize bearings, or replace the crankshaft.

Crankshaft Specifications

Main Bearing Journals	6SY and 8SY
Standard Diameter	107.978 - 108.000 mm (4.2511 - 4.2520 in.)
Undersize 1 Diameter	107.728 - 107.750 mm (4.2412 - 4.2421 in.)
Undersize 2 Diameter	107.428 - 107.450 mm (4.2294 - 4.2303 in.)
Undersize 3 Diameter	107.228 - 107.250 mm (4.2216 - 4.2224 in.)
Undersize 4 Diameter	106.978 - 107.000 mm (4.2117 - 4.2126 in.)
Oil Hole Radius	4.75 - 4.85 mm (0.187 - 0.191 in.)
Surface Quality	0.25 Ra

Connecting Rod Journals	6SY and 8SY
Standard Diameter	86.978 - 87.000 mm (3.4247 - 3.4252 in.)
Undersize 1 Diameter	86.728 - 86.750 mm (3.4247-3.4153 in.)
Undersize 2 Diameter	86.478 - 86.500 mm (3.4046 - 3.4055 in.)
Undersize 3 Diameter	86.228 - 86.250 mm (3.3948 - 3.3957 in.)
Undersize 4 Diameter	85.978 - 86.000 mm (3.3850 - 3.3858 in.)
Hole Recess Radius	4.8 - 5.2 mm (0.189 - 0.205 in.)
Surface Quality	0.25 Ra (roughness average)
Maximum Width	56.05 mm (2.207 in.)
Oil Clearance	0.051 - 0.114 mm (0.0020-0.0045 in.)

Cylinder Block and Crankshaft

ENGINE

Thrust Bearing	6SY and 8SY
Standard Thickness	3.37 - 3.43 mm (0.133 - 0.135 in.)
Oversize 1 Thickness	3.45 - 3.51 mm (0.136 - 0.138 in.)
Oversize 2 Thickness	3.50 - 3.56 mm (0.138 - 0.140 in.)
Oversize 3 Thickness	3.63 - 3.69 mm (0.143 - 0.145 in.))
Oversize 4 Thickness	3.88 - 3.94 mm (0.153 - 0.155 in)
End Play	0.138 - 0.380 mm (0.0054 - 0.0149 in.)

Recondition the Crankshaft

If any the crankshaft journals do not meet specifications, it may be possible to grind any or all of them to an undersize. The connecting rod bearings, main bearings and thrust bearing inserts are available undersize. If the journals are ground undersize, the finishing standards must be adhered to.

Checking and Grinding

- When regrinding, stated undersizes must be complied with. Suitable bearings are available for these sizes.

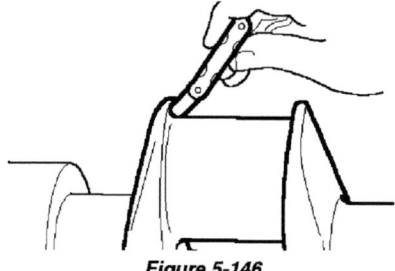

Figure 5-146

- It is important that the fillet radius of the journals is correct (**Figure 5-146**).
- After grinding the journals, the oil hole should be rounded off and polished.

Inspect the Cylinder Block

Reconditioning

Heat arising from the main bearings seizing and rotating in the cylinder block will change the properties of the material in the cylinder block. These cylinder blocks must be discarded.

If the main bearing seizes but does not rotate in the cylinder block, the cylinder block can be overhauled. The main bearing bore roundness must be within specifications. Machining out-of-round main bearing seats is not recommended.

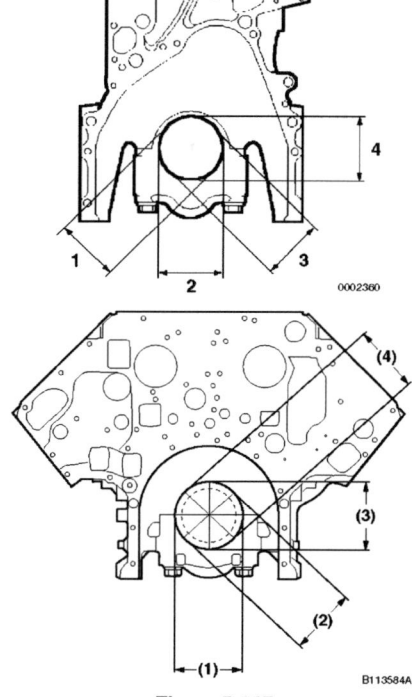

Figure 5-147

ENGINE

Cylinder Block and Crankshaft

1. Remove all main bearing inserts. Ensure the bearing seating surfaces are free of any debris. Install the main bearing caps and tighten to 50 N·m (37 ft-lb) plus 90°.
2. Measure the diameter of each main bearing bore at four different positions **(Figure 5-147)**.

Specifications

Main Bearing Bore Diameter	
Standard	112.200-112.222 mm (4.4173-4.4182 in.)
Out-of-Round (Maximum)	0.016 mm (0.0006 in.)

3. Ensure that oil passages are clear and unobstructed.
4. Check for discoloration or evidence of cracks. If a fracture is suspected, use the color check method or the Magnaflux method to determine if the cylinder block is fractured.

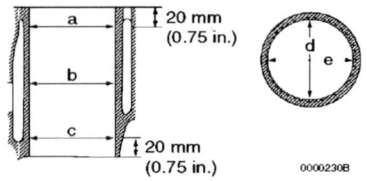

Figure 5-148

5. Measure cylinders for roundness, taper, and inspect for evidence of scoring. Consider honing or replacing the damaged liner(s) if the measurements are not within specification.
6. Take measurements at three places *(a, b, c)*, and in two directions *(d and e)* in each cylinder.

Install Crankshaft

NOTICE: Ensure the bearing inserts and bearing mounting surfaces are absolutely clean and free of oil.

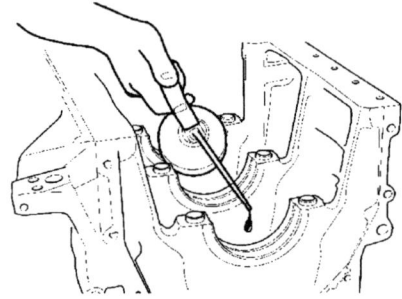

Figure 5-149

1. Install the main bearing inserts in the cylinder block and main bearing caps. Apply a generous amount of clean engine oil **(Figure 5-149)** to the bearing inserts and crankshaft journals. Ensure all oil holes are properly aligned.
2. Install thrust bearings.

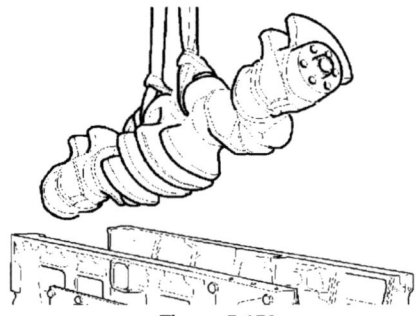

Figure 5-150

3. Carefully lower the crankshaft into place.
NOTICE: The main bearing caps are marked and must be installed in their original positions.

Cylinder Block and Crankshaft | ENGINE

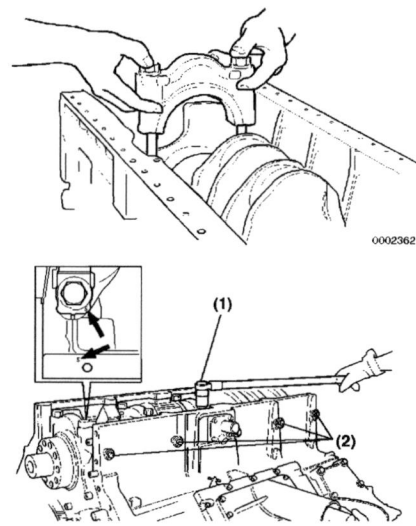

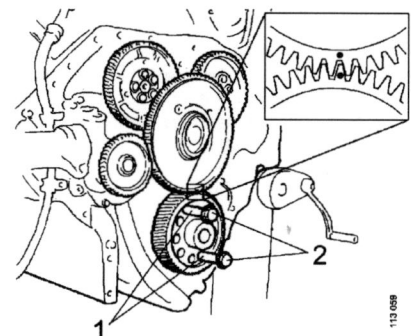

Figure 5-151

Figure 5-152

4. Install main bearing caps. Lubricate and tighten bearing cap bolts (**Figure 5-151, (1)**) to specification.

5. **8SY:** Lubricate and install main bearing side bolts (**Figure 5-151, (2)**) and tighten to specifications.

Main Bearing Bolt Torque

Item	6SY	8SY
Main Bearing Cap Bolts (torque-turn)	S/N: 6 513 632 and before: 50 N·m (37 ft-lb) plus 90°	90 N·m (66 ft-lb) plus 90°
	S/N: 6 513 633 and later: 200 N·m (148 ft-lb) plus 90°	
Main Bearing Side Bolts	-	180 N·m (133 ft-lb)

6. Install crankshaft gear and temporarily retain using two flywheel bolts (**Figure 5-152, (2)**) and 50 mm (2 in.) spacers (**Figure 5-152, (1)**). Ensure the timing marks are aligned. *See Crankshaft Gear on page 5-69.*

7. Install pistons and connecting rods. Install piston cooling nozzles. *See Install the Piston and Connecting Rod on page 5-45.*

8. Install oil pump, oil suction pipe with strainer and the oil sump. *See Oil Pump on page 8-14.*

9. Install spacing sleeve on crankshaft journal. Install driver and crankshaft damper. Tighten to 135 N·m (100 ft-lb).

10. Install new seal in front cover/housing. *See Replace the Front Crankshaft Seal on page 5-90.*

11. Install front seal housing using a new gasket. *See Install the Front Gear Housing - 8SY on page 5-62.*

12. Install belt pulley and tighten bolts to:
    - **6SY:** 110 N·m (81 ft-lb)
    - **8SY:** 92 N·m (68 ft-lb)

13. Install flywheel housing. *See Install the Flywheel Housing on page 5-53.*

14. Install flywheel. *See Install the Flywheel on page 5-54.*

15. Install cylinder heads. *See Install the Cylinder Head on page 5-34.*

ENGINE

Cylinder Block and Crankshaft

Replace the Front Crankshaft Seal

1. Remove belt(s), crankshaft damper and belt pulley. *NOTICE: **8SY engines**: The crankshaft seal seals against the hub of the belt pulley. Use care not to damage the sealing surface of pulley **(Figure 5-153)**.*

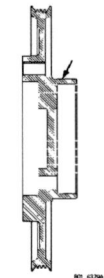

Figure 5-153

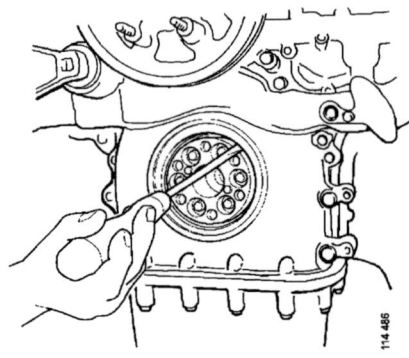

Figure 5-155

3. Pull or pry seal from the cover **(Figure 5-155)**. Take care to avoid damaging the seal mounting surface in the cover.
4. Wipe the sealing surface in the cover clean.

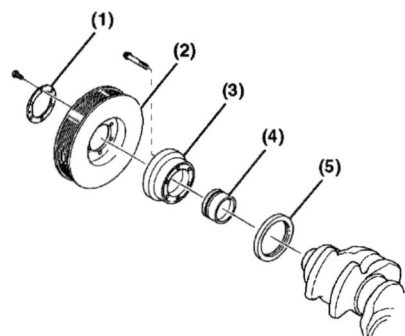

1 – Washer
2 – Pulley
3 – Driver
4 – Spacing Sleeve
5 – Seal

Figure 5-154

2. **6SY:** Remove driver bolts and remove driver **(Figure 5-154, (3))**. Use care not to damage the sealing surface of driver.

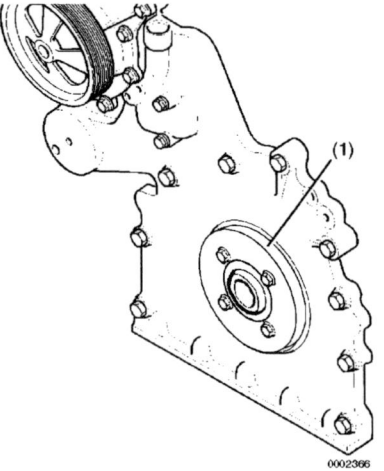

EXHAUST MANIFOLD

Replacing Gaskets

1. **WARNING!** *Make sure that all connections are tightened to specifications after repair is made to the exhaust system.* Remove the bolts between the exhaust manifold and the turbocharger connection pipe.
2. Remove the bolts and remove the exhaust manifold.
3. Scrape away the gaskets from the exhaust manifolds and cylinder head.
4. Lubricate the joints with heat-resistant grease and install new gaskets.
5. Install new O-rings in the water seals.
6. Install the water-cooled exhaust manifold. Tighten bolts to:
   - **6SY:** 59 N·m (44 ft-lb)
   - **8SY:** 63 N·m (46 ft-lb)
7. Install new O-rings and seal. Connect the turbocharger pipe. Tighten the bolts to 63 N·m (46 ft-lb).

Figure 5-156

5. NOTICE: The crankshaft seal must be installed dry and must not be lubricated. The sleeve in the seal should be left in place until the seal is installed. Place new seal on seal installer **(Figure 5-156, (1))** and press in place by tightening the bolts alternately. The seal is correctly installed when the tool contacts the cover.
6. Remove the tool by threading the bolts into the threaded holes of the special tool.
7. Wipe clean the sealing surface of the driver (6SY) or belt pulley (8SY).
8. **6SY:** Install a new seal on the end surface of the driver and push the driver onto the spacing sleeve on the end of the crankshaft.
9. **6SY:** Install the driver to the crankshaft flange and tighten the flange bolts to 135 N·m (100 ft-lb).
10. **6SY:** Install crankshaft damper and belt pulley. Tighten to 110 N·m (81 ft-lb).
11. **8SY:** Install belt pulley. Tighten to 92 N·m (68 ft-lb).
12. Install belt(s). *See Replace Alternator Belt on page 11-9* for the correct belt routing.

ENGINE

LIFTING THE ENGINE

6SY Engines

1. Disconnect negative (-) battery cable.
2. Drain engine oil and coolant.
3. Detach engine from reverse gear.
4. Detach the pipe between the seawater pump and heat exchanger. Remove the seawater pump.
5. Remove turbocharger oil pipes.
6. Remove starter motor wiring and alternator wiring.
7. Remove wiring to the control unit.
8. Remove fuel connection. *See Replace the Fuel Feed Pump on page 6-13.*
9. Disconnect pipe to the gearbox cooler or reversing gear oil cooler.
10. Fasten lifting chain (OEM Part No. 98 094) **(Figure 5-157, (1))** to the rear lifting eyes. DANGER! *ALWAYS use lifting equipment with sufficient capacity to lift the marine engine. Additional equipment is necessary to lift the marine engine and marine gear together.*
    DANGER! *NEVER stand under hoisted engine. If the hoist mechanism fails, the engine will fall on you, causing death or serious injury.* CAUTION! *Avoid injury or equipment damage due to engine falling. ALWAYS secure the engine solidly to prevent the engine from falling during service.*
11. Fasten lever block (OEM Part No. 587 308) **(Figure 5-157, (2))** to the front lifting eye.
12. Disconnect all engine mounts. *NOTICE: The lifting eyes are designed for a maximum inclination angle of 30° when lifting the engine.*

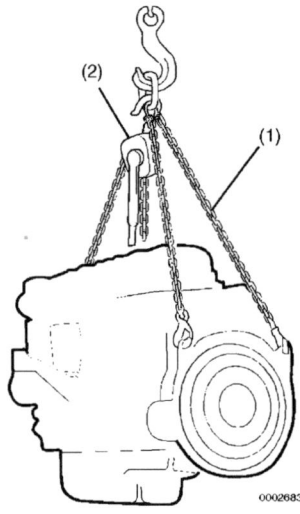

Figure 5-157

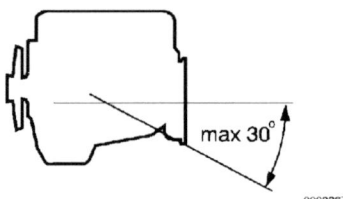

Figure 5-158

13. Carefully lift engine using the lever block to adjust the angle of the engine **(Figure 5-158)**. DANGER! *NEVER stand under hoisted marine engine. If the hoist mechanism fails, the marine engine will fall on you.*
14. Place engine on suitable engine support or attach to an engine repair stand of sufficient weight capacity. WARNING! *ALWAYS secure the engine solidly to prevent injury or damage to parts due to the engine falling during work on the engine.*

8SY Engines

1. Disconnect negative (-) battery cable.
2. Drain engine oil and coolant.

Attaching Engine to Repair Stand

ENGINE

3. Detach engine from reverse gear.
4. Detach the pipe between the seawater pump and heat exchanger. Remove the seawater pump.
5. Remove turbocharger oil pipes.
6. Remove starter motor wiring and alternator wiring.
7. Remove wiring to the control unit.
8. Remove fuel connection. *See Replace the Fuel Feed Pump on page 6-13.*
9. Disconnect connecting pipe to the gearbox cooler or reversing gear oil cooler.
10. Attach two lifting eyes (OEM Part No. 1 360 442) (or similar tool) onto the flywheel housing over the center in the 10 o'clock to 2 o'clock position.
11. Fasten lifting chain (OEM Part No. 98 094) to the rear lifting eyes.
12. Fasten lever block (OEM Part No. 587 308) to the front lifting eye. *NOTICE: The engine lifting eyes are sized for lifting the engine only, not the engine together with connected equipment (gearbox, reverse gear, etc.) or frame. All three lifting eyes must be used.*
13. Disconnect all engine mounts. *NOTICE: The lifting eyes are designed for a maximum inclination angle of 20° when lifting the engine.*
14. Carefully lift engine using the lever block to adjust the angle of the engine.
15. Place engine on suitable engine support or attach to an engine repair stand of sufficient weight capacity. **WARNING!** *ALWAYS secure the engine solidly to prevent injury or damage to parts due to the engine falling during work on the engine.*

ATTACHING ENGINE TO REPAIR STAND

When attaching and engine to a repair stand, be sure to use a stand of adequate capacity to safely support the engine to be repaired and that it is attached to the engine. **CAUTION!** *Avoid injury or equipment damage due to engine falling.* *ALWAYS secure the engine solidly to prevent the engine from falling during service.*

ENGINE   **Attaching Engine to Repair Stand**

This Page Intentionally Left Blank

Section 6

FUEL SYSTEM

Page

Safety Precautions	6-3
Introduction	6-3
Specifications	6-4
Special Service Tools	6-5
Fuel System Components	6-6
Fuel Delivery Components	6-6
Fuel Injector Components	6-7
Tests and Adjustments	6-7
Adjust the Unit Injectors	6-7
Measure the Fuel Feed Pump Pressure	6-7
Test the Fuel Pressure Relief Valve	6-8
Repair	6-8
Remove the Unit Injector	6-8
Install the Unit Injector	6-11
Replace the Fuel Feed Pump	6-13
Replace the Fuel Filter and Fuel Filter / Water Separator	6-14
Replace Return Fuel Line	6-15
Bleed the Fuel System	6-17

FUEL SYSTEM

This Page Intentionally Left Blank

FUEL SYSTEM

SAFETY PRECAUTIONS

⚠ WARNING
Fire Hazard

Diesel fuel is flammable and explosive under certain conditions. NEVER put diesel fuel or other flammable material such as oil, hay or dried grass near the engine during engine operation or shortly after shutdown.

Never use a shop rag to catch the fuel.

ALWAYS put an approved fuel container under the opening whenever you remove any fuel system component (such as changing the fuel filter). Dispose of waste properly.

Wipe up all spills immediately.

High-Pressure Hazard

Avoid injury from escaping fuel under pressure. NEVER check for a fuel leak with your hands. ALWAYS use a piece of wood or cardboard.

INTRODUCTION

This section of the *Service Manual* describes the procedures necessary to remove, install, and adjust the PDE31 and PDE32 unit injectors and their associated system components as used on the Yanmar 6SY and 8SY engines.

FUEL SYSTEM

SPECIFICATIONS

Test and Adjustment Specifications

Inspection Item		Specification	Reference Page
PDE31 Unit Injector Height		66.8 - 67.0 mm (2.63 - 2.64 in.)	See Adjusting Unit Injectors on page 5-19
PDE32 Unit Injector Height		69.8 - 70.0 mm (2.75 - 2.76 in.)	
Fuel Pressure	Minimum at 500 rpm	4.5 bar (65 psi)	See Measure the Fuel Feed Pump Pressure on page 6-7
	Minimum at 1900 rpm	5.5 bar (80 psi)	
Fuel Pressure Relief Valve Pressure	Minimum (Hand Pumping)	4.5 bar (65 psi)	See Test the Fuel Pressure Relief Valve on page 6-8
	Maximum at 1500 rpm	7.5 bar (109 psi)	
Return Line Tubing	6 mm OD	Minimum Internal Diameter of Bend	35 mm (1.38 in.)	See Replace Return Fuel Line on page 6-15
	12 mm OD		95 mm (3.74 in.)	

Special Torque Chart

Component		Tightening Torque	Lubricating Oil Application (Thread Portion and Seat Surface)	Reference Page
Rocker Arm Adjusting Screw Locknut		39 N·m (29 ft-lb)	-	See Adjust Valve and Unit Injector Clearances on page 5-18
Rocker Arm Shaft Bolt		105 N·m (77 ft-lb)	Not Applied	See Install the Unit Injector on page 6-11
Unit Injector Fork Clamp Bolt (torque-turn)		20 N·m (133 in.-lb) plus 75°	Not Applied	
Injector Electrical Terminal Screw		2 N·m (283 in.-oz)	Not Applied	
Rocker Cover Bolt (Upper and Lower Cover)		26 N·m (19 ft-lb)	Not Applied	
Return Line Nut	6 mm OD Tubing	10 N·m (89 in.-lb)	-	See Replace Return Fuel Line on page 6-15
	12 mm OD Tubing	20 N·m (177 in.-lb)	-	

Special Service Tools　　　　　　　　　　　　　　　　　　　　　　　**FUEL SYSTEM**

SPECIAL SERVICE TOOLS

Note: The tool numbers used in this section are either Yanmar or Scania part numbers. Yanmar part numbers are referred to as **Yanmar Part No.** and Scania part numbers are referred to as **OEM Part No.** Tools not having part numbers must be acquired locally.

No.	Tool Name	Applicable Model and Tool Size	Illustration
1	Unit Injector Adjustment Tool (For Adjusting Unit Injectors)	OEM Part No. 99 414 - PDE31 OEM Part No. 99 442 - PDE32	0002672
2	Flywheel Turning Tool	OEM Part No. 99 309	0002660
3	Slide Hammer (For Removing Unit Injectors)	OEM Part No. 87 596	0002655
4	Fuel Pressure Gauge (For Measuring Fuel System Pressure)	OEM Part No. 98 113	
5	Torque Screwdriver (For Connecting Cables to Injector)	OEM Part No. 288 179	

FUEL SYSTEM

FUEL SYSTEM COMPONENTS

Fuel Delivery Components

6SY Engines

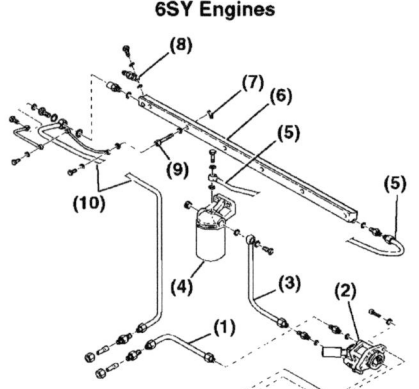

1 – Fuel Supply Line
2 – Fuel Feed Pump
3 – Fuel Supply to Filter
4 – Fuel Filter
5 – Fuel Supply to Fuel Manifold
6 – Fuel Manifold
7 – Gasket
8 – Bleeder Valve
9 – Banjo Bolt
10 – Fuel Return Line

Figure 6-1

8SY Engines

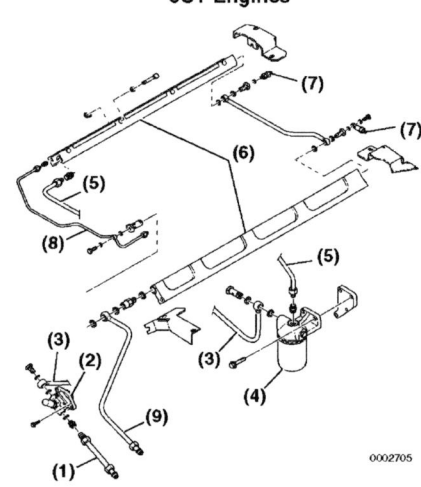

1 – Fuel Supply Line
2 – Fuel Feed Pump
3 – Fuel Supply to Filter
4 – Fuel Filter
5 – Fuel Supply to Left Fuel Manifold
6 – Fuel Manifold (2 used)
7 – Bleeder Valve
8 – Fuel Leak-Off Line
9 – Fuel Return Line

Figure 6-2

Fuel Injector Components

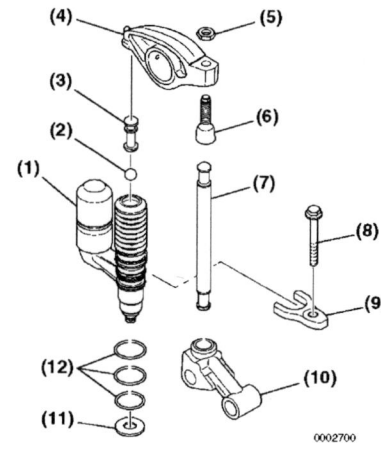

1 – Unit Injector Assembly
2 – Ball
3 – Link
4 – Rocker Arm
5 – Jam Nut
6 – Adjusting Screw
7 – Pushrod
8 – Clamp Fork Bolt
9 – Clamp Fork
10 – Roller Tappet
11 – Gasket
12 – O-Ring

Figure 6-3

FUEL SYSTEM

TESTS AND ADJUSTMENTS

NOTICE: All work that involves opening the fuel system must be completed as follows:

- Bleed the system. *See Bleed the Fuel System on page 6-17.*
- Start engine and check for leaks. Allow engine to run until it is running smoothly.
- Check and delete any fault codes that are registered in the control unit after the work has been completed.

Adjust the Unit Injectors

Unit injectors and valves should be adjusted at the same time. *See Adjust Valve and Unit Injector Clearances on page 5-18 for procedures.*

Measure the Fuel Feed Pump Pressure

Procedure

1. Replace fuel filter and bleed fuel system before measuring.

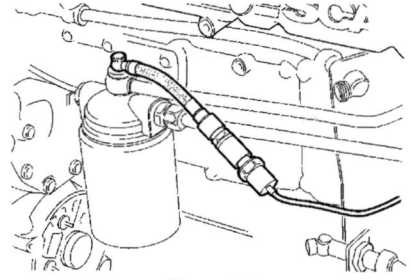

Figure 6-4

2. Connect a pressure gauge to the fuel filter outlet connection as shown in **Figure 6-4**.
3. Start engine and set speed to 500 rpm. Read and record pressure.
4. Increase engine speed to 1900 rpm. Read and record pressure.

FUEL SYSTEM
Repair

Specifications

Inspection Item	RPM	Pressure (Min.)
Fuel Feed Pump Pressure	500 rpm	4.5 bar (65 psi)
	1900 rpm	5.5 bar (80 psi)

Results

- If pressure reading is below specification, inspect fuel line connections, pressure relief valve, fuel filter and feed pump.

Test the Fuel Pressure Relief Valve

Procedure

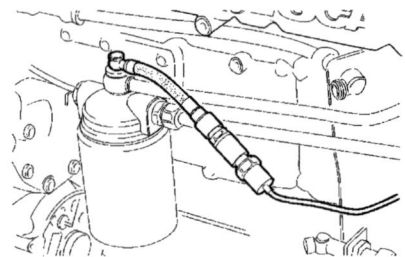

Figure 6-5

1. Connect a pressure gauge to the fuel filter outlet connection as shown in **Figure 6-5**.
2. Turn the key switch to the ON position. Do not start the engine at this time.
3. Operate the hand pump while reading the pressure gauge. Read and record pressure.
4. Start the engine and increase the speed to 1500 rpm. Read and record pressure.

Specifications

Inspection Item	RPM	Pressure
Fuel Pressure Relief	Hand-Operated	4.5 bar (65 psi) (Min.)
	1500 rpm	7.5 bar (109 psi) (Max.)

Results

- If test pressure reading is not within specifications, the fuel pressure relief valve must be replaced.

REPAIR

NOTICE: All work that involves opening the fuel system must be completed as follows:

- Bleed the system. *See Bleed the Fuel System on page 6-17.*
- Start engine and check for leaks. Allow engine to run until it is running smoothly.
- Check and delete any fault codes that are registered in the control unit after the work has been completed.

Remove the Unit Injector

1. Disconnect the battery(s), negative (-) cable first.
2. Shut off all valves in the fuel supply system. **CAUTION!** *Ensure that no fuel enters the cylinder from the disconnected fuel system components. If fuel runs into the combustion chamber, it must be removed immediately using a pump.*

6SY Engines

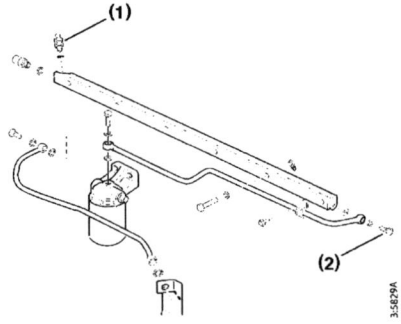

Figure 6-6

Repair

FUEL SYSTEM

8SY Engines

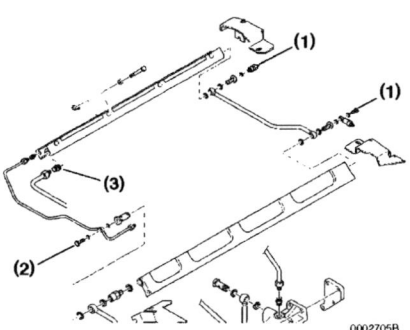

Figure 6-7

3. Open bleeder valve(s) **(Figure 6-6, (1)) or (Figure 6-7, (1))** and drain fuel system by loosening banjo bolt **(Figure 6-6, (2)) or (Figure 6-7, (2))** on opposite end of fuel manifold. On 8SY engines, also loosen union **(Figure 6-6, (3)) or (Figure 6-7, (3))**.
4. Clean rocker cover and surrounding area.
5. Remove upper rocker cover. *See Remove and Install Rocker Covers on page 5-23.*

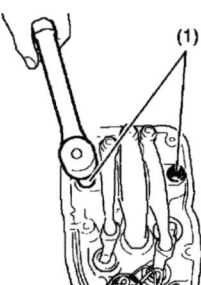

Figure 6-8

6. Remove bolts **(Figure 6-8, (1))** retaining the rocker arm shaft. Alternately loosen each bolt until valve tension is relieved. **WARNING!** *Never lean over the engine when removing the rocker arm shaft. The unit injector spring is under considerable tension and can unexpectedly come loose, causing personal injury.*

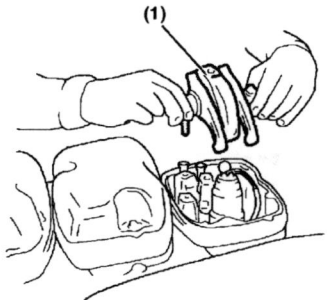

Figure 6-9

Note: If the spring comes loose from the unit injector, the unit injector must be replaced.

7. Remove rocker arm shaft assembly **(Figure 6-9, (1))**. **CAUTION!** *Identify all parts and their location using an appropriate method. It is important that all parts are returned to the same position during the reassembly process.*

FUEL SYSTEM   Repair

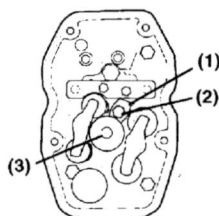

Figure 6-10

1 – Fork Clamp
2 – Fork Clamp Bolt
3 – Unit Injector

8. Remove unit injector fork clamp bolt **(Figure 6-10, (2))** and fork clamp **(Figure 6-10, (1))**.

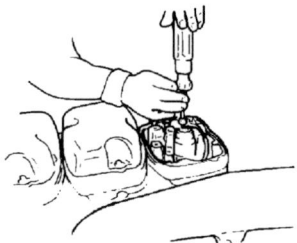

Figure 6-11

9. Disconnect electrical wires from unit injector. The screws cannot be removed **(Figure 6-11)**.

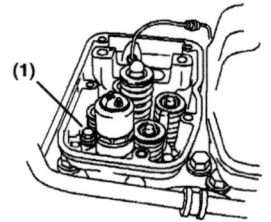

Figure 6-12

10. Remove one lower rocker cover bolt **(Figure 6-12, (1))** to provide easier positioning of the slide hammer. *NOTICE: If the slide hammer is placed directly under the solenoid valve, there is a risk of breaking the solenoid valve.*

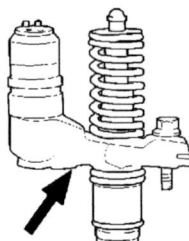

Figure 6-13

11. Rotate unit injector counterclockwise until it stops. Position slide hammer under solenoid valve at the approximate location **(Figure 6-13)**. *NOTICE: Never lift the unit injector by the spring. The spring can come loose resulting in the need to replace the unit injector.*

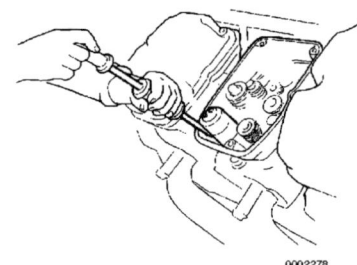

Figure 6-14

12. Remove unit injector using a slide hammer. If unit injector is stuck, tap carefully with rubber mallet on the solenoid valve housing **(Figure 6-14)**.

13. If injector gasket did not come out with injector, remove it from the bottom of the injector seat. *NOTICE: The unit injector must not be disassembled. Replace the entire unit as necessary.*

Repair

FUEL SYSTEM

Install the Unit Injector

1. Make sure that the old gasket is not at the bottom of the injector seat. Clean the sealing surfaces in the injector seat.

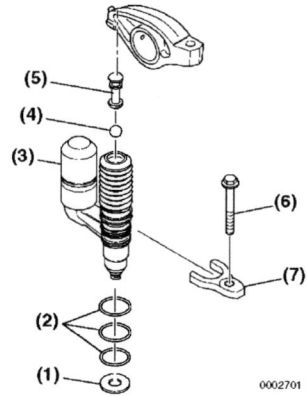

1 – Gasket
2 – O-Ring
3 – Unit Injector
4 – Ball
5 – Link
6 – Bolt
7 – Fork Clamp

Figure 6-15

2. Lubricate the unit injector O-rings with O-ring grease (OEM Part No.1 402 039 or equivalent). NOTICE: Always install new O-rings and sealing washer when installing a unit injector. Make sure all sealing surfaces are clean.

3. Install new gasket on unit injector. The rubber insert of the gasket will keep gasket in place on the unit injector.

Note: Ensure fork clamp and bolt are dry and free of oil.

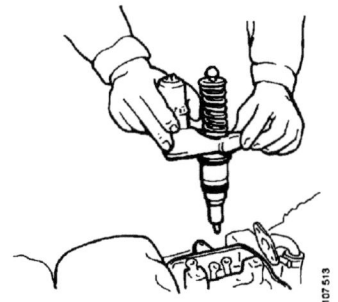

Figure 6-16

4. Place the bolt in the fork clamp. Place the fork clamp in position on the unit injector and insert the injector into the cylinder head. Press the unit injector down by hand as far as possible **(Figure 6-16)**. NOTICE: NEVER hit the unit injector spring with a mallet. Doing so will disengage the spring retainer and render the injector unusable.

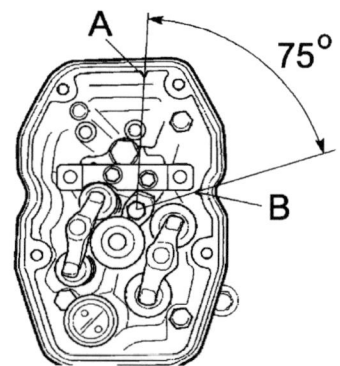

Figure 6-17

5. Torque-turn tighten the bolt to 20 N·m (133 in.-lb) plus an additional 75°. There are two marks **(Figure 6-17, (A and B))** on the lower rocker cover with a 75° angle between them.

FUEL SYSTEM

Repair

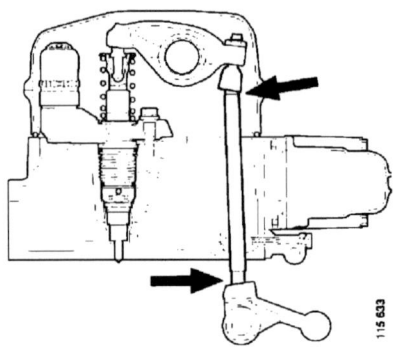

Figure 6-18

6. Install the rocker shaft and rockers. Tighten the bolts to 105 N·m (77 ft-lb).

7. Ensure the pushrods are in their correct positions, including the injector ball and link. Ensure the unit injector pushrod is firmly secured in its lower position by the retaining ring **(Figure 6-18)**.

8. Adjust the unit injector. *See Adjust Valve and Unit Injector Clearances on page 5-18.*

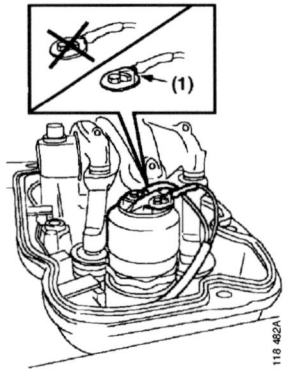

Figure 6-19

NOTICE: *Ensure injector wire terminals are installed with the bosses* **(Figure 6-19, (1))** *facing up.*

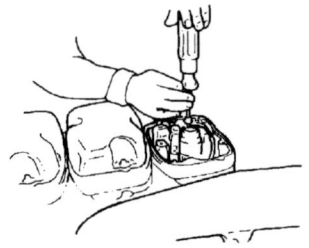

Figure 6-20

9. Connect wires on the unit injectors. Their relative position is not important. Use torque screwdriver *588 179* (or similar tool) to tighten screws to 2 N·m (283 in.-oz) **(Figure 6-20)**.
NOTICE: *Tighten screws to correct torque. The entire unit injector must be replaced if screws shear off due to over tightening.*

10. Install upper rocker cover and tighten bolts to 26 N·m (19 ft-lb). *See Remove and Install Rocker Covers on page 5-23.*

6SY Engines

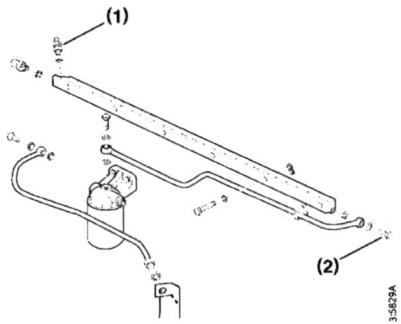

Figure 6-21

FUEL SYSTEM

8SY Engines

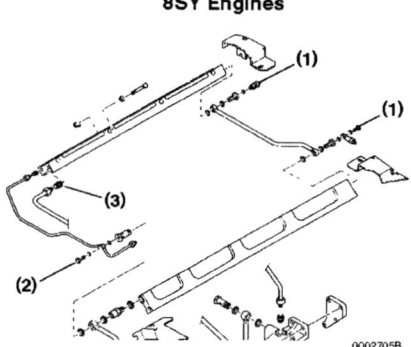

Figure 6-22

6SY Engines

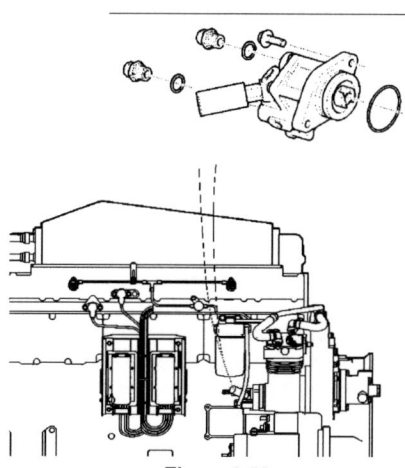

Figure 6-23

8SY Engines

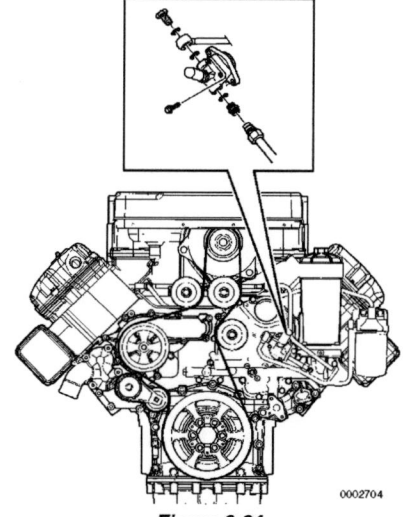

Figure 6-24

11. Close bleeder valve(s) **(Figure 6-21, (1))** or **(Figure 6-22, (1))** and tighten banjo bolt(s) **(Figure 6-21, (2))** or **(Figure 6-22, (2))**.
12. Turn on fuel supply valves.
13. Fill and bleed fuel system. *See Bleed the Fuel System on page 6-17.*
14. Connect the battery(s), negative (-) cable last.
15. Start the engine and check for fuel leaks. Allow the engine to run until it is running smoothly.
16. Check and delete any fault codes that are registered in the control unit after the work has been completed. *See Fault Codes on page 13-18.*

Replace the Fuel Feed Pump

1. Disconnect the battery(s), negative (-) cable first.
2. Shut off all valves in fuel supply system.
3. Clean outside of fuel feed pump.

FUEL SYSTEM

Repair

4. Remove supply and pressure lines from fuel feed pump. Install caps or plugs on all open fittings to prevent contamination of the fuel system.
5. Remove two bolts and remove the fuel feed pump.
6. Place a new O-ring onto the fuel feed pump and lubricate with O-ring grease (OEM Part No.1 402 039 or equivalent).
7. Install fuel feed pump.
8. Connect the suction and pressure lines.
9. Bleed fuel system. *See Bleed the Fuel System on page 6-17.*
10. Start the engine and check for leaks.
11. Check and delete any fault codes that are registered in the control unit after the work has been completed. *See Fault Codes on page 13-18.*

If the fuel feed pump refuses to prime:

The fuel feed pump may not prime because it is working against fuel remaining in the fuel system. Perform the following steps:

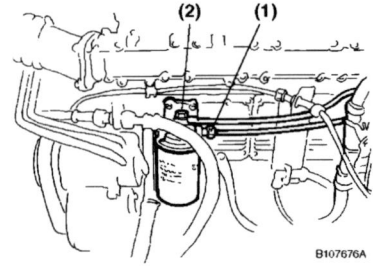

1 – Inlet Pipe
2 – Outlet Pipe

Figure 6-25

1. Detach the inlet pipe **(Figure 6-25, (1))** at the fuel filter. **WARNING!** *Wear eye protection. The fuel system is under pressure and fuel could spray out when you remove any fuel system component.*

2. Operate the hand pump until resistance is felt and the fuel begins to flow from the pipe.
3. **If pump still refuses to prime:** Disconnect the feed pump outlet pipe **(Figure 6-25, (2))**. Pump until fuel begins to run out of the pipe.
4. Bleed the fuel system. *See Bleed the Fuel System on page 6-17.*

Replace the Fuel Filter and Fuel Filter / Water Separator

Replace the Fuel Filter

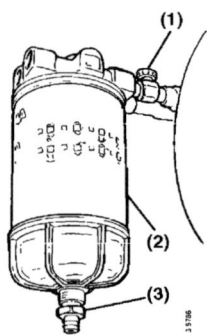

Figure 6-26

1. Close the fuel tank cock **(Figure 6-26, (1))**.
2. Loosen the drain plug **(Figure 6-26, (3))** and drain off any water and dirt collected inside. *NOTICE: If the fuel filter / water separator is positioned higher than the fuel level in the fuel tank, water may not drip out when the fuel filter / water separator drain cock is opened. If this happens, turn the air vent screw on the top of the fuel filter / water separator 2-3 turns counterclockwise. Be sure to tighten the air vent screw after the water has drained out.*

Repair

FUEL SYSTEM

6SY Engines

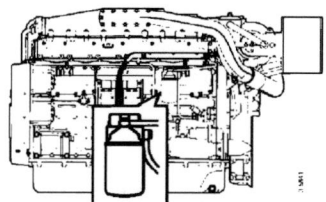

Figure 6-27

8SY Engines

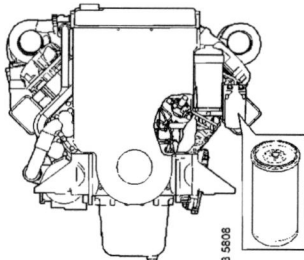

Figure 6-28

3. Clean the outside of the filter and remove it by turning it counterclockwise.
4. Install a new Yanmar filter and tighten by hand.
5. Bleed the fuel system. *See Bleed the Fuel System on page 6-17.*

Replace the Fuel Filter / Water Separator

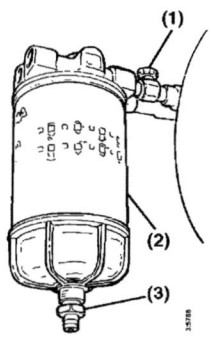

Figure 6-29

1. Close the fuel tank cock **(Figure 6-29, (1))**.
2. Loosen the drain plug **(Figure 6-29, (3))** at the bottom of the fuel filter / water separator and drain off any water and dirt.
3. Turn the filter container **(Figure 6-29, (2))** counterclockwise to remove.
4. Remove the old filter. Lubricate the seal, insert the new filter into the container and hand-tighten.
5. Turn the filter container clockwise to install.
6. Open the fuel tank cock **(Figure 6-29, (1))**.
7. After reassembling the fuel filter / water separator, vent air from the fuel system. *See Bleed the Fuel System on page 6-17.*

Replace Return Fuel Line

1. Disconnect the battery(s), negative (-) cable first.
2. Shut off all valves in the fuel supply system.
3. Open the bleeder valve and drain the fuel system by loosening the banjo screw on the back of the fuel manifold. Catch fuel in an appropriate container.

FUEL SYSTEM

Repair

6SY Engines

Specifications

Tubing Diameter	Minimum Internal Diameter of Bend
6 mm Union Nut	35 mm (1.38 in.)
12 mm Union Nut	95 mm (3.74 in.)

Replacing Plastic Tubing on a Union

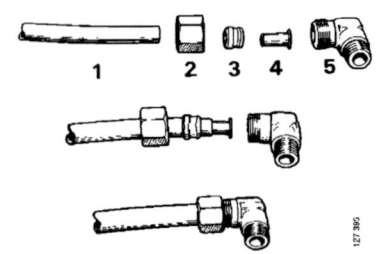

1 – Plastic Tube
2 – Union Nut
3 – Ferrule
4 – Insert Sleeve
5 – Union

Figure 6-30

1. Remove tubing to be replaced and use as pattern to cut the new tubing to length.
   NOTICE: Avoid sharp bends when installing plastic tubing. If the tubing is bent into a diameter smaller than specified, a kink may develop in the tubing and restrict the fuel flow.
2. Install union nut, ferrule and insert sleeve in end of tubing.
3. Insert tubing into union until it bottoms.
4. Hold tubing securely in the union and install union nut. Tighten union nut to specification.

Specifications

Tubing Diameter	Torque
6 mm	10 N·m (89 in.-lb)
12 mm	20 N·m (177 in.-lb)

Replacing Plastic Tubing on a Banjo Union

1. Remove tubing to be replaced.

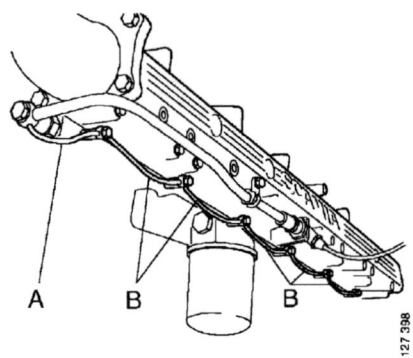

Figure 6-31

2. Cut plastic tubing with pipe cutter (OEM Part No. 587 258 or similar tool) to length shown in **Figure 6-31**:

   (Figure 6-31, (A)) Length = 106 mm (4.17 in.)

   (Figure 6-31, (B)) Length = 151 mm (5.94 in.)

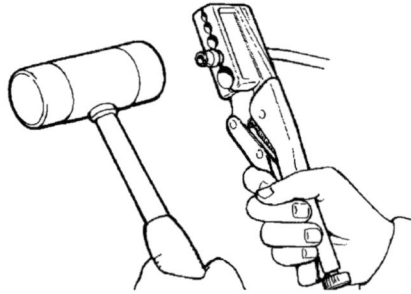

Figure 6-32

3. Hold plastic tubing tightly with pliers (OEM Part No. 587 956 or similar tool) and install the union.
4. Tap the union onto the tubing using a plastic mallet **(Figure 6-32)**. *NOTICE: Do not use a metal hammer. Damage to the union will result.*

Repair

FUEL SYSTEM

8SY Engines

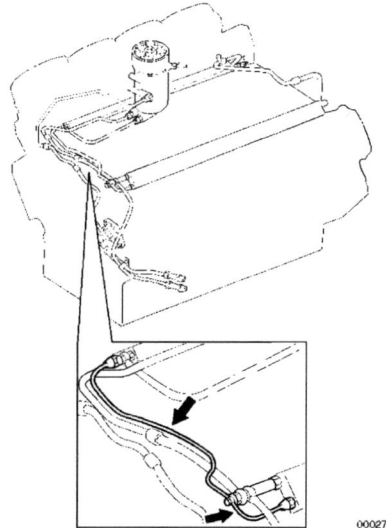

Figure 6-33

NOTICE: The return line is pre-shaped and must not be replaced with bulk plastic tubing because of the risk of wear against other parts. The return line is pre-shaped and is available as a replacement part. See parts catalog for correct part number. Install as shown **(Figure 6-33)**.

Bleed the Fuel System

The fuel system needs to be bled under the following conditions:

- Before starting the engine for the first time.
- After running out of fuel and fuel has been added to the fuel tank.
- After fuel system maintenance such as changing the fuel filter and draining the fuel filter / water separator, or replacing a fuel system component.

6SY Engines

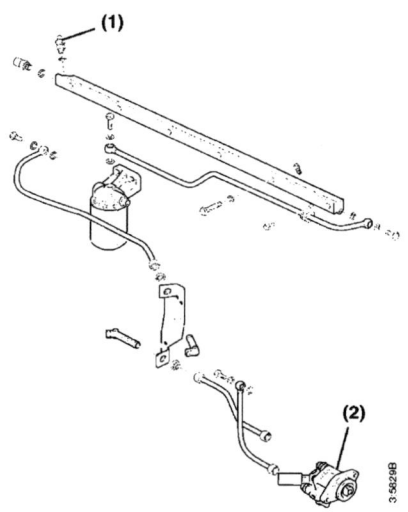

Figure 6-34

FUEL SYSTEM   Repair

8SY Engines

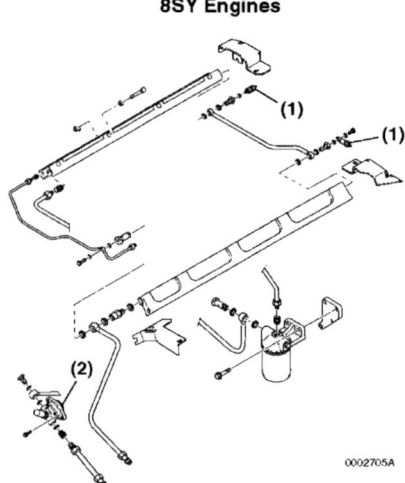

Figure 6-35

1. Install a transparent plastic hose on each fuel rail bleeder valve. Place the hoses in an appropriate container.
2. Open the bleeder valve **(Figure 6-34, (1)) or (Figure 6-35, (1))** and operate the hand pump **(Figure 6-34, (2)) or (Figure 6-35, (2))** until fuel flows without air bubbles. This may take 130 - 150 pump strokes. **WARNING!** *Place an approved container under the air bleed port when you prime the fuel system. Never use a shop rag to catch the fuel. Wipe up any spills immediately. ALWAYS close the air bleed port after you complete priming the system.*
3. Close the bleeder valves and remove the hoses.
4. Dispose of waste fuel properly.

5. Continue hand pumping until there is resistance:
   - Approximately 20 strokes after replacing the fuel filter
   - Approximately 50 strokes after replacing a fuel injector
6. Start the engine and check for leaks. *NOTICE: NEVER hold the key in the START position for longer than 15 seconds or the starter motor will overheat.*

If the engine fails to start after bleeding:
- Open the bleeder valves again and operate the hand pump until fuel without air bubbles flows out.
- Tighten the bleeder valves. Start the engine and check for leaks.

Section 7

COOLING SYSTEM

	Page
Introduction	7-3
Specifications	7-4
Special Service Tools	7-5
Tests and Adjustments	7-7
Pressure Testing Cooling System and Filler Cap	7-7
Testing the Thermostat	7-8
Repair	7-8
Drain, Flush and Fill the Engine with Engine Coolant	7-8
Venting the Cooling System - 8SY Engines Only	7-9
Coolant Pump Removal	7-10
Install Coolant Pump	7-11
Remove and Install Pulley	7-11
Change the Coolant Pump Seal	7-12
Remove and Install Thermostat	7-14
Remove and Install Fresh Water Charge Air Cooler	7-15
Remove and Install Seawater Charge Air Cooler - 6SY Engines Only	7-18
Seawater Pump	7-24
Check or Replace the Zinc Anodes	7-28

COOLING SYSTEM

This Page Intentionally Left Blank

COOLING SYSTEM

Introduction

INTRODUCTION

This section of the *Service Manual* describes the procedures necessary to service the 6SY and 8SY marine engine cooling systems.

See *Engine Piping Diagrams on page 3-6* for cooling system flow information.

NOTICE

Only use the engine coolant specified. Other engine coolants may affect warranty coverage, cause an internal buildup of rust and scale and / or shorten engine life.

Prevent dirt and debris from contaminating the engine coolant. Carefully clean the radiator cap and the surrounding area before you remove the cap.

NEVER mix different types of engine coolants. This may adversely affect the properties of the engine coolant.

COOLING SYSTEM

SPECIFICATIONS

Note: All pressure specifications are with engine at normal operating temperature.

Test and Adjustment Specifications

Inspection Item	Model	Specification			Reference Page
Cooling System Test Pressure	All	0.4 - 0.5 bar (5.8 - 7.3 psi)			See Pressure Testing Cooling System and Filler Cap on page 7-7
Filler Cap Test Pressure	All	0.4 - 0.6 bar (5.8 - 8.7 psi)			
Thermostat		Marking	Starts Opening	Fully Open	See Testing the Thermostat on page 7-8
	6SY	75°C	73 - 77°C (163 - 171°F)	87°C (189°F)	
	8SY	75°C	73 - 77°C (163 - 171°F)	87°C (189°F)	

Repair Specifications

Coolant Recovery Tank Level - Cold Engine		50 mm (2 in.) Below Filler
Coolant Pump Impeller Installation Distance		13.3 - 13.7 mm (0.524 - 0.539 in.)
Volume Including Heat Exchanger and Reserve Tank	6SY	40 L (10.5 gal)
	8SY	75 L (20 gal)

Special Torque Chart

Component		Torque	Lubricating Oil Application	Reference Page
Charge Air Cooler Bolt		26 N·m (230 in.-lb)	Not Applied	See Remove and Install Fresh Water Charge Air Cooler on page 7-15
Upper Manifold Housing Bolt	6SY	26 N·m (230 in.-lb)	Not Applied	
	8SY	50 N·m (37 ft-lb)		
Inlet Pipe V-Clamp	M6 Screw	8 N·m (71 in.-lb)	Not Applied	
	M8 Screw	20 N·m (177 in.-lb)	Not Applied	
Heat Exchanger Retaining Nut		50 N·m (37 ft-lb)	Not Applied	See Remove and Install the Heat Exchanger on page 7-20
Seawater Pump Gear Nut		100 N·m (74 ft-lb)	Not Applied	See Seawater Pump on page 7-24

Special Service Tools COOLING SYSTEM

SPECIAL SERVICE TOOLS

Note: The tool numbers used in this section are either Yanmar or Scania part numbers. Yanmar part numbers are referred to as **Yanmar Part No.** and Scania part numbers are referred to as **OEM Part No.** Tools not having part numbers must be obtained locally.

No.	Tool Name	Applicable Model and Tool Size	Illustration
1	Cooling System Tester (For Pressure-Testing the Cooling System and Filler Cap)	OEM Part No. 587 048	
2	Puller (Used for Removing Belt Pulley)	OEM Part No. 587 315	
3	Drift (Used for Removing Belt Pulley)	OEM Part No. 87 664	
4	Puller (For Removing Coolant Pump Impeller)	OEM Part No. 98 736	
5	Drift For Removing Coolant Pump Impeller)	OEM Part No. 87 664	
6	Seal Installer (For Installing Seal in Coolant Pump)	OEM Part No. 99 117	

COOLING SYSTEM

Measuring instruments

No.	Tool Name	Applicable Model and Tool Size	Illustration
7	Impeller Puller (For Removing Seawater Pump Impeller)	OEM Part No. 98 482	

Measuring instruments

No.	Instrument Name	Application	Illustration
1	Calipers	For measuring outside diameters, depth, thickness and width	0000836
2	Torque Wrench	For tightening nuts and bolts to the specified torque	0000840

Tests and Adjustments

COOLING SYSTEM

TESTS AND ADJUSTMENTS

Pressure Testing Cooling System and Filler Cap

Cooling System

Use a cooling system tester with connections compatible with the Yanmar SY series cooling system, such as Leitenberger TVK 138/3 (OEM Part No. 587 048 or similar tool).

1. Remove the coolant recovery tank filler cap.
   WARNING! ***NEVER remove the coolant filler cap if the engine is hot. Steam and hot engine coolant will escape and seriously burn you. Allow the engine to cool before attempting to remove the filler cap.***
2. Check that the lugs and sealing flange on the filler pipe are undamaged and free from anything that might prevent a good seal.
3. Check that the coolant level is correct. Fill with coolant as necessary. *See Drain, Flush and Fill the Engine with Engine Coolant on page 7-8.*

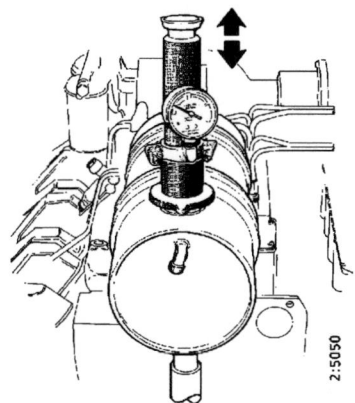

Figure 7-1

4. Install the tester and adapter in place of the radiator cap.

5. Pump until the pressure is 0.4 - 0.5 bar (5.8 - 7.3 psi) **(Figure 7-1)**.
6. If the pressure drops, there is leakage in the system. Start by checking all hoses and pipe connections.

Filler Cap

Note: Applies to cooling system with pressure cap.

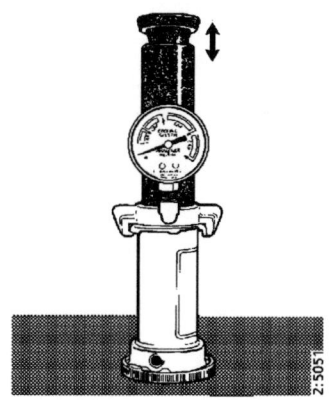

Figure 7-2

1. Connect the cap to the cooling system tester using the adapter for the cap.
2. Pump up the pressure until the cap opens **(Figure 7-2)**.
3. The tester needle should stop between 0.4 - 0.6 bar (5.8 - 8.7 psi) for pressure caps with an opening pressure of 0.5 bar (7.3 psi).

COOLING SYSTEM

Repair

Testing the Thermostat

1. The design temperature for the thermostat is stamped into the thermostat body. Find and record this number.
2. Immerse one thermostat at a time in a container of water. Suspend it so that it does not come into contact with the walls or bottom of the container.
3. Slowly heat the water and monitor the temperature with a thermometer. Stir the water.
4. Check that the thermostat begins to open at the specified temperature, and that it is fully open at the temperature given in the specifications.

If it does not open at the specified temperature, it should be replaced.

Specifications

Marking	Starts Opening	Fully Open
75°C	73 - 77°C (163 - 171°F)	87°C (189°F)

REPAIR

Drain, Flush and Fill the Engine with Engine Coolant

Cooling performance drops when coolant is contaminated with rust and scale. The coolant must be replaced periodically because its properties deteriorate over time.

1. Remove the filler cap from the coolant recovery tank. **WARNING!** *NEVER remove the coolant filler cap if the engine is hot. Steam and hot engine coolant will escape and seriously burn you. Allow the engine to cool sufficiently before attempting to remove the filler cap.* NOTICE: Prevent dirt and debris from contaminating engine coolant. Carefully clean the heat exchanger cap and surrounding area before you remove the cap.

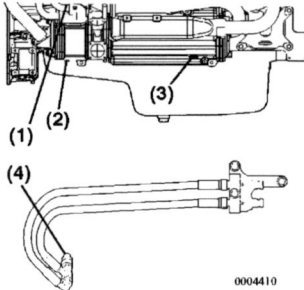

Figure 7-3

2. Drain the coolant:
   - Open the two drain taps on the two hoses (**Figure 7-3, (4)**) fastened in the side cover on the ride side of the block (**Figure 7-3, (1)**).
   - Open the drain tap located on the lower left side of the block (**Figure 7-3, (2)**).
   - Remove the two plugs (**Figure 7-3, (3)**) below the heat exchanger (if equipped).
3. Close the drain taps and reinstall the heat exchanger plugs (if equipped).

Repair

COOLING SYSTEM

4. Fold the hoses and attach them to the bracket.

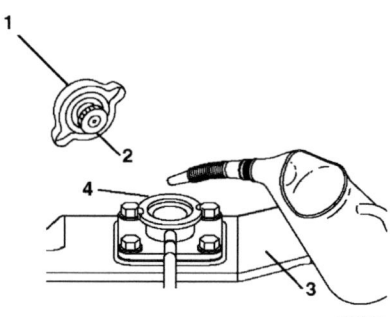

Figure 7-4

5. Inspect the cap gasket **(Figure 7-4, (2))** and flange on the filler pipe **(Figure 7-4, (4))** for damage.
6. Check the rubber hose connecting the coolant recovery tank to the heat exchanger. Be sure the hose is securely connected and there is no looseness or damage.
7. Pour coolant mix slowly into the heat exchanger **(Figure 7-4, (3))** to prevent the formation of air pockets. Fill until the coolant overflows from the filler port.
8. Install the fill cap and tighten firmly.
9. Remove the coolant recovery tank cap and fill with coolant mix to approximately 50 mm (2 in.) below the full line. Replace cap. Never fill to the full line.
10. **6SY Engines:** After filling an empty cooling system, test-run the engine for about five minutes and check the engine coolant level again.
11. **8SY Engines:** After filling an empty cooling system, vent the system. *See Venting the Cooling System - 8SY Engines Only on page 7-9.*

Venting the Cooling System - 8SY Engines Only

1. Remove the filler cap from the coolant recovery tank. **WARNING!** *NEVER remove the coolant filler cap if the engine is hot. Steam and hot engine coolant will escape and seriously burn you. Allow the engine to cool sufficiently before attempting to remove the filler cap.* NOTICE: *Prevent dirt and debris from contaminating engine coolant. Carefully clean the heat exchanger cap and surrounding area before you remove the cap.*

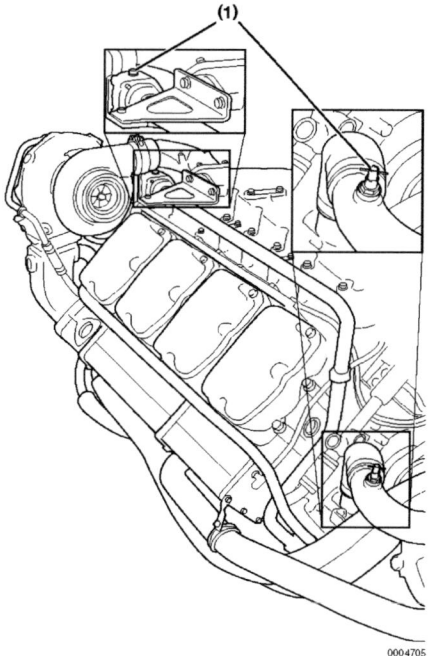

Figure 7-5

2. Start the engine and loosen the two bleed screws **(Figure 7-5, (1))**.

COOLING SYSTEM   Repair

3. When coolant with no air bubbles starts to flow, tighten the bleed screws. *NOTICE: Dispose of waste properly.*
4. Run the engine until it is hot and the thermostat opens.
5. Add more coolant if necessary. *NOTICE: NEVER add cold coolant to a hot engine. Serious engine damage may result.*
6. Install coolant recovery tank cap.

Coolant Pump Removal

6SY Engine

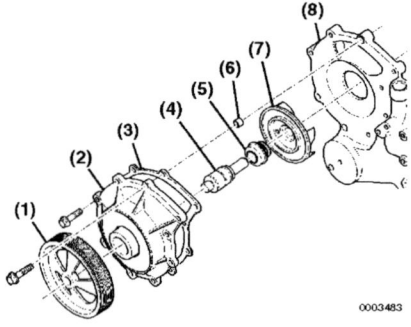

1 – Pulley
2 – Pump Housing
3 – Gasket
4 – Shaft with Bearing
5 – Mechanical Seal Assembly
6 – Guide Sleeve
7 – Impeller
8 – Front Cover

Figure 7-6

8SY Engine

1 – Pulley
2 – Pump Housing
3 – Shaft with Bearing
4 – Mechanical Seal Assembly
5 – Impeller
6 – Guide Sleeve
7 – Gasket
8 – Front Cover
9 – Gasket
10 – Gasket

Figure 7-7

1. Remove the coolant recovery tank filler cap. **WARNING!** *NEVER remove the coolant filler cap if the engine is hot. Steam and hot engine coolant will escape and seriously burn you. Allow the engine to cool before attempting to remove the filler cap.*
2. Drain coolant from engine:
   - **6SY:** Open the drain cock on the right-hand side of the engine block, and remove two plugs from the underside of the heat exchanger.
   - **8SY:** Remove two plugs from the underside of the heat exchanger.
3. Remove the belt guard.

Repair

COOLING SYSTEM

4. Remove the alternator belt. *See Replace Alternator Belt on page 11-9.*
5. Remove the coolant pump assembly from front cover.

Install Coolant Pump

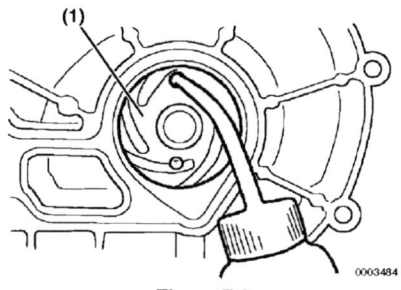

Figure 7-8

1. The seal on the coolant pump must be lubricated with paraffin oil before being installed:
   - Spray oil through the holes in the impeller **(Figure 7-20, (1))**. Try to aim the oil toward the shaft.
   - Rotate the impeller 180°.
   - Spray oil into the other hole.
   - Rotate the impeller a few turns to ensure that the oil has coated the entire seal.
2. Ensure that the mating surfaces on the pump and pump housing are clean. Install the pump and a new gasket.
3. Install the alternator belt. *See Replace Alternator Belt on page 11-9.*
4. Install the belt guard.
5. Fill engine block with coolant. *See Drain, Flush and Fill the Engine with Engine Coolant on page 7-8.*
6. Start the engine and check for coolant leaks. Check the level of the coolant and fill as necessary.

Remove and Install Pulley

1. Remove coolant pump from engine. *See Venting the Cooling System - 8SY Engines Only on page 7-9.*

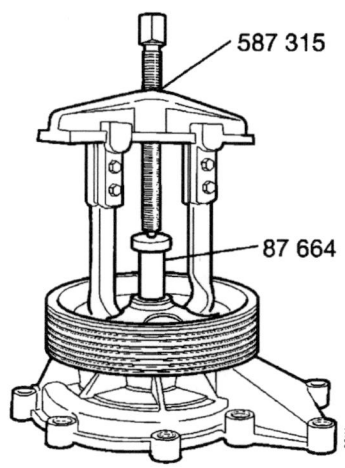

Figure 7-9

2. Remove the pulley using puller (OEM Part No. 587 315 or similar tool) and drift (OEM Part No. 87 664 or similar tool). *NOTICE: Support the bottom end of the pump shaft when pressing pulley into place. Failure to do so could result in the pump shaft position moving, resulting in a coolant leak or seal damage.*

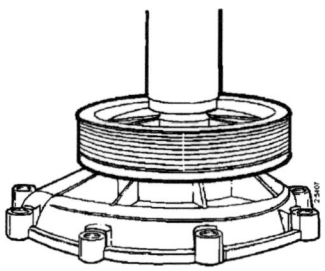

Figure 7-10

COOLING SYSTEM
Repair

3. Press the pulley onto the shaft until it is flush with the shaft end face.

Change the Coolant Pump Seal

1. Remove coolant pump from engine. *See Venting the Cooling System - 8SY Engines Only on page 7-9.*
2. Place the pump with pulley on a flat surface. *NOTICE: Support the bottom end of the pump shaft when pressing pulley into place. Failure to do so could result in the pump shaft position moving, resulting in a coolant leak or seal damage.*

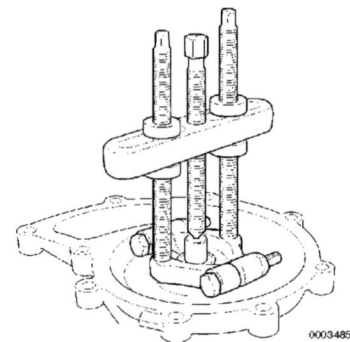

Figure 7-12

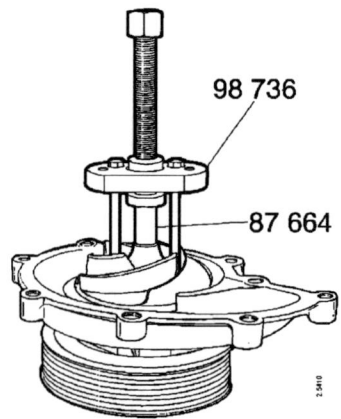

Figure 7-11

3. Remove the impeller using puller (OEM Part No. 98 736), two M8 x 65 mm bolts and drift (OEM Part No. 87 664 or similar tools).

4. Remove the seal using puller (OEM Part No. 587 516 and OEM Part No. 587 518 or similar tools). The seal will divide into two parts with the outer ring remaining in the coolant pump **(Figure 7-12)**.

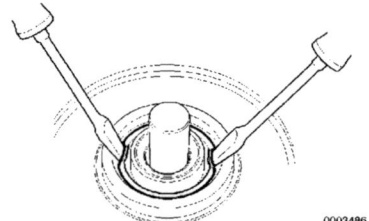

Figure 7-13

5. Remove the outer ring by heating the area around the seal with a hot air gun to release the locking agent. *NOTICE: Do not damage the pump housing sealing surface.*
6. Bend up the edge of the outer ring with two screwdrivers and remove the ring **(Figure 7-13)**.

COOLING SYSTEM

7. Apply sealing agent (OEM Part No. 561 200 or similar) to the inside and outside of the sealing ring (brass sleeve). Make sure that no sealing agent gets onto other sealing surfaces.
   NOTICE: Use sealing agent sparingly. Excess sealing agent can cause the two mating seal surfaces to become glued together. Seals which have sealing agent pre-applied should not have more sealing agent applied to them.

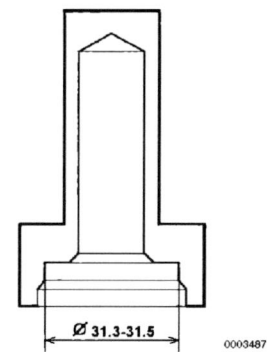

Figure 7-15

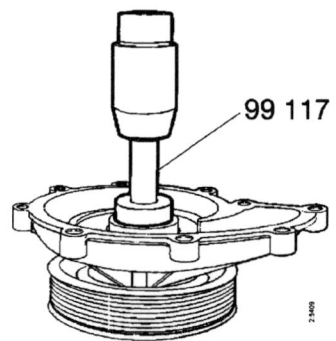

Figure 7-14

8. *NOTICE: It is very important that tool OEM Part No. 99 117 is used. It is designed to correctly preload the spring which holds the seal.* Press in the new seal using OEM Part No. 99 117 until the edge of the brass sleeve abuts against the pump housing. Keep it under pressure for about 10 seconds **(Figure 7-14)**.

9. *NOTICE: If you have the old-style OEM Part No. 99 117, it must be modified to install the new seal. If the seal is installed with a tool that has not been modified, the seal will break which will result in leakage. Modify the tool to the dimensions shown in* **Figure 7-15**.

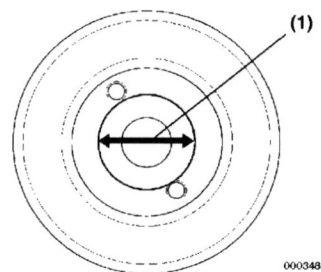

Figure 7-16

10. Measure the seal recess diameter **(Figure 7-16, (1))**. If it measures 30.7 mm, it must be enlarged to 33.0 mm using a lathe. *NOTICE: If the impeller seal recess diameter* **(Figure 7-16, (1))** *in the housing is 30.7 mm, it must be modified to install a new seal. Otherwise the seal will be damaged which will result in leakage.*

COOLING SYSTEM   Repair

11. Support the bottom end of the impeller shaft to prevent movement of the impeller shaft.
    NOTICE: Failure to support the bottom end of the pump shaft could result in the pump shaft position moving, resulting in a coolant leak or seal damage.

6SY Thermostat Removal

6SY Engine

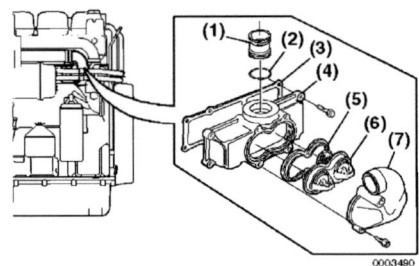

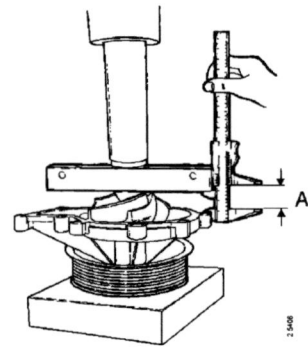

Figure 7-17

12. Press on the impeller using drift (OEM Part No. 99 117) until the distance between the pump housing gasket surface and the impeller shaft surface **(Figure 7-17, (A))** is 13.3 - 13.7 mm (0.524 - 0.539 in.).

1 – Connection Pipe
2 – O-Ring
3 – Gasket
4 – Thermostat Housing
5 – Seal
6 – Thermostat
7 – Thermostat Housing Cover

Figure 7-18

1. Remove the clamp ring and water lines between thermostat housing and charge air cooler.
2. Remove the tube from the front cover to the heat exchanger.
3. Remove bolts from the connection housing at the back of the front cover and remove it along with the charge air thermostat housing, bypass pipe and outlet pipe from the heat exchanger.
4. Remove the thermostat housing cover along with the inlet pipe to the heat exchanger.
5. Remove the thermostat.
6. Test thermostat as required. *See Testing the Thermostat on page 7-8.*

Remove and Install Thermostat

Drain a sufficient amount of coolant from the system to get coolant level below thermostat.
CAUTION! *Wear eye protection and rubber gloves when you handle Long Life engine coolant. If contact with the eyes or skin should occur, flush eyes and wash immediately with clean water.*

- **6SY:** Open the drain cock on the right side of the engine block, and removing two plugs from the underside of the heat exchanger.
- **8SY:** Remove two plugs from the underside of the heat exchanger.

Repair

COOLING SYSTEM

Thermostat Removal - 8SY

8SY Engine

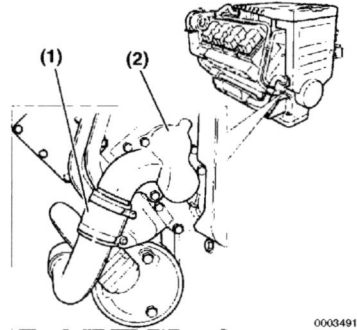

1 – Connection Pipe
2 – Thermostat Housing Cover

Figure 7-19

1. Remove the hose from the thermostat housing cover.
2. Remove the thermostat housing cover and remove the thermostat.
3. Test thermostat as required. *See Testing the Thermostat on page 7-8.*

Thermostat Installation - All Engines

1. Clean the thermostat housing and check that nothing can obstruct the function of the thermostat(s).
2. Place the thermostat(s) in the housing. Install new gaskets and install the thermostat housing.
3. Install all pipes and connections that were removed.
4. Fill the system with coolant. *See Drain, Flush and Fill the Engine with Engine Coolant on page 7-8.*
5. Start the engine and check for coolant leaks. Check the level of the coolant and fill as necessary.

Remove and Install Fresh Water Charge Air Cooler

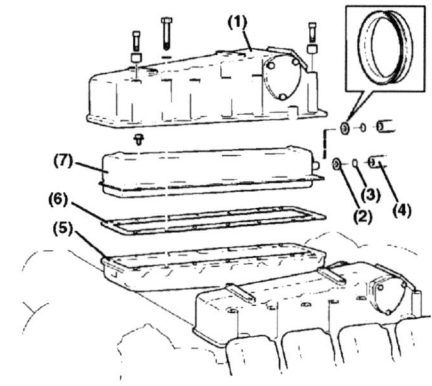

1 – Upper Intake Housing
2 – Seal
3 – O-Ring
4 – Coolant Pipe
5 – Lower Intake Manifold
6 – Gasket
7 – Intake Air Cooler

Figure 7-20

Note: 8 SY engine shown.

1. Drain coolant from the engine:
   - **6SY:** Open the drain cock on the right side of the engine block, and removing two plugs from the underside of the heat exchanger.
   - **8SY:** Remove two plugs from the underside of the heat exchanger.
2. **8SY:** Remove the connection pipe between upper intake manifold housings.
3. Disconnect the pipe between intake manifold and turbocharger.
4. **6SY:** Remove the charge air thermostat housing from intake manifold. Cap the fittings to prevent coolant spillage.

COOLING SYSTEM   Repair

5. **8SY:** Disconnect inlet and outlet water lines from charge air cooler fittings. Cap the fittings to prevent coolant spillage.
6. Remove the upper intake manifold housing.
   NOTICE: Take care to ensure that no coolant spills from the element into the intake manifold.
7. Remove the charge air cooler assembly from each intake manifold.
8. Clean the element using paraffin-based engine detergent only. *NOTICE: NEVER use caustic soda to clean the components.*
9. Clean and degrease the sealing surfaces on the upper and lower intake manifold housings.
10. Install charge air cooler(s) and a new gasket. Tighten bolts to 26 N·m (230 in.-lb).
11. Install upper intake manifold(s). Tighten bolts to:
    6SY: 26 N·m (230 in.-lb)
    8SY: 50 N·m (37 ft-lb)
12. **8SY:** Install connection pipe between intake manifolds.
13. **8SY:** Connect coolant hoses to charge air coolers.
14. **6SY:** Install thermostat housing to front of intake manifold with new gasket and O-rings.
15. Install and secure all remaining air inlet pipes and hoses. Tighten V-clamps to:
    - M6 Screw: 8 N·m (71 in.-lb)
    - M8 Screw: 20 N·m (177 in.-lb)
16. Fill the system with coolant. *See Drain, Flush and Fill the Engine with Engine Coolant on page 7-8.*
17. Start the engine and check for coolant leaks. Check the level of the coolant and fill as necessary.

Repair   **COOLING SYSTEM**

This Page Intentionally Left Blank

COOLING SYSTEM

Repair

Remove and Install Seawater Charge Air Cooler - 6SY Engines Only

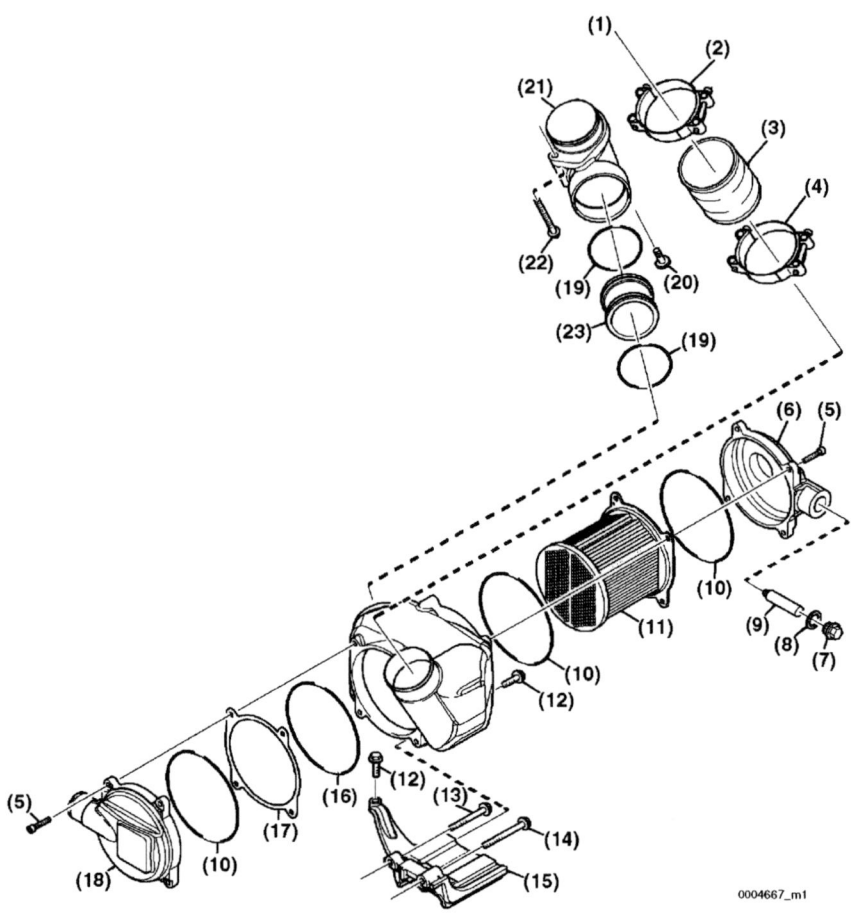

Figure 7-21

COOLING SYSTEM

Repair

1 – To Intake Manifold
2 – Hose Clamp
3 – Hose
4 – Hose Clamp
5 – Screw (8 used)
6 – Cover
7 – Plug
8 – Sealing Ring
9 – Zinc Anode
10 – O-Ring
11 – Seawater Charge Air Cooler Core
12 – Flange Screw (M10 x 50 mm) (3 used)
13 – Flange Screw (M10 x 50 mm)
14 – Flange Screw (M10 x 100 mm)
15 – Bracket
16 – O-Ring
17 – Flange
18 – Cover
19 – O-Ring
20 – Flange Screw (M10 x 50 mm)
21 – Charge Air Pipe
22 – Flange Screw (M10 x 100 mm)
23 – Holder

COOLING SYSTEM Repair

Remove and Install the Heat Exchanger

6SY Engines

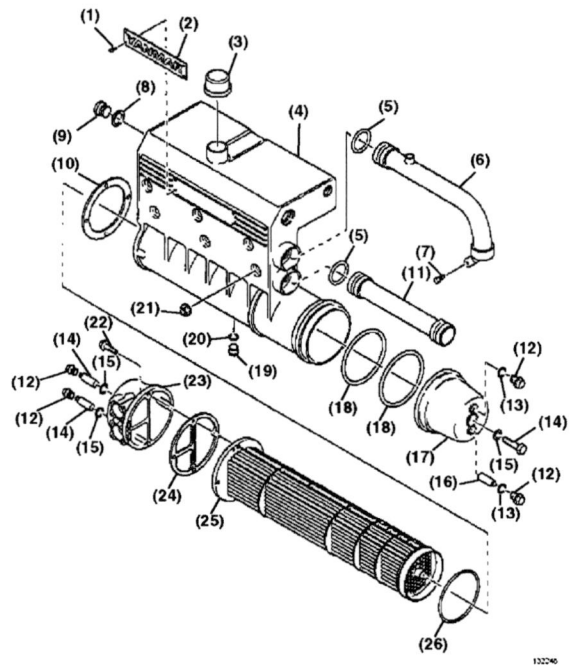

1 – Screw
2 – Nameplate
3 – Filler Cap
4 – Heat Exchanger Housing
5 – O-Ring
6 – Return Pipe to Coolant Pump
7 – Bolt
8 – Gasket
9 – Plug
10 – Gasket
11 – Outlet Pipe from Engine
12 – Bolt
13 – Seal
14 – Bolt
15 – Seal
16 – Anode (3 used)
17 – Front Cover
18 – O-Ring
19 – Drain Plug
20 – Gasket
21 – Flange Nut
22 – Bolt
23 – Rear Cover
24 – Gasket
25 – Cooler Core
26 – O-Ring

Figure 7-22

Repair   **COOLING SYSTEM**

1. Drain coolant from the engine.
2. Drain the seawater circuit by removing the cover from the seawater pump and the connections from the heat exchanger outlet.
3. Disconnect the coolant pipes from the charge air cooler. Disconnect the pipe between the front cover and the heat exchanger.
4. Remove the connection housing at the coolant pump inlet along with the return pipe from the heat exchanger.
5. Remove the thermostat housing cover and the outlet pipe to the heat exchanger.
6. Remove the seawater inlet flange from the heat exchanger.
7. Remove the vent pipe from the coolant recovery tank.
8. Remove the flange nuts and lift off the complete heat exchanger assembly.
9. Remove the rear cover and pull out the cooler element.
10. Use paraffin-based engine detergent to clean the cooler element. *NOTICE: NEVER use caustic soda to clean the components.*
11. Any internal deposits in the tubes can be removed using a round rod.

Note: Always install new gaskets and O-rings.

12. Lubricate and install a new O-ring **(Figure 7-22, (26))** inside the housing and install the cooler core. *NOTICE: Make sure all O-rings are correctly installed in their grooves. Failure to do so will result in leaks causing oil and coolant to mix.*
13. Install the front and rear covers using new O-rings and gaskets.
14. Install the heat exchanger assembly on the engine. Tighten the flange nuts to 50 N·m (37 ft-lb).
15. Install the coolant inlet and outlet pipes, thermostat housing cover, connection housing, charge air cooler coolant pipes and thermostat housing.
16. Fill the system with coolant. *See Drain, Flush and Fill the Engine with Engine Coolant on page 7-8.*
17. Start the engine and check for coolant leaks. Check the level of the coolant and fill as necessary.

COOLING SYSTEM

Repair

8SY Engines

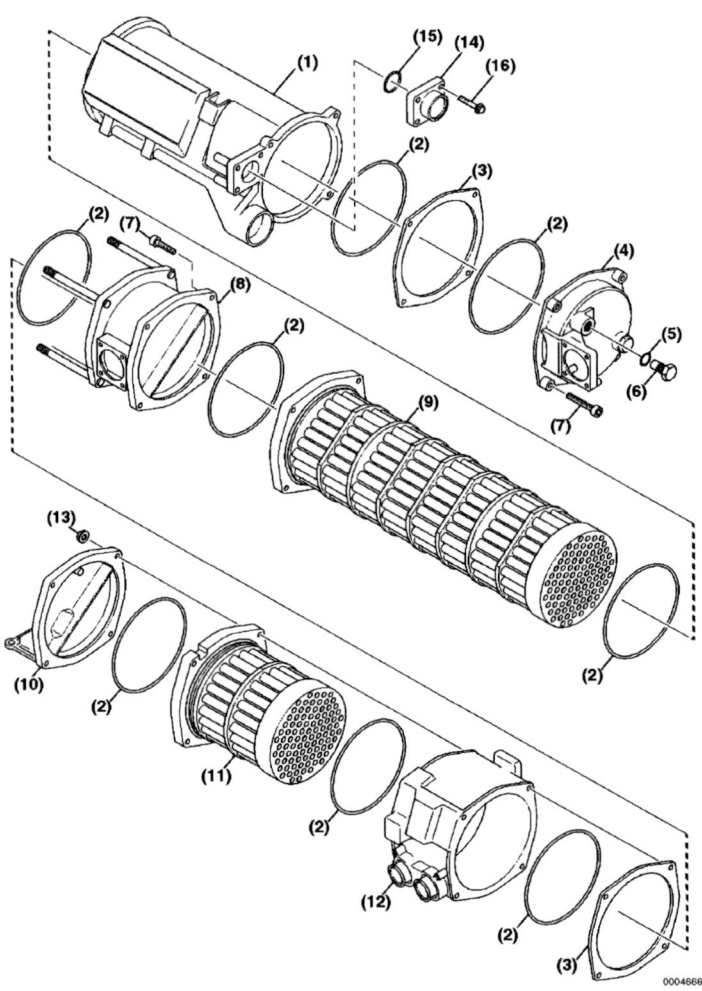

Figure 7-23

Repair

COOLING SYSTEM

1 – Heat Exchanger Housing, Main Section
2 – O-Ring (8 used)
3 – Flange (2 used)
4 – Cover
5 – Sealing Ring
6 – Plug
7 – Screw (M8 x 35 mm) (4 used)
8 – Housing
9 – Heat Exchanger Core
10 – Cover
11 – Heat Exchanger Core
12 – Housing
13 – Flange Nut (M8) (4 used)
14 – Flange
15 – O-Ring
16 – Screw (M8 x 30 mm) (4 used)

COOLING SYSTEM

Repair

1. Drain coolant from the engine.
2. Drain the seawater circuit by removing the cover from the seawater pump and the connections from the heat exchanger outlet.
3. Disconnect all connections to the heat exchanger and to the reverse gear oil cooler, if installed.
4. Remove the heat exchanger.
5. Remove the rear cover and pull out the charge air cooling element.
6. Remove the charge air section housing, intermediate section housing and front cover.
7. Remove the main section element. It may be necessary to tap the element carefully in order to loosen it.
8. Use paraffin-based engine detergent to clean the elements. *NOTICE: NEVER use caustic soda to clean the components.*
9. Any internal deposits in the tubes can be removed using a round rod.

Note: Always install new gaskets and O-rings.

10. Lubricate and install the O-rings on the elements and assemble in reverse order. *NOTICE: Make sure all O-rings are correctly installed in their grooves. Failure to do so will result in leaks causing oil and coolant to mix.*
11. Fill the system with coolant. *See Drain, Flush and Fill the Engine with Engine Coolant on page 7-8.*
12. Start the engine and check for coolant leaks. Check the level of the coolant and fill as necessary.

Seawater Pump

Replace the Impeller

1. Drain the seawater circuit by removing the cover from the seawater pump.
2. **8SY:** Detach the outlet pipe.
3. Remove the rubber washer from the center of the impeller.

6SY Engines

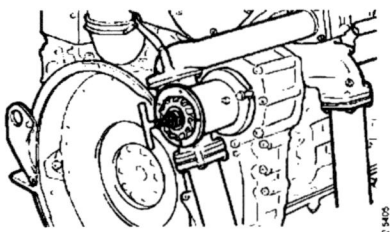

Figure 7-24

8SY Engines

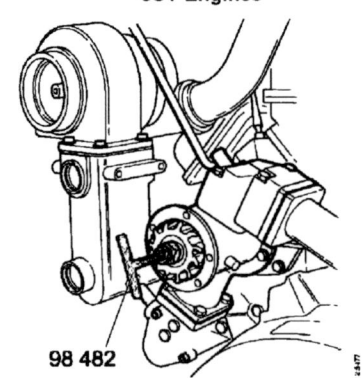

98 482

Figure 7-25

4. Extract the impeller using puller (OEM Part No. 98 482 or similar tool).

Repair

COOLING SYSTEM

Note: When installing the new impeller, bend the vanes in the same direction as on the old one.

5. Install the new impeller and the rubber washer. Attach the cover using a new gasket.

Remove and Disassemble Seawater Pump

1. Remove the inlet and outlet connections from the pump.
2. Remove the securing screws from the timing gear cover and remove the pump.

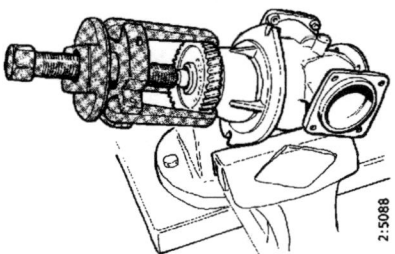

Figure 7-26

3. Clamp the pump housing in a soft-jawed vise. Remove the nut and remove the gear using a universal puller **(Figure 7-26)**.

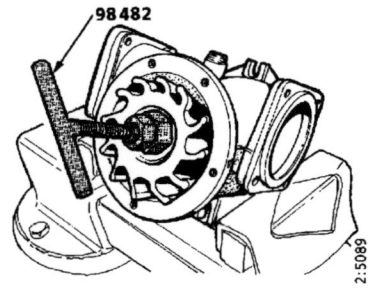

Figure 7-27

4. Remove the impeller cover and gasket.
5. Extract the impeller using puller (OEM Part No. 98 482 or similar tool) **(Figure 7-27)**.

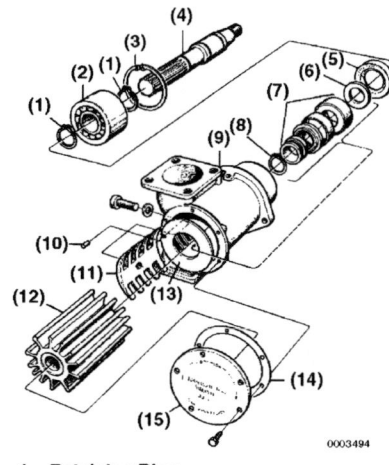

1 – Retaining Ring
2 – Ball Bearing
3 – Retaining Ring
4 – Shaft
5 – Lip Seal
6 – Deflector Ring
7 – Mechanical Seal
8 – Retaining Ring
9 – Pump Housing
10 – Pin
11 – Comb
12 – Impeller
13 – Wear Washer
14 – Gasket
15 – Impeller Cover

Figure 7-28

6. Remove the comb and wear washer.

COOLING SYSTEM   Repair

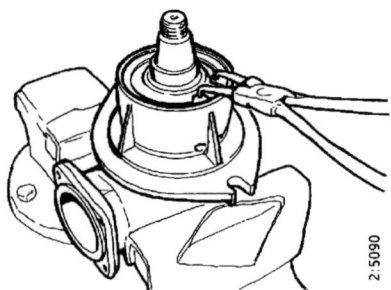

Figure 7-29

7. Remove the retaining ring from the housing **(Figure 7-29)**.

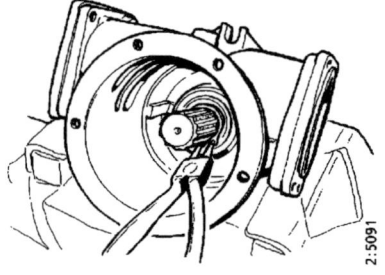

Figure 7-30

8. Remove the retaining ring from the shaft on the impeller side of the bearing **(Figure 7-30)**. Tap the shaft and bearing out of the housing.
9. Remove the ceramic ring and rubber sleeve from the seat on the water side. Remove the deflector ring. Tap out the lip seal.

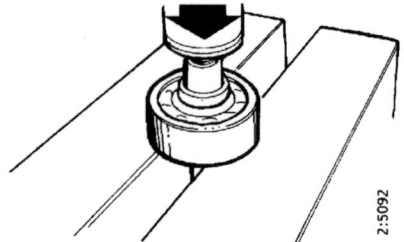

Figure 7-31

10. Remove the retaining rings from both sides of the bearing and place the shaft and bearing in a press between parallel pieces. Press the shaft out of the bearing **(Figure 7-31)**.

Inspect the Seawater Pump

Clean all parts except the mechanical seal components and check:

- That the splines on the shaft are not damaged.
- That the bearing can be easily rotated and is not damaged, and that it has not rotated on the shaft or in the housing.
- That the comb is not too worn or defective.

Replace parts which are defective or worn.

COOLING SYSTEM

Assemble the Seawater Pump

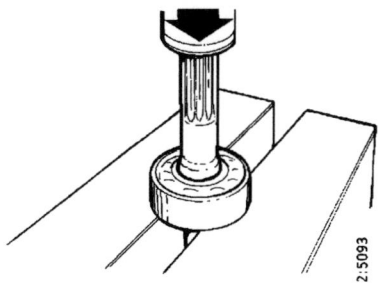

Figure 7-32

1. Place the bearing on parallel pieces in a press so that the inner race is also supported. Press the shaft to the correct position **(Figure 7-32)** and install the retaining rings.

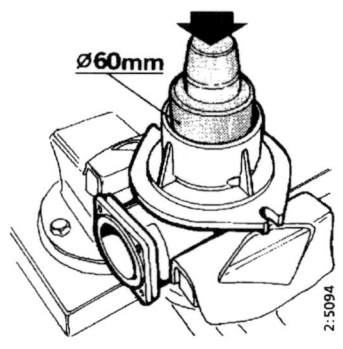

Figure 7-33

2. Mount the pump housing in a soft-jawed vise. Use a drift or tube with an outside diameter of 60 mm and tap a new seal into the housing. Install the seal so that the lip faces out **(Figure 7-33)**.

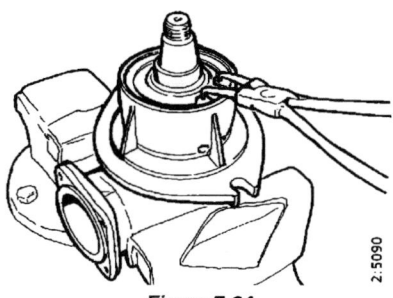

Figure 7-34

3. Tap the shaft and bearing into the housing until the bearing is against the shoulder in the housing. Install the retaining ring **(Figure 7-34)**.

4. Turn the housing in the vise. Push the deflector ring as far onto the shaft as possible.

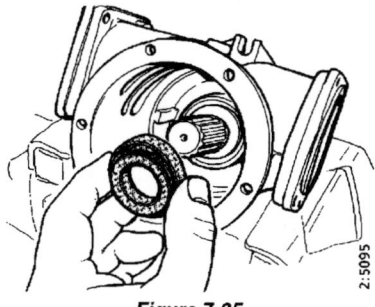

Figure 7-35

5. Install a new mechanical seal onto the shaft as follows:

   - Press the rubber sleeve into the seat in the housing **(Figure 7-35)**.
   - Apply a little oil around the outside of the ceramic ring and press it into the rubber sleeve with the flat surface facing out.
   - Push the rest of the mechanical seal components onto the shaft with the ceramic ring installed first.
   - Press the seal assembly in past the retaining ring groove and install a new retaining ring

COOLING SYSTEM

Repair

6. Install a new wear washer. Install a new copper washer onto the comb retaining screw and attach the comb.
7. Install the impeller and fasten the cover with a new gasket.
8. Lightly tap the gear onto the end of the shaft. Tighten the nut to 100 N·m (74 ft-lb).
9. Make sure that the overflow holes in the pump housing are open.

Check or Replace the Zinc Anodes

6SY Engines

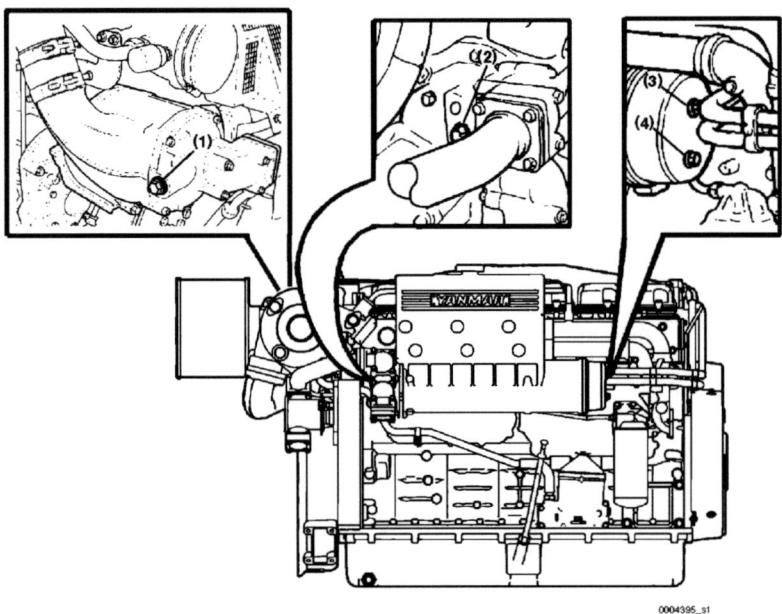

Figure 7-36

Repair   **COOLING SYSTEM**

8SY Engines

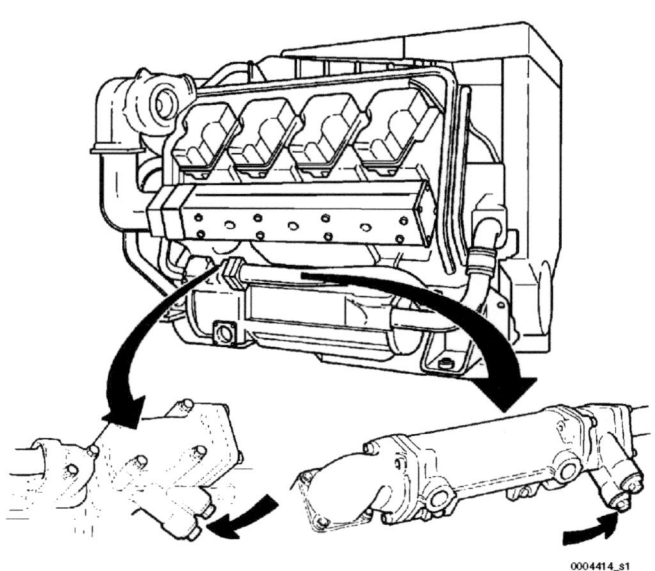

Figure 7-37

1. Drain the seawater cooling circuit and check the anodes.
2. Scrape off all loose material on the anodes.
3. A new anode is 63 mm (2.50 in.) long with a diameter of 17 mm (11/16 in.). Replace an anode if less than half of the anode remains.
   NOTICE: NEVER use thread sealer or thread sealing tape when installing zinc anodes. Anodes must make good metal-to-metal contact to perform properly.

   NOTICE: If operation is continued with an anode less than half of the new anode length, corrosion of the seawater coolant system will occur and water leakage or parts breakage will result.

Note: If the anodes are extremely corroded, check them more frequently.

COOLING SYSTEM Repair

This Page Intentionally Left Blank

Section 8

LUBRICATION

	Page
Introduction	8-3
Specifications	8-3
Special Service Tools	8-4
Tests and Adjustments	8-5
Check the Engine Oil Pressure	8-5
Repair	8-6
Remove and Install the Oil Cooler	8-6
Remove and Install Oil Cleaning Components	8-9
Replace the Engine Oil Filter - 8SY	8-11
Clean the Centrifugal Engine Oil Cleaner	8-11
Oil Pump	8-14

LUBRICATION

This Page Intentionally Left Blank

Introduction | **LUBRICATION**

INTRODUCTION

This section of the Service Manual describes the procedures necessary to service the 6SY and 8SY lubrication systems.

SPECIFICATIONS

Note: All pressure specifications are with engine at normal operating temperature.

Test and Adjustment Specifications

Inspection Item	Model	Test RPM	Specification
Oil Pressure	6SY	Idle	1.6 bar (23 psi)
		1000 rpm	2.5 bar (36 psi)
		2000 rpm	4.5 - 6.0 bar (65 - 87 psi)
	8SY	Idle	1.4 bar (20 psi)
		1000 rpm	3.0 bar (43 psi)
		2000 rpm	3.5 - 5.5 bar (51 - 80 psi)
Oil Pressure Relief Valve Spring Free Length	6SY	-	61.4 mm (2.417 in.)

Repair Specifications

Maximum Thickness of Deposits on Walls of Centrifugal Oil Cleaner Bowl	20 mm (0.75 in.)

Special Torque Chart

Component		Tightening Torque	Lubricating Oil Application	Reference Page
Oil Cooler-to-Cover Bolt		26 N·m (230 in.-lb)	Not Applied	See Remove and Install the Oil Cooler on page 8-6
Oil Cleaner Rotor Shaft		34 N·m (25 ft-lb)	See Footnote*	See Clean the Centrifugal Engine Oil Cleaner on page 8-11
Rotor Bowl Nut		Hand-tighten	Not Applied	
Centrifugal Oil Cleaner Cover Lock Nut		15 N·m (133 in.-lb)	Not Applied	
Oil Filter Housing Cover	8SY Engine	25 N·m (221 in.-lb)	Not Applied	See Replace the Engine Oil Filter - 8SY on page 8-11
Oil Sump Bolt		30 N·m (22 ft-lb)	Not Applied	See Installation of Oil Pump on page 8-15
Oil Pump Mounting Bolt		26 N·m (230 in.-lb)	Applied	
Oil Sump Drain Plug		80 N·m (59 ft-lb)	Not Applied	

*Apply medium-strength thread lock and sealer to threads.

LUBRICATION   Special Service Tools

SPECIAL SERVICE TOOLS

Note: The tool numbers used in this section are either Yanmar or Scania part numbers. Yanmar part numbers are referred to as **Yanmar Part No.** and Scania part numbers are referred to as **OEM Part No.** Tools not having part numbers must be obtained locally.

No.	Tool Name	Part Number	Illustration
1	Rotor Shaft Socket (For Removing and Installing Centrifugal Oil Cleaner Rotor Shaft)	OEM Part No. 98 421	
2	Lifting Eyes (Used to Lift Engine)	OEM Part No. 99 398	

Measuring Instruments

No.	Instrument Name	Application	Illustration
1	Torque Wrench	For tightening nuts and bolts to the specified torque	

Tests and Adjustments

LUBRICATION

TESTS AND ADJUSTMENTS

Check the Engine Oil Pressure

Note: The oil pressure relief valve is not a safety valve.

Perform an engine oil pressure check if there is any indication of low oil pressure.

1. Start the engine and allow it to warm to normal operating temperature.
2. Stop the engine. **WARNING!** *ALWAYS keep your hands and other body parts away from hot engine surfaces such as the muffler, exhaust pipe, turbocharger (if equipped) and engine block during operation and shortly after you shut the engine down. These surfaces are extremely hot while the engine is operating and could cause burns.*

Sensor Location - 6SY

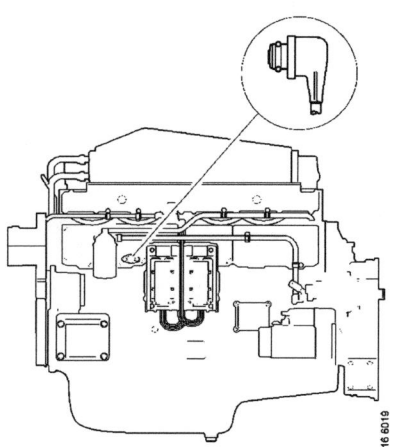

Figure 8-1

Sensor Location - 8SY

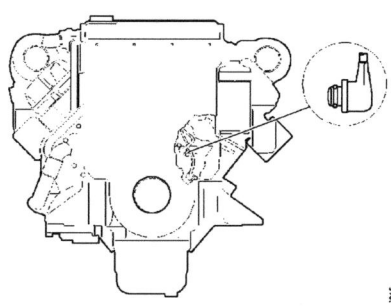

Figure 8-2

3. Remove the oil pressure sensor.
4. Install a mechanical oil pressure gauge in the oil pressure sensor port.
5. Start the engine and read the pressure gauge:
   - If the mechanical oil pressure test gauge indicates good oil pressure, replace the faulty oil pressure sensor or faulty oil pressure gauge.
   - If the mechanical oil pressure test gauge indicates low oil pressure, troubleshoot the lubrication system to locate the cause of the low oil pressure. *See Low Oil Pressure on page 13-6*. Repair as necessary.

Inspection Item		Test RPM	Specification
Engine Oil Pressure	6SY	Idle	1.6 bar (23 psi)
		1000 rpm	2.5 bar (36 psi)
		2000 rpm	4.5 - 6.0 bar (65 - 87 psi)
	8SY	Idle	1.4 bar (20 psi)
		1000 rpm	3.0 bar (43 psi)
		2000 rpm	3.5 - 5.5 bar (51 - 80 psi)

LUBRICATION

Repair

REPAIR

Remove and Install the Oil Cooler

6SY Engines

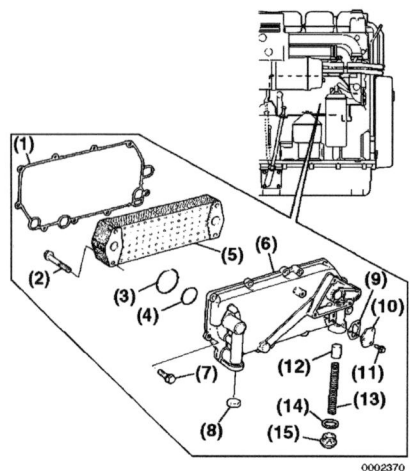

1 – Gasket
2 – Flange Bolt
3 – O-Ring
4 – O-Ring
5 – Oil Cooler
6 – Oil Cooler Cover
7 – Flange Bolt
8 – Core Plug
9 – Gasket
10 – Cover
11 – Bolt
12 – Piston
13 – Spring
14 – Gasket
15 – Plug

Figure 8-3

1. Drain engine coolant into a suitable container.
2. Disconnect turbocharger lube line.
3. Remove the oil filter.

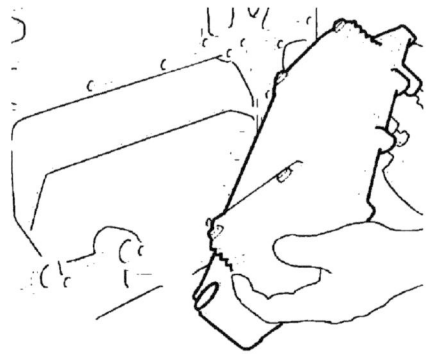

Figure 8-4

4. Remove the side cover and oil cooler from the cylinder block.

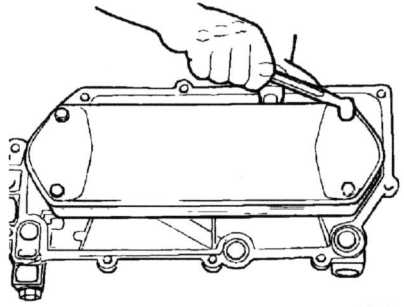

Figure 8-5

5. Remove four bolts securing the oil cooler to the side cover.
6. Remove the oil cooler.

Repair   **LUBRICATION**

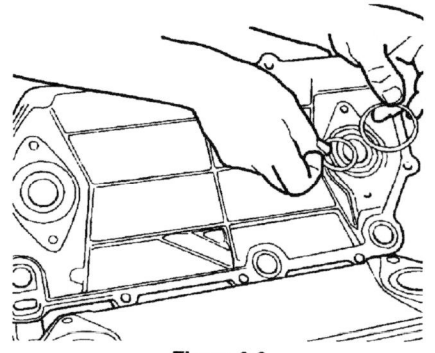

Figure 8-6

7. Install four new O-rings.
8. Arrach the oil cooler to the side cover. Tighten bolts to 26 N·m (230 in.-lb).
9. Install the oil cooler assembly and new gasket to the cylinder block.
10. Fill the engine with coolant.

8SY Engines

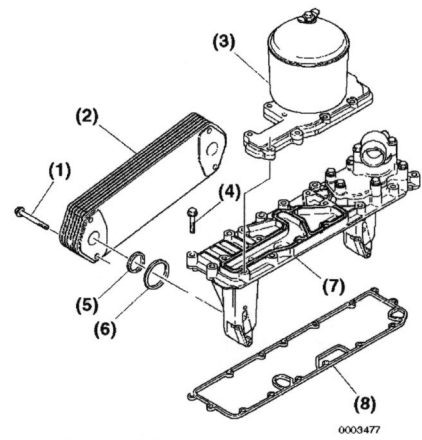

1 – Flange Bolt
2 – Oil Cooler
3 – Centrifugal Oil Cleaner Assembly
4 – Flange Bolt
5 – O-Ring
6 – O-Ring
7 – Oil Cooler Cover
8 – Gasket

Figure 8-7

1. Drain engine coolant into a suitable container.
2. Remove catwalk.
3. Remove pipe between charge air coolers.
4. Remove connection pipe to the closed crankcase ventilation.
5. Remove centrifugal oil cleaner assembly.
   NOTICE: Lift oil cooler and cover assembly straight up without tipping to prevent oil from dripping into the cooling system.
6. Remove the oil cooler cover and oil cooler assembly from the cylinder block.

LUBRICATION   Repair

15. Connect the closed crankcase ventilation pipe.
16. Fill the engine with coolant.

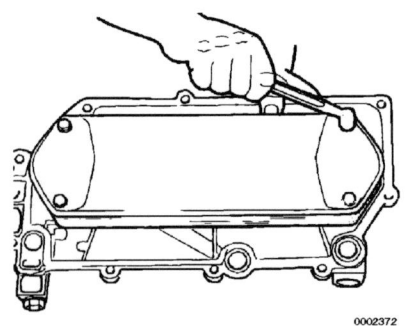

Figure 8-8

7. Remove four bolts securing the oil cooler to the side cover **(Figure 8-8)**.
8. Remove the oil cooler.

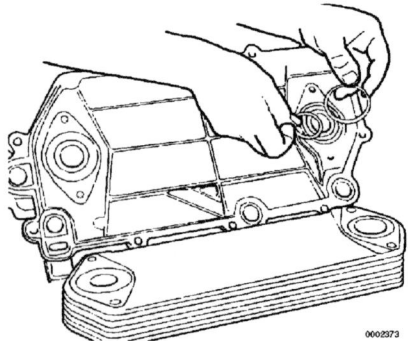

Figure 8-9

9. Install two new O-rings on each end of housing.
10. Attach the oil cooler to the cover. Tighten bolts to 26 N·m (230 in.-lb).
11. Install the oil cooler and cover assembly and new gasket to the cylinder block.
12. Clean and install the centrifugal oil cleaner. *See Clean the Centrifugal Engine Oil Cleaner on page 8-11.*
13. Install pipe between charge air coolers.
14. Install catwalk.

Repair

LUBRICATION

Remove and Install Oil Cleaning Components

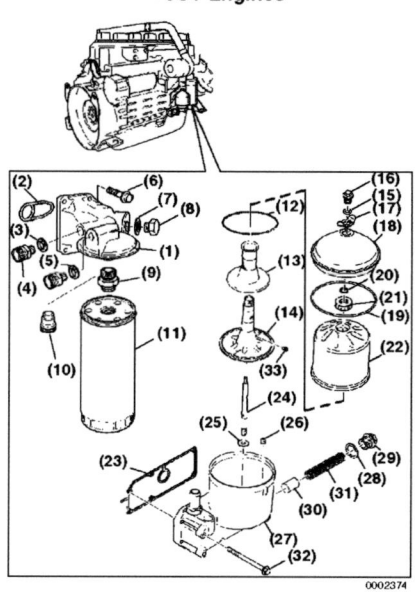

Figure 8-10

6SY Engines

1 – Filter Head
2 – Gasket
3 – Seal
4 – Straight Union
5 – Gasket
6 – Flange Bolt
7 – Gasket
8 – Plug
9 – Union
10 – Overflow Valve
11 – Spin-on Oil Filter
12 – O-Ring
13 – Strainer
14 – Centrifugal Filter Rotor
15 – O-Ring
16 – Locknut
17 – Lifting Eye
18 – Centrifugal Oil Cleaner Cover
19 – O-Ring
20 – Snap Ring
21 – Nut
22 – Centrifugal Rotor Bowl
23 – Gasket
24 – Shaft
25 – Washer
26 – Plug
27 – Centrifugal Oil Cleaner Housing
28 – Gasket
29 – Plug
30 – Piston
31 – Spring
32 – Flange Bolt
33 – Nozzle

LUBRICATION Repair

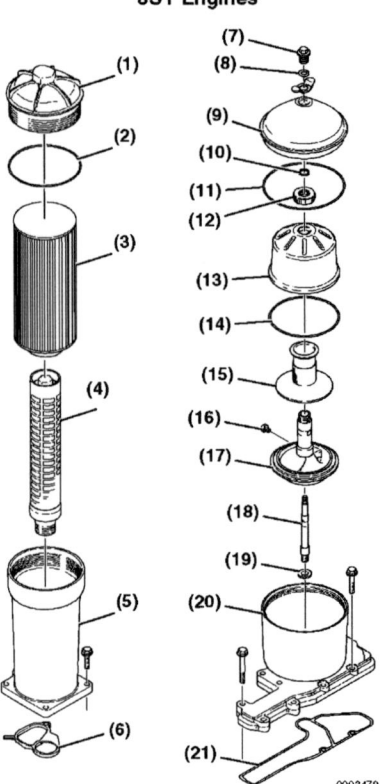

8SY Engines

1 – Filter Cover
2 – O-Ring
3 – Filter Element
4 – Tube
5 – Filter Housing
6 – Gasket
7 – Locknut
8 – O-Ring
9 – Centrifugal Oil Cleaner Cover
10 – Snap Ring
11 – O-Ring
12 – Nut
13 – Centrifugal Rotor Bowl
14 – O-Ring
15 – Nozzle
16 – Strainer
17 – Centrifugal Filter Rotor
18 – Shaft
19 – Washer
20 – Centrifugal Oil Cleaner Housing
21 – Gasket

Figure 8-11

Repair

LUBRICATION

Replace the Engine Oil Filter - 8SY

NOTICE: The centrifugal oil cleaner must be cleaned when replacing the engine oil filter.

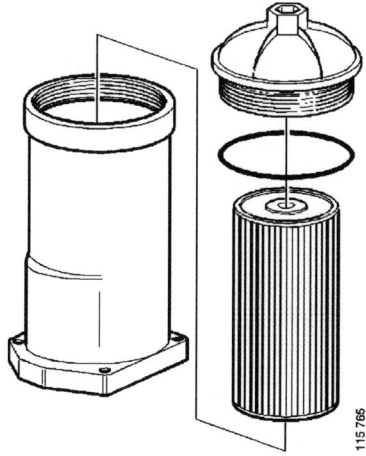

Figure 8-12

NOTICE: Do not use an adjustable wrench or other open-end tool as there is a risk of damaging the filter cover.

1. Remove the filter cover using a 6-point socket or box-end wrench.
2. Lift out the filter housing cover with filter element attached. The filter housing will drain automatically once the filter has been removed.
3. Remove the old filter from the cover by carefully bending it to one side.
4. Make sure all oil has drained from the filter housing. Wipe the oil filter housing and cover clean.
5. Install a new O-ring on the cover. Lubricate the O-ring with clean engine oil.
6. Press a new filter element onto the snap fastener in the cover.
7. Install the filter cover and filter. Tighten to 25 N·m (221 in.-lb).
8. Start the engine and inspect the filter housing for leaks.

Clean the Centrifugal Engine Oil Cleaner

During routine cleaning of the oil cleaner, a small amount of dirt deposits will accumulate in the rotor bowl.

If little or no deposits have accumulated, the rotor is not spinning. The cause must be immediately investigated.

If dirt deposits exceed 20 mm (0.75 in.) when the filter is cleaned at the recommended intervals, the rotor bowl should be cleaned more often.

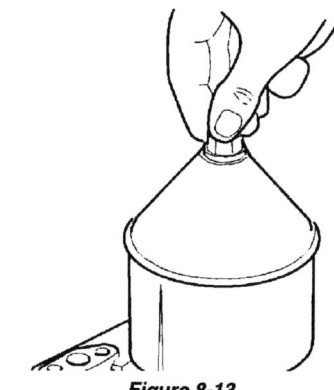

Figure 8-13

1. Remove the outer cover **(Figure 8-13)**.
2. Lift out the rotor bowl and rotor as an assembly. Wipe off the outside of the rotor bowl.

LUBRICATION   Repair

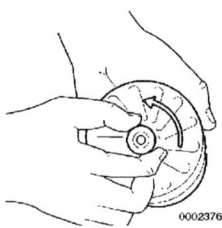

Figure 8-14

3. Loosen the rotor nut as follows to prevent damaging the bearing (**Figure 8-14**).

   - **6SY:** Loosen nut approximately one and a half turns.
   - **8SY:** Loosen nut approximately three turns.

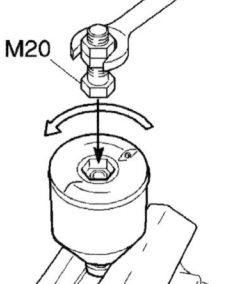

Figure 8-15

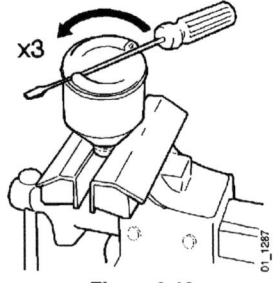

Figure 8-16

- If the rotor nut is difficult to loosen, clamp the nut in a vise and turn the rotor one and a half turns counterclockwise by hand, or use an M20 bolt as shown in **Figure 8-15** and **Figure 8-16**. *NOTICE: NEVER clamp the rotor in a vise. NEVER strike the rotor bowl. Doing so may cause damage resulting in imbalance.*

4. Hold the rotor bowl and tap on the rotor nut with your hand or a plastic hammer to loosen the rotor from the bowl.

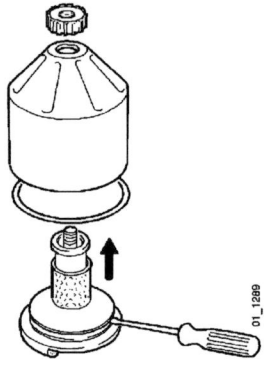

Figure 8-17

5. Remove the nut and rotor bowl from the rotor (**Figure 8-17**).
6. Remove the strainer located on the rotor. If the strainer is stuck, pry carefully at the bottom between the rotor and the strainer (**Figure 8-17**).

Figure 8-18

7. Scrape away the deposits inside the bowl with a knife (**Figure 8-18**).

Repair

LUBRICATION

8. Wash the parts using an appropriate cleaning solvent.
9. Inspect the two nozzles on the rotor. Make sure they are not blocked or damaged. Replace any damaged nozzles.
10. Inspect the bearings for damage or roughness.

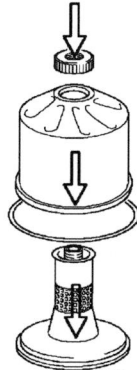

Figure 8-19

11. Install a new O-ring in the rotor bowl.
12. Assemble the parts and hand-tighten the rotor bowl nut (**Figure 8-19**).

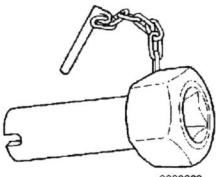

Figure 8-20

13. Make sure the rotor shaft is tight in the housing. If the shaft is loose:
    - Remove the rotor shaft and clean the threads in the housing and on the shaft using a suitable solvent.
    - Apply locking compound (OEM Part No. 561 200 or similar tool) to the threads of the rotor shaft.
    - Install the rotor shaft and washer. Tighten using socket (OEM Part No. 98 421 or similar tool) to 34 N·m (25 ft-lb) (**Figure 8-20**).

    Note: It may be necessary to modify socket OEM Part No. 98 421 as follows:
    - Drill out the threads of an M20 nut so that it fits on the drive end of the socket.
    - Weld the nut onto the socket. The socket will fit the old centrifugal oil cleaner after modification.

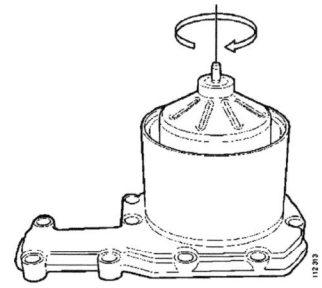

Figure 8-21

Note: Note: 8SY components shown. 6SY is similar.

14. Install the rotor and spin the rotor by hand to make sure it rotates freely (**Figure 8-21**).

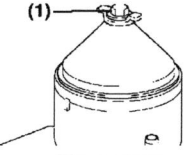

Figure 8-22

15. Install a new O-ring on the housing cover lock nut. Install the washer and locknut (**Figure 8-22, (1)**). Tighten locknut to 15 N·m (133 in -lb)

LUBRICATION
Repair

Oil Pump

The oil pump contains no serviceable parts. If the oil pump is damaged or leaks, it must be replaced as an assembly.

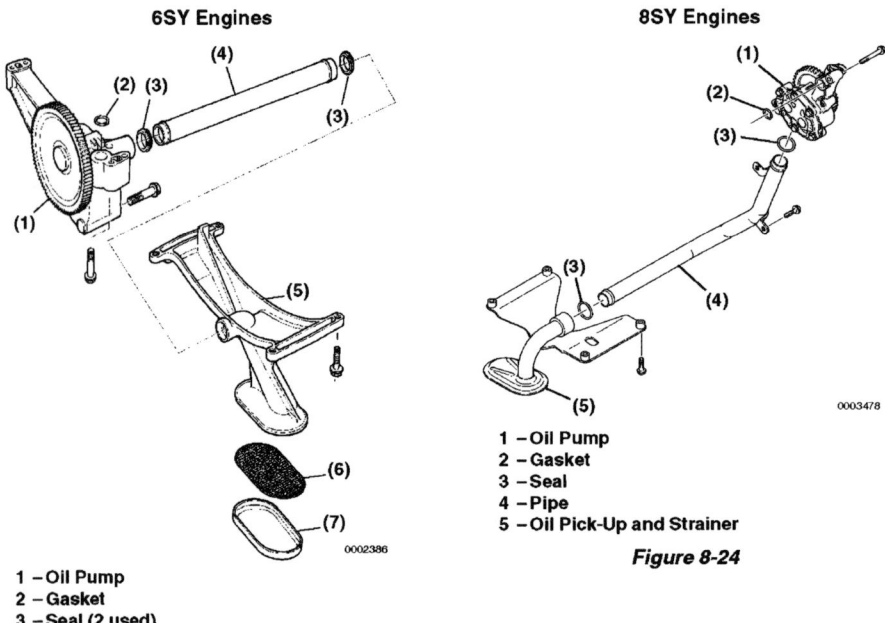

1 – Oil Pump
2 – Gasket
3 – Seal (2 used)
4 – Pipe
5 – Oil Pick-Up
6 – Strainer
7 – Ring

Figure 8-23

1 – Oil Pump
2 – Gasket
3 – Seal
4 – Pipe
5 – Oil Pick-Up and Strainer

Figure 8-24

Repair

LUBRICATION

Removal of Oil Pump

1. Drain oil from oil sump.
2. Remove debris from the magnet. Install and tighten oil plug to 80 N·m (59 ft-lb).
3. Remove oil sump.
4. **8SY Engine:** Support engine using lifting eyes (OEM Part No. 99 318 or similar tool) and a suitable hoist. **DANGER! *ALWAYS use lifting equipment with sufficient capacity to lift the marine engine. Additional equipment is necessary to lift the marine engine and marine gear together.***
5. **8SY Engine:** Remove the flywheel housing. See *Remove the Flywheel Housing on page 5-53*.
6. Remove oil strainer assembly and suction pipe.
7. Remove oil pump.

Installation of Oil Pump

1. Install oil pump assembly using a new O-ring between oil pump and cylinder block. Tighten bolts to 26 N·m (230 in.-lb).
2. Install suction pipe and strainer using new O-rings.
3. **8SY Engine:** Install flywheel housing and flywheel. See *Install the Flywheel Housing on page 5-53*.
4. Install oil sump. Tighten bolts to 30 N·m (22 ft-lb).
5. Fill crankcase to proper level with new engine oil.

LUBRICATION Repair

This Page Intentionally Left Blank

Section 9

TURBOCHARGER

	Page
Introduction	9-3
General Information	9-3
Oil Leaks	9-3
Foreign Bodies	9-3
Air and Exhaust Leaks	9-3
Oil Filter	9-3
Cleaning the Compressor Wheel	9-3
Specifications	9-4
Special Service Tools	9-5
Component Location	9-6
6SY Engines	9-6
8SY Engines	9-7
Tests and Adjustments	9-8
Measuring Charge Pressure	9-8
Repair	9-8
If the Turbocharger Does Not Operate:	9-8
Remove Turbocharger	9-9
Inspect the Turbocharger	9-10
Measure the Radial and Axial Clearance	9-10
Install the Turbocharger	9-12

TURBOCHARGER

This Page Intentionally Left Blank

INTRODUCTION

This section of the Service Manual describes the disassembly, inspection, and reassembly of turbochargers used on 6SY and 8SY engines.

GENERAL INFORMATION

NOTICE: Observe strict cleanliness at all times when working on the turbocharger. Never leave connections for oil inlets or outlets unprotected. Foreign bodies in the bearing housing will lead to turbocharger breakdown.

Oil Leaks

A blocked air filter creates excess vacuum in the air inlet line. There is then a risk of oil mist being drawn from the bearing housing.

If the sealing ring on the turbine side is worn, the exhaust gases will be blue when idling.

If the oil outlet pipe from the turbocharger is damaged, there is risk of oil leaking out.

Foreign Bodies

Foreign bodies in the turbine or compressor, even as small as a grain of sand or metal shavings, will ruin the vanes. This will lead to imbalance and bearing wear. Engine power will drop.

NOTICE: Never attempt to straighten a damaged vane. It may break off when running and the turbocharger may stop operating completely, causing serious damage to the engine.

Air and Exhaust Leaks

Even small leaks in the line between the air filter and the turbocharger will cause dirt to be deposited on the compressor wheel. The charge pressure will be reduced, resulting in increased exhaust temperature and smoke, which will reduce the service life of the engine.

Leaks in the exhaust line between the cylinder head and the turbocharger will also result in loss of charging pressure.

Oil Filter

The turbocharger rotates at high speed, sometimes above 100,000 rpm.

The turbocharger relies on the engine lubrication system for clean oil. It is vital that scheduled oil and filter changes be performed and the centrifugal oil cleaner be cleaned to provide maximum turbocharger life. If the oil filter becomes plugged, oil will pass through a bypass valve without being filtered, resulting in shortened turbocharger and engine life. Always use original Yanmar oil filters to ensure maximum turbocharger and engine service life.

Cleaning the Compressor Wheel

1. Remove the compressor cover. *NOTICE: The compressor wheel must not be removed from the shaft. Imbalance may occur when it is reassembled.*
2. Clean the compressor wheel with white spirit and a brush.
3. Install the compressor cover and measure the charging pressure again.

TURBOCHARGER

SPECIFICATIONS

Test and Adjustment Specifications

Inspection Item		Limit		Reference Page
Turbocharger Boost Pressure	6SY	Minimum - *	Maximum - *	See Measuring Charge Pressure on page 9-8
	8SY	Minimum - *	Maximum - *	
Turbocharger Shaft Radial Clearance	6SY	0.198 - 0.564 mm (0.0078 - 0.0222 in.)		See Measure the Radial and Axial Clearance on page 9-10
	8SY	0.611 mm (0.0240 in.)		
Turbocharger Shaft Axial Clearance	6SY	0.025 - 0.106 mm (0.001 - 0.004 in.)		
	8SY	0.102 mm (0.004 in.)		

* Not available at time of publication

Special Torque Chart

Component		Torque	Lubricant Application (Thread Portion and Seat Surface)	Reference Page
Turbocharger-to-Exhaust Manifold Bolt	6SY	50 N·m (37 ft-lb)	High-Temperature Grease	See Install the Turbocharger on page 9-12
	8SY	63 N·m (46 ft-lb)		
Turbocharger-to-Exhaust Pipe Bolt		24 N·m (212 in.-lb)	Not Applied	
Turbocharger-to-Intake Pipe V-Clamp	M6 Bolt	8 N·m (71 in.-lb)	Not Applied	
	M8 Bolt	20 N·m (177 in.-lb)	Not Applied	

Special Service Tools **TURBOCHARGER**

SPECIAL SERVICE TOOLS

Note: The tool numbers used in this section are either Yanmar or Scania part numbers. Yanmar part numbers are referred to as **Yanmar Part No.** and Scania part numbers are referred to as **OEM Part No.** Tools not having part numbers must be obtained locally.

No.	Instrument Name	Application	Illustration
1	Dial Indicator	Measure shaft end play	0000831
2	Dial Indicator	Measure shaft side play	0000832
3	Magnetic Stand	For holding the dial indicator when measuring	0000833
4	Torque Wrench	For tightening nuts and bolts to the specified torque	0000840

TURBOCHARGER

COMPONENT LOCATION

6SY Engines

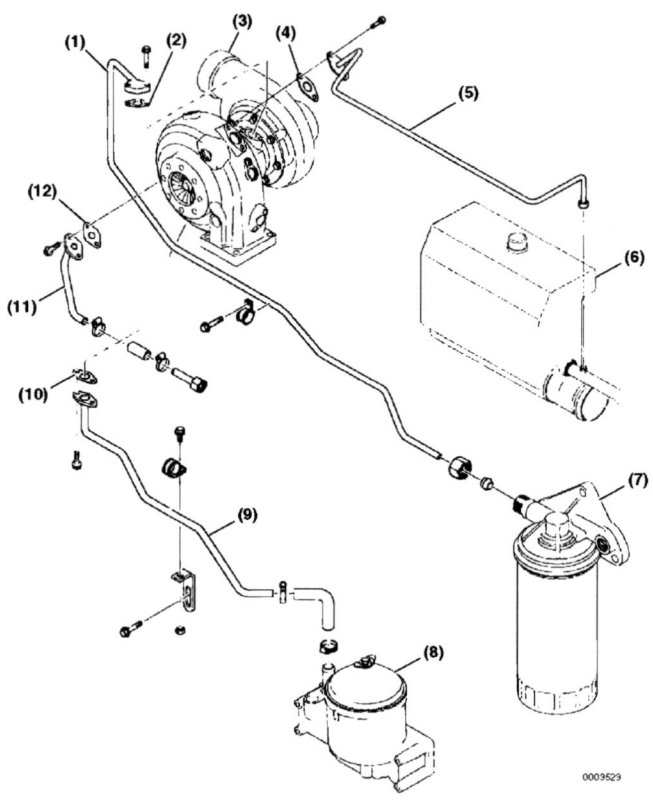

1 – Oil Supply Line
2 – Gasket
3 – Turbocharger
4 – Gasket
5 – Coolant Return Line
6 – Heat Exchanger Assembly
7 – Engine Oil Filter
8 – Centrifugal Oil Cleaner
9 – Oil Return Line
10 – Gasket
11 – Coolant Supply Line
12 – Gasket

Figure 9-1

Component Location

TURBOCHARGER

8SY Engines

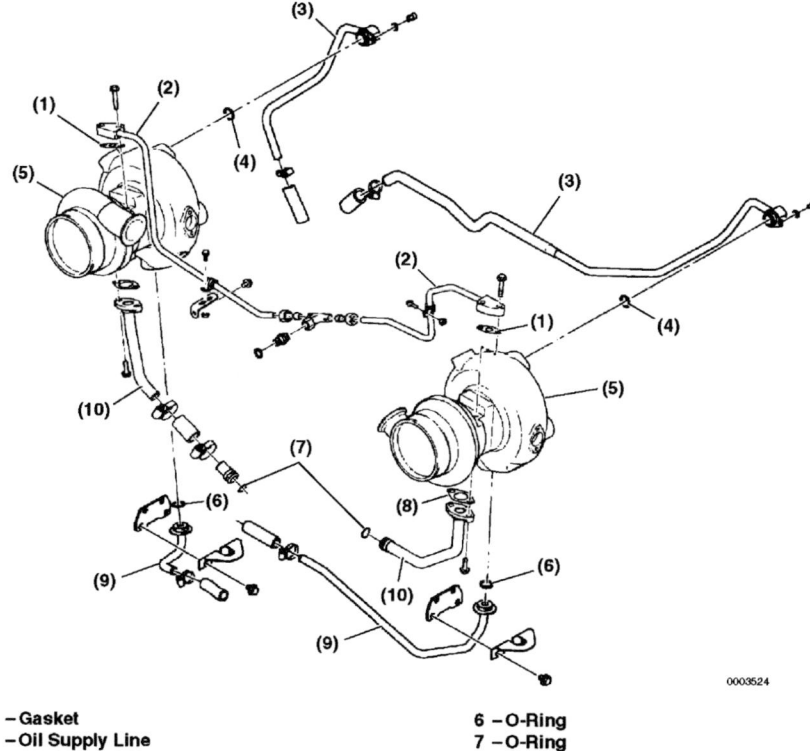

1 – Gasket
2 – Oil Supply Line
3 – Coolant Return Line
4 – O-Ring
5 – Turbocharger
6 – O-Ring
7 – O-Ring
8 – Gasket
9 – Coolant Supply Line
10 – Oil Return Line

Figure 9-2

TURBOCHARGER

TESTS AND ADJUSTMENTS

Measuring Charge Pressure

The turbocharger charge pressure can be measured using console digital display.

Low charge pressure can be due to compressor wheel or turbine wheel damage, or dirt in the compressor housing.

REPAIR

If the Turbocharger Does Not Operate:

1. Check that there is no leakage or loose objects in the line between the air cleaner and turbocharger.
2. Check that there are no loose particles in the exhaust or intake manifolds.
3. Check that all valves are intact.
4. Check the oil return line from the turbocharger for blockage or deformity.
5. Check the oil supply line to the turbocharger for any blockage, deformation and leakage under pressure.
6. Check the condition and part number of the oil filter.
7. Check that the air filter is not blocked and that there are no other reasons for an abnormal increase of vacuum in the intake system.
8. Check that engine output is correct. Excessively high output reduces the service life of the turbocharger.

Repair

TURBOCHARGER

Remove Turbocharger

NOTICE: Observe strict cleanliness at all times when working on the turbocharger. Never leave connections for oil inlets or outlets unprotected. Foreign bodies in the bearing housing will lead to turbocharger breakdown.

6SY Engines

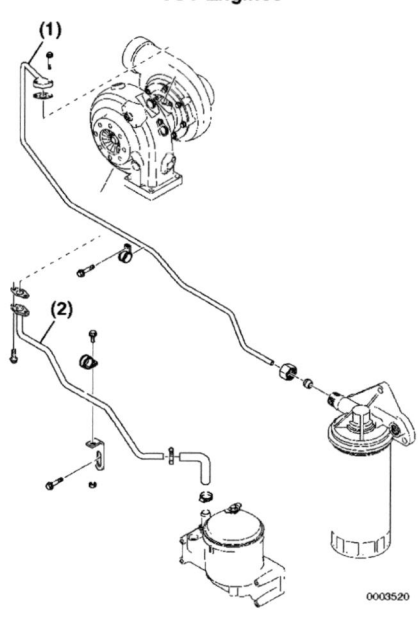

Figure 9-3

8SY Engines

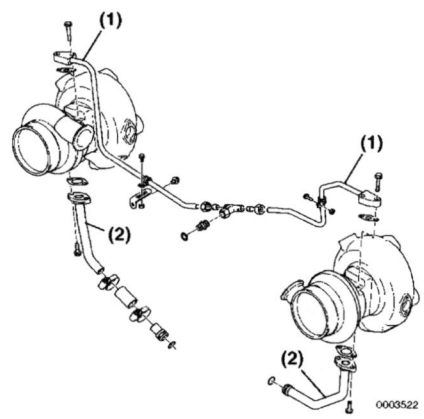

Figure 9-4

9. Remove the oil supply (**Figure 9-3, (1)**) or (**Figure 9-4, (1)**) and return (**Figure 9-3, (2)**) or (**Figure 9-4, (2)**) lines from the turbocharger. Plug or cap all connections.

10. Drain one half of the coolant from the closed cooling system until the coolant level is below the level of the turbocharger.

TURBOCHARGER
Repair

6SY Engines

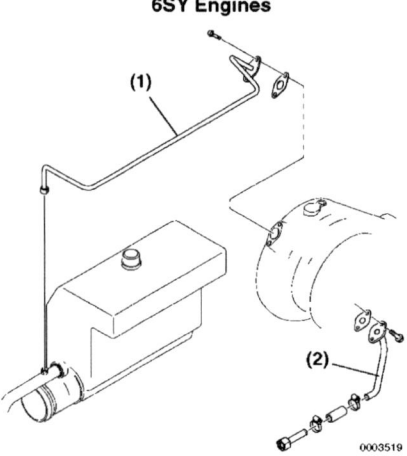

Figure 9-5

8SY Engines

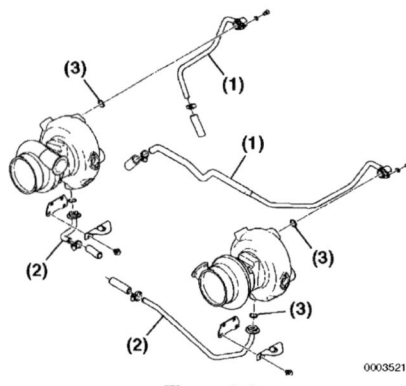

Figure 9-6

11. Remove the coolant supply (**Figure 9-5, (2)**) or (**Figure 9-6, (2)**) and return (**Figure 9-5, (1)**) or (**Figure 9-6, (1)**) lines from the turbocharger. Plug or cap all connections.

12. Remove and discard O-rings (**Figure 9-5, (3)**) or (**Figure 9-6, (3)**).

13. Disconnect the exhaust pipe, induction pipe and charge air cooler pipe from the turbocharger.

14. Remove the nuts retaining the turbocharger and remove the turbocharger.

Inspect the Turbocharger

Inspect the turbine and compressor wheels for evidence of dirt, excess carbon build-up or damage from a foreign object. Dirt and carbon can be removed using a solvent-based cleaner. Damage to either the turbine or compressor wheels will require replacement of the turbocharger assembly.

NOTICE: Never attempt to straighten a damaged vane. It may break off when running and the turbocharger may stop operating completely, causing serious damage to the engine.

Cleaning the Compressor

- Disassemble the compressor housing and clean with mineral spirits and a brush.

- Replace the O-ring if it is damaged. Assemble the compressor housing and measure the charging pressure again.

Measure the Radial and Axial Clearance

In general, measuring the radial and axial clearance gives no indication of the remaining service life of the turbocharger.

When the turbocharger seems to be functioning poorly or noisily, measuring the charging pressure or radial and axial clearance can indicate whether the turbocharger is at fault.

It is advisable to remove the turbocharger to measure axial and radial clearances. Attach the turbocharger to a steel plate, which will also serve as a base for the magnetic stand holding the dial indicator.

Repair

TURBOCHARGER

Radial Clearance

Take readings on both the turbine and compressor wheels.

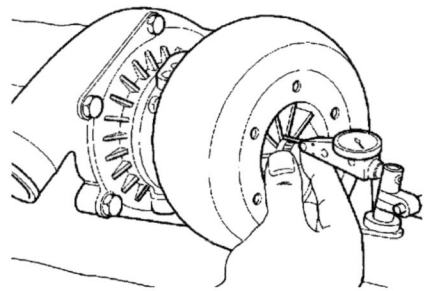

Figure 9-7

1. Place the tip of the dial indicator rocker against the turbine / compressor wheel.

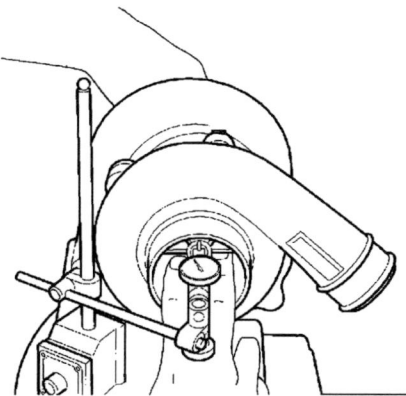

Figure 9-8

2. Pull up both ends of the shaft. Take a reading.
3. Press down both ends of the shaft. Take a reading. The difference between the readings is the radial clearance.
4. Repeat the test three times on each side.
5. If any of the wheels makes contact with the housing, despite the radial clearance reading, the turbocharger must be replaced.

Axial Clearance

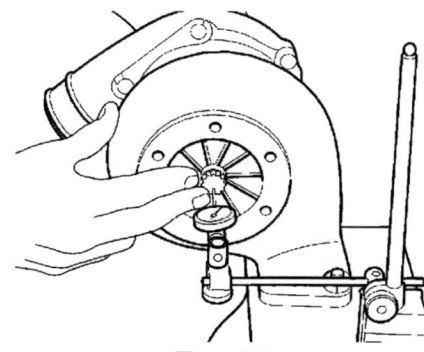

Figure 9-9

1. Place the tip of the dial indicator against the end of the shaft.
2. Press the shaft longitudinally back and forth and take a reading at the end positions. The difference between the readings is the axial clearance.
3. Repeat the test three times.

Specifications

Inspection Item	Engine	Limit
Turbocharger Shaft Radial Clearance	6SY	0.198 - 0.564 mm (0.0078 - 0.0222 in.)
	8SY	0.611 mm (0.0240 in.)
Turbocharger Shaft Axial Clearance	6SY	0.025 - 0.106 mm (0.001 - 0.004 in.)
	8SY	0.102 mm (0.004 in.)

TURBOCHARGER   Repair

Install the Turbocharger

Note: When installing the turbocharger, replace all gaskets with new ones. Change the oil filter and clean the centrifugal oil cleaner.

1. Clean the connecting flange on the exhaust manifold of all old gasket material.
2. Install a new gasket. Lubricate the turbocharger mounting studs with temperature resistant lubricant, OEM Part No. 561 205 (or similar tool). Install the turbocharger on the exhaust manifold and tighten nuts to:
   - **6SY:** 50 N·m (37 ft-lb)
   - **8SY:** 63 N·m (46 ft-lb)

8SY Engines

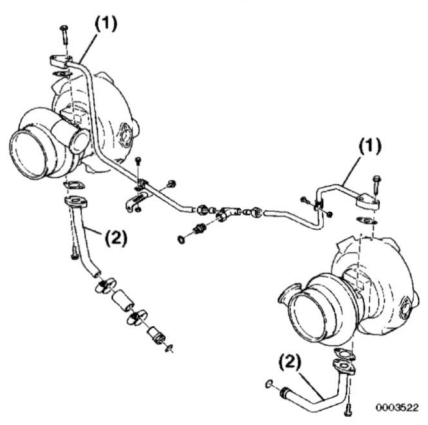

Figure 9-11

3. Connect the oil supply (**Figure 9-10, (1)**) or (**Figure 9-11, (1)**) and return (**Figure 9-10, (2)**) or (**Figure 9-11, (2)**) lines.

6SY Engines

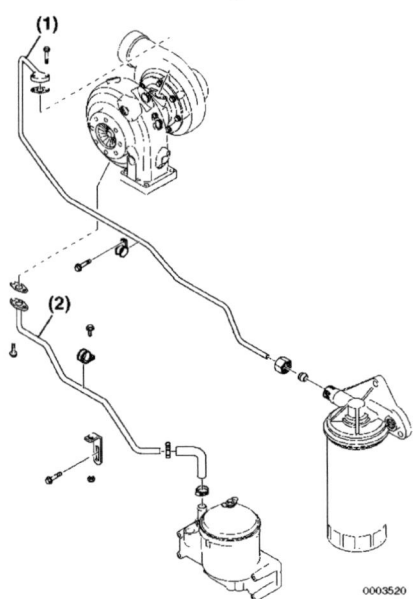

Figure 9-10

Repair

TURBOCHARGER

6SY Engines

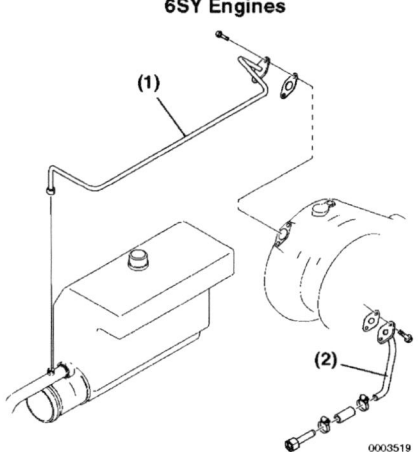

Figure 9-12

8SY Engines

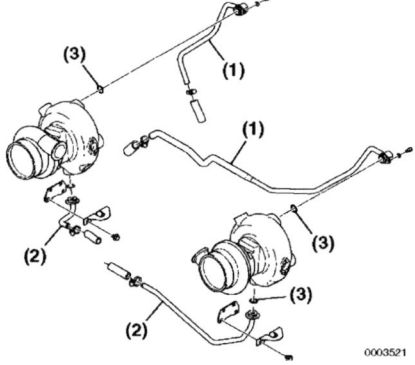

Figure 9-13

5. Connect the charge air pipe, induction pipe and exhaust pipe. Tighten to:
   - **V-Clamp - M6 Bolt:** 8 N·m (71 in.-lb)
   - **V-Clamp - M8 Bolt:** 20 N·m (177 in.-lb)
   - **Exhaust Pipe Flange Bolt:** 24 N·m (212 in.-lb)
6. Install a new oil filter and clean the centrifugal oil cleaner.
7. Start the engine and keep speed at idle until normal oil pressure is reached. *NOTICE: DO NOT raise engine speed above idle until normal oil pressure is reached. Damage to the turbocharger bearings and other engine components could result.*
8. Start the engine and check for oil, water and exhaust leakage.

4. Install new O-rings **(Figure 9-12, (3))** or **(Figure 9-13, (3))** and connect the coolant supply **(Figure 9-12, (2))** or **(Figure 9-13, (2))** and return **(Figure 9-12, (1))** or **(Figure 9-13, (1))** lines.

TURBOCHARGER   Repair

This Page Intentionally Left Blank

Section 10

STARTER MOTOR

	Page
Before You Begin Servicing	10-3
Introduction	10-4
Starter Motor Specifications	10-5
Starter Motor Troubleshooting	10-6
Remove and Install Starter Motor	10-7
Repair Starter Motor - Bosch JE	10-8
Components	10-8
Brush Replacement	10-10
Replace Solenoid	10-11

STARTER MOTOR

This Page Intentionally Left Blank

BEFORE YOU BEGIN SERVICING

⚠ WARNING

ALWAYS turn off the battery switch (if equipped) or disconnect the negative battery cable before servicing the electrical system.

ALWAYS check the electrical harnesses for cracks, abrasions, and damaged or corroded connectors. ALWAYS keep the connectors and terminals clean.

NOTICE

NEVER engage the starter motor while the engine is running. Damage to the starter motor pinion and / or ring gear will result.

STARTER MOTOR

INTRODUCTION

This section of the *Service Manual* covers the servicing of starter motor. Yanmar Part No. 165000-29830 is standard equipment on 6SY and 8SY model engines and is used in this section to show the service procedures for a representative starter motor. For specific part detail, see the *Yanmar Parts Catalog* for the engine being serviced.

STARTER MOTOR SPECIFICATIONS

Repair Specifications

Item	Bosch JE
Power	6.7 kW (4942 ft-lb/s)
Direction of Rotation (Viewed toward flywheel housing)	Counterclockwise
Brush Length (Minimum)	17.5 mm (0.689 in.)
Brush Spring Pressure	47 - 53 N (10.5 - 12.0 lbf)
Solenoid Pull-in Winding Resistance	0.5 ohms
Solenoid Hold-in Winding Resistance	2.5 ohms
Armature Radial Run-out (Maximum)	0.10 mm (0.004 in.)
Commutator Radial Run-out (Maximum)	0.03 mm (0.001 in.)
Commutator Diameter (Minimum)	42.5 mm (1.673 in.)

Special Torque Chart

Item	Bosch JE
Battery Positive (+) Cable	24 - 32 N·m (17 - 24 ft-lb)
Control Cable	2 - 3 N·m (18 - 27 in.-lb)
Ground Cable-to-Starter Housing	16 - 20 N·m (142 - 177 in.-lb)

STARTER MOTOR

Starter Motor Troubleshooting

STARTER MOTOR TROUBLESHOOTING

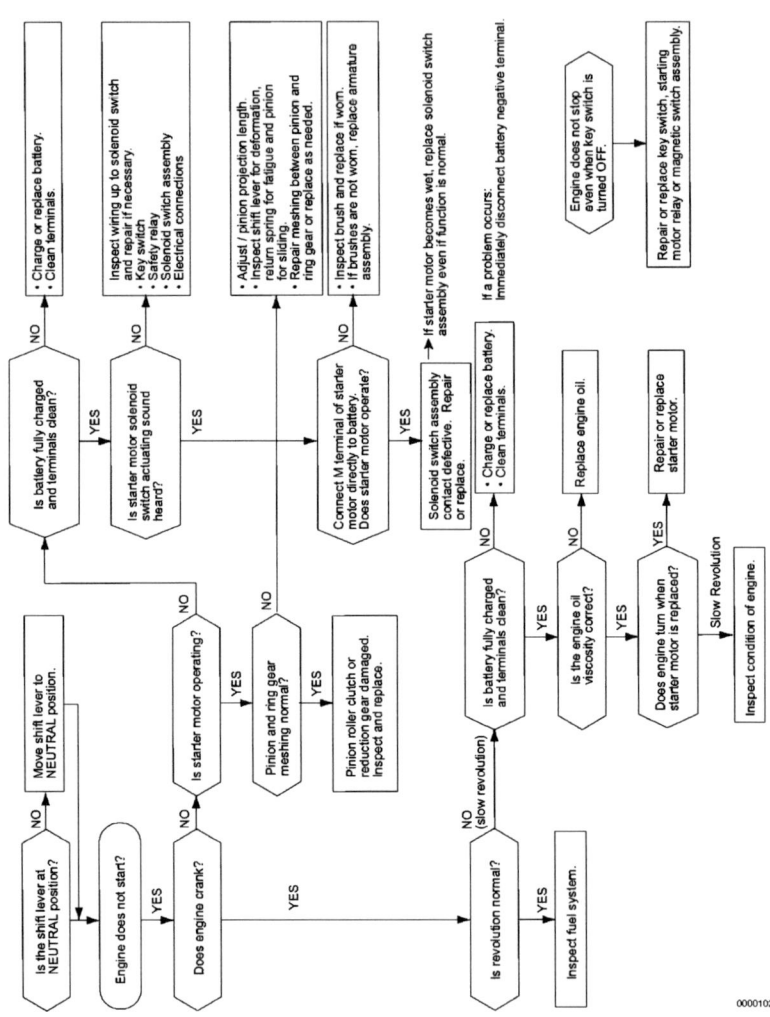

Figure 10-1

REMOVE AND INSTALL STARTER MOTOR

1. Disconnect the battery(s), negative (-) cable first or turn off the battery master switch.

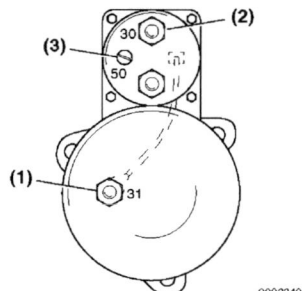

Figure 10-2

Note: The dotted conductor wire shows ground connection for the solenoid switch on 2-pin starter motors.

2. Disconnect ground cable **(Figure 10-2, (1))** if used.
3. Disconnect positive (+) cable **(Figure 10-2, (2))** and primary wire **(Figure 10-2, (3))**.
4. Move cables to one side.
5. Remove bolts holding the starter motor to the flywheel housing.
6. Carefully remove the starter motor. **WARNING! The starter motor is heavy. Use care when removing the starter motor.**
7. Inspect the starter motor. NOTICE: Check the starter pinion for damage. If the starter pinion is damaged, the flywheel ring gear must also be checked for damage.
8. Clean the starter mounting area of the flywheel housing.
9. Install the starter motor.
10. Clean the cable connections.
11. Connect the cables to the appropriate terminals:

- Primary wire **(Figure 10-2, (3))**. Tighten to 2 - 3 N·m (18 - 27 in.-lb).
- Battery positive (+) **(Figure 10-2, (2))**. Tighten to 24 - 32 N·m (17 - 24 ft-lb).
- Ground cable **(Figure 10-2, (3))**. Tighten to 16 - 20 N·m (142 - 177 in.-lb).

12. Connect the battery, negative (-) cable first, or return the master switch to the ON position.
13. Install any panels or housings removed to access the starter.
14. Operate starter to verify operation.

STARTER MOTOR

REPAIR STARTER MOTOR - BOSCH JE

Components

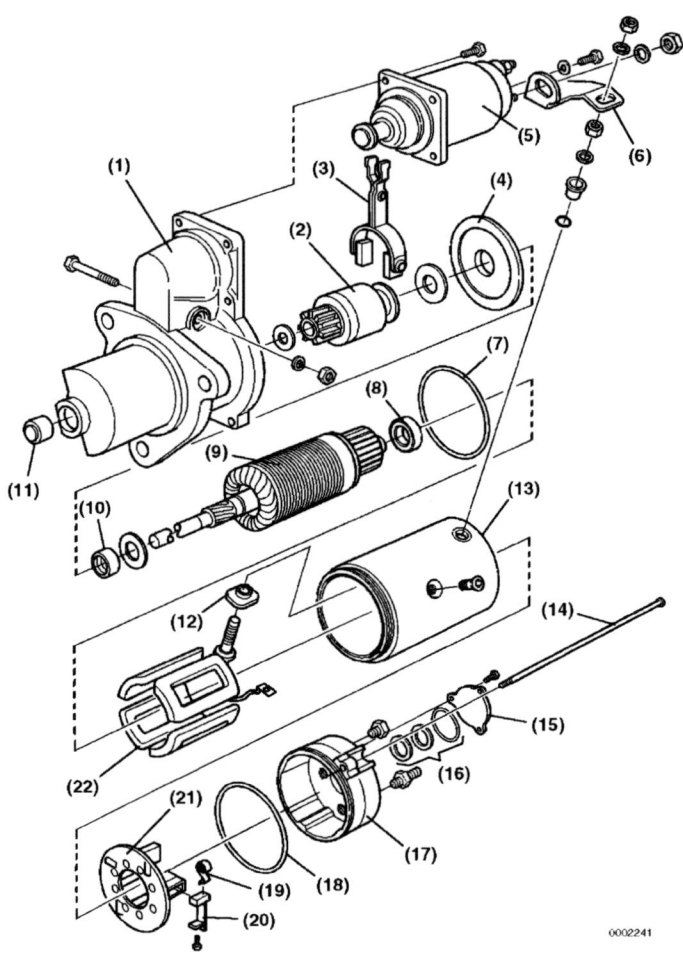

Figure 10-3

Repair Starter Motor - Bosch JE   **STARTER MOTOR**

1 – Front Housing
2 – Pinion Gear
3 – Engaging Lever
4 – Intermediate Bearing
5 – Solenoid Assembly
6 – Conducting Bar
7 – O-Ring
8 – Bearing
9 – Armature
10 – Bearing
11 – Bearing
12 – Electrical Stud and Insulator
13 – Field Housing
14 – Through-Bolt
15 – Rear Cover
16 – Shim Washers and Gasket
17 – Rear Bearing Housing
18 – O-Ring
19 – Brush Spring
20 – Brush Kit
21 – Brush Holder Assembly
22 – Field Winding

STARTER MOTOR

Brush Replacement

Equipment Required
Four spring locks are required to replace the brushes and springs. Make from thin sheet metal cut into four pieces approximately 20 x 40 mm.

Repair
1. Remove starter. *See Remove and Install Starter Motor on page 10-7.*

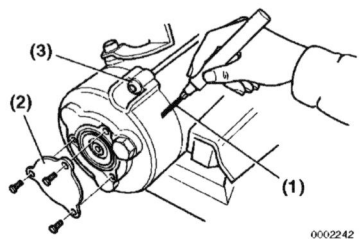

Figure 10-4

2. Mark the position **(Figure 10-4, (1))** of the rear bearing housing with a marker.
3. Remove the rear cover **(Figure 10-4, (2))**.
4. Remove the through-bolts **(Figure 10-4, (3))** and rear bearing housing.

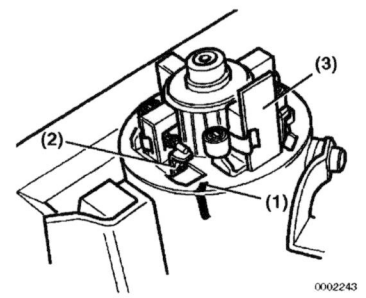

Figure 10-5

5. Mark the position of the brush holder **(Figure 10-5, (1))**.

Repair Starter Motor - Bosch JE

6. Remove positive brush wire connection screws **(Figure 10-5, (2))**.
7. Install the spring locks **(Figure 10-5, (3))** to relieve spring pressure on the brushes.
8. Remove the brush holder and brushes.
9. Inspect the commutator for damage, burned areas, or wear.

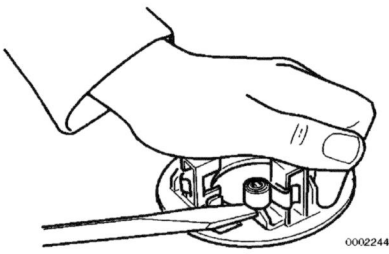

Figure 10-6

10. Remove the brushes and springs using a screwdriver **(Figure 10-6)**. **CAUTION!** *The brush springs are under considerable tension when installing or removing from the brush housing and can unexpectedly come out. ALWAYS wear safety glasses when repairing the recoil starter.*
11. Place new brushes in the brush holder. Do not install the springs yet.
12. Install the brush holder and align the mark made during disassembly. Connect the brush wires.

STARTER MOTOR

Repair Starter Motor - Bosch JE

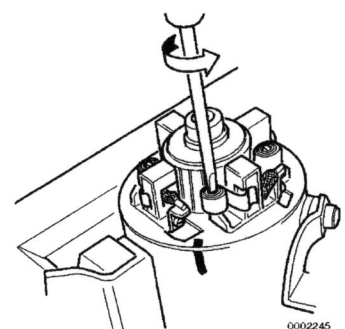

Figure 10-7

13. Install new springs. Use a small screwdriver in the center of the spring to coil it and slide it onto the post **(Figure 10-7)**.
    - Set the brush in position.
    - Coil the spring one half turn.
    - Press the center of the spring onto the post.
14. Install the end housing using the spring locks to relieve spring pressure on the brushes. Align the marks made during disassembly.
15. Install the rear cover and seal.
16. Install starter. *See Remove and Install Starter Motor on page 10-7.*

Replace Solenoid

1. Remove starter. *See Remove and Install Starter Motor on page 10-7.*

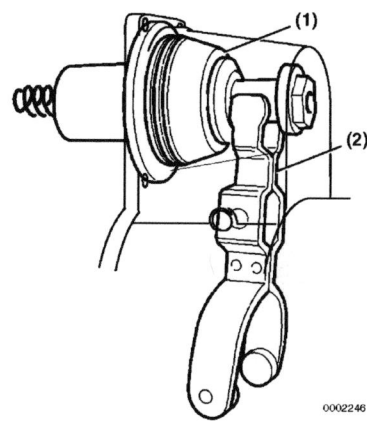

Figure 10-8

2. Remove the solenoid conducting bar.
3. Remove four bolts and the solenoid housing.
4. Remove the plunger assembly **(Figure 10-8, (1))**.
5. Apply heat-resistant grease to the plunger surfaces that engage the coupling lever **(Figure 10-8, (2))**.
6. Install the plunger assembly making sure that it engages the coupling lever.
7. Lightly lubricate the plunger with a heat-resistant grease.
8. Install the solenoid housing and secure with four screws.
9. Install the conducting bar and tighten terminal nuts to specification.
10. Install starter. *See Remove and Install Starter Motor on page 10-7.*

STARTER MOTOR

Repair Starter Motor - Bosch JE

This Page Intentionally Left Blank

Section 11

ALTERNATOR

Page

Before You Begin Servicing	11-3
Introduction	11-4
Specifications	11-5
Calculating Alternator Capacity	11-6
Alternator and Charging System Troubleshooting	11-6
Test and Inspection	11-7
Output Test	11-7
Brush Length	11-8
Rotor	11-8
Repair	11-9
Replace Alternator Belt	11-9

ALTERNATOR

This Page Intentionally Left Blank

BEFORE YOU BEGIN SERVICING

⚠ WARNING

ALWAYS turn off the battery switch (if equipped) or disconnect the negative battery cable before servicing the electrical system.

ALWAYS check the electrical harnesses for cracks, abrasions, and damaged or corroded connectors.
ALWAYS keep the connectors and terminals clean.

NOTICE

NEVER operate the engine if the alternator is producing unusual sounds. Damage to the alternator will result.

NEVER turn the battery switch OFF while the engine is operating. Damage to the alternator will result.

NEVER reverse the positive (+) and negative (-) ends of the battery cable. The alternator diode and stator coil will be damaged.

NEVER use a high-pressure wash directly on the alternator. Water will damage the alternator and result in inadequate charging.

NEVER operate the engine if the alternator is producing unusual sounds. Damage to the alternator will result.

NEVER turn the battery switch OFF while the engine is operating. Damage to the alternator will result.

NEVER use a high-pressure wash directly on the alternator. Water will damage the alternator and result in inadequate charging.

ALTERNATOR

INTRODUCTION

This section of the *Service Manual* describes servicing of the 6SY and 8SY charging systems.

Yanmar 6SY and 8SY marine engines can be equipped with one or two alternators, depending on system requirements.

- Ensure correct polarity when connecting the batteries. The alternator diodes will be damaged if the polarity is reversed.

- It is not necessary to disconnect any leads to the alternator for electric welding. Attach the welder's ground clamp as close as possible to the welding point.

SPECIFICATIONS

Repair Specifications

Item	Bosch (65A)	Bosch (140A)
Manufacturer's Number	N1-28V 20/65A	T1-28V 70/14A
Output at 6000 RPM (alternator speed)	1800W	*
System Voltage	24 V, Negative Ground	24V, Negative Ground
Drive Ratio	3.5:1	*
Output Test Amperage @ 28 V	*	*
Output Test Voltage	27.5-28.5 V	*
Brush Length (Minimum)	7.5 mm (0.295 in.)	*
Slip Ring Diameter (Minimum)	26.8 mm (1.055 in.)	*
Rotor Resistance	8.4 - 8.8 ohms	*
Stator Resistance	0.3 ohm	*

*Not available at time of publication

Special Torque Chart

Item	Bosch 65A	Bosch 140A
Belt Pulley Nut	65 N·m (48 lb·ft)	*

*Not available at time of publication

ALTERNATOR

CALCULATING ALTERNATOR CAPACITY

Some engines or aggregates have a considerable level of equipment with high current consumption.

It is essential that the alternator capacity is adapted to the consumption in question. If the alternator capacity is too low, battery life will be impaired and cause possible starting difficulties.

The alternator must be able to deliver an excess charge of at least 10 A. In principle, the batteries are intended for starting the engine.

1. Add together the engine or aggregate current consumers that can be engaged simultaneously when in operation. Add to this value at least 10 A.

Example:

If there is a consumption of 40 A, the alternator must be capable of outputting 50 A.

1. Determine the relevant type of operation. Long-term service has fewer stops and therefore requires a lower alternator capacity than an engine or aggregate with many stops. Look up the required alternator capacity in the diagram on the right.

The current generated by the alternator is dependent on the engine speed. The table below shows the approximate current delivered by the alternator at various engine speeds.

Alternator Current Output (approximate) with 3.5:1 Drive Ratio

RPM		Bosch (65A)
Engine	Alternator	Output (Amps)
500	1750	31
600	2100	40
700	2450	46
800	2800	50
900	3150	53
1000	3500	56
1100	3850	58
1200	4200	60
1300	4550	61
1400	4900	63
1500	5250	64
1600	5600	64
1700	5950	65
1800	6300	65
1900	6650	66
2000	7000	66
2100	7350	67
2200	7700	67
2300	8050	67
2400	8400	67

ALTERNATOR AND CHARGING SYSTEM TROUBLESHOOTING

If a fault code is present that indicates a malfunction in the alternator or charging system, follow the procedures in the *Fault Codes on page 13-18*.

ALTERNATOR

TEST AND INSPECTION

Output Test

1. Connect a calibrated test instrument with load resistor as illustrated in **(Figure 11-1)**. *NOTICE: NEVER operate the engine with the batteries disconnected. Damage to the alternator will result.*

Note: A digital clip-on ammeter can also be connected to the B+ wire at the alternator for a more precise reading.

2. Start the engine and let it run for a few minutes before carrying out the test.
3. Increase the engine speed to 1715 rpm, (6000 rpm alternator speed). Apply current to the load resistor. Record voltage and current output.

Note: The following steps must be performed with fully charged batteries.

4. Remove the load and allow the engine to run until the alternator is delivering approximately 5A at the battery.
5. Again record voltage.

Specifications

Inspection Item	Bosch (65A)
Test Output Amperage @ 28 V	*
Test Output Voltage	27.5 - 28.5 V

*Not available at time of publication.

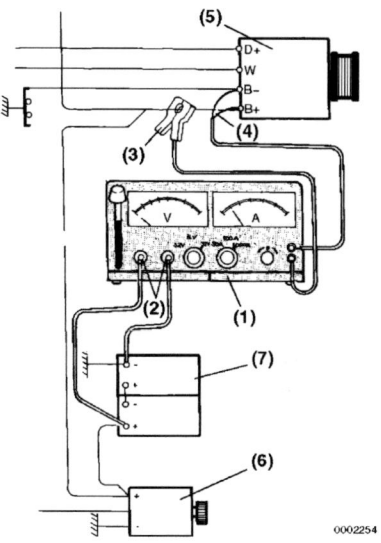

1 – Test Instrument Equipped with Voltmeter, Ammeter and Load Resistor
2 – Connection to Load Resistor
3 – Clip for Current Reading
4 – Connection to Voltmeter
5 – Alternator
6 – Starter Motor
7 – Batteries

Figure 11-1

ALTERNATOR

Test and Inspection

Brush Length

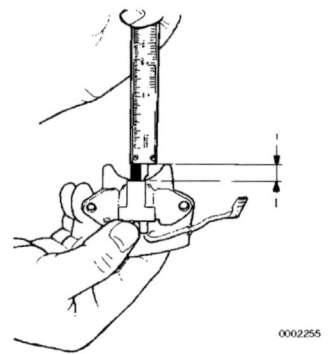

Figure 11-2

The brush holder is attached to the charge regulator. The brushes must be checked for damage and length. The ends must be bright and rounded so they fit against the slip rings.

Brush length is measured between the end of the brush and the brush holder.

Specifications

Inspection Item	Bosch 65A
Brush Length (minimum)	7.5 mm (0.295 in.)

Rotor

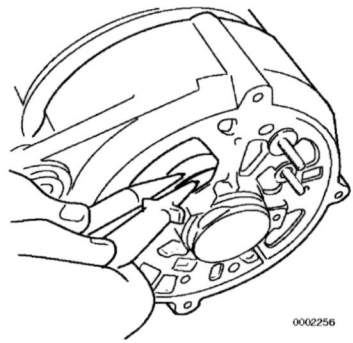

Figure 11-3

Slip Rings

The slip rings must be bright metal across their whole surface. Dull slip rings indicate bad contact with the brushes. The slip rings can be accessed after removing the charge regulator.

Resistance

Measure the rotor resistance using an ohmmeter between the slip rings.

Specifications

Inspection Item	Bosch 65A
Rotor Resistance	8.4 - 8.8 ohms

When measuring between the slip rings and the core, the ohmmeter must show infinite resistance (at least 10 megaohms).

ALTERNATOR

REPAIR

Replace Alternator Belt

6SY Engines

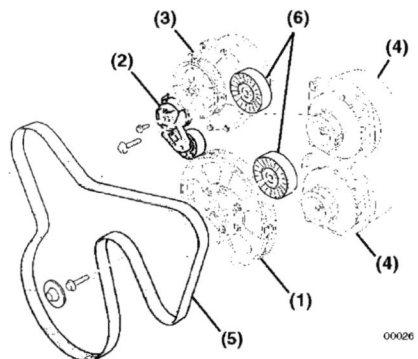

1 – Crankshaft Belt Pulley
2 – Belt Tensioner
3 – Coolant Pump
4 – Alternator
5 – Alternator Belt
6 – Idler Roller

Figure 11-4

Note: 6SY with dual alternators shown.

8SY Engines

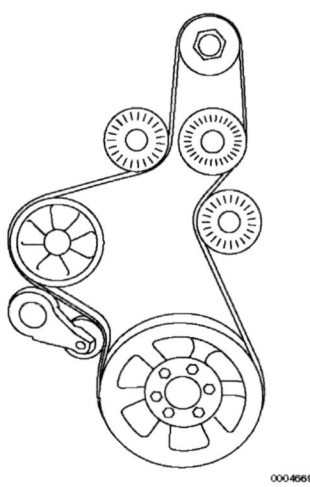

Figure 11-5

1. Install a 1/2-inch drive breaker bar in the square hole of the belt tensioner.
2. Rotate the tensioner to relieve belt tension. Remove belt.
3. Installation is the reverse of removal.

ALTERNATOR   Repair

This Page Intentionally Left Blank

Section 12

EMS

	Page
Introduction	12-3
Specifications	12-3
Special Service Tools	12-3
Function Description - Engine Management System (EMS S6)	12-4
General	12-4
Component Location	12-5
Engine Speed Sensors - T28 and T29	12-7
Charge Air Pressure and Temperature Sensor - T26	12-8
Coolant Temperature Sensor - T27	12-10
Oil Pressure Sensor - T25	12-11
EMS S6 Control Unit E44	12-12
EMS S6 Control Unit Connections	12-13
Repair	12-17
Replace the EMS S6 Control Unit	12-17
Remove the EMS S6 Wiring	12-17
Installing EMS S6 Wiring	12-20

EMS

This Page Intentionally Left Blank

Introduction

EMS

INTRODUCTION

This section of the *Service Manual* describes the operation of and procedures to replace the components of the Engine Management System as used on the Yanmar 6SY and 8SY marine engines.

Specifications

Special Torque Chart

Component	Tightening Torque	Lubricating Oil Application (Thread Portion and Seat Surface)	Reference Page
Injector Electrical Terminal Screw	2 N·m (283 in.-oz)	Not Applied	See Installing EMS S6 Wiring on page 12-20
Rocker Cover Bolt (Upper and Lower Cover)	26 N·m (19 ft-lb)	Not Applied	

SPECIAL SERVICE TOOLS

Note: The tool numbers used in this section are either Yanmar or Scania part numbers. Yanmar part numbers are referred to as **Yanmar Part No.** and Scania part numbers are referred to as **OEM Part No.** Tools not having part numbers must be acquired locally.

No	Tool Name	Applicable Model and Tool Size	Illustration
1	Torque Screwdriver (For Connecting Cables to Injector)	OEM Part No. 288 179	

FUNCTION DESCRIPTION - ENGINE MANAGEMENT SYSTEM (EMS S6)

General

Figure 12-1 illustrates the components and systems with which the EMS S6 control unit communicates.

Communication with certain components must take place via a coordinator (Teleflex i8310).

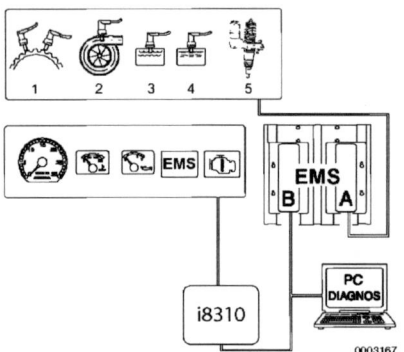

1 – Engine Speed Sensors (2 used)
2 – Charge Air Pressure and Temperature Sensor
3 – Coolant Temperature Sensor
4 – Oil Pressure Sensor
5 – Unit Injector Solenoid Valves (one per cylinder)

Figure 12-1

Function Description - Engine Management System (EMS S6) **EMS**

Component Location

6SY Engines

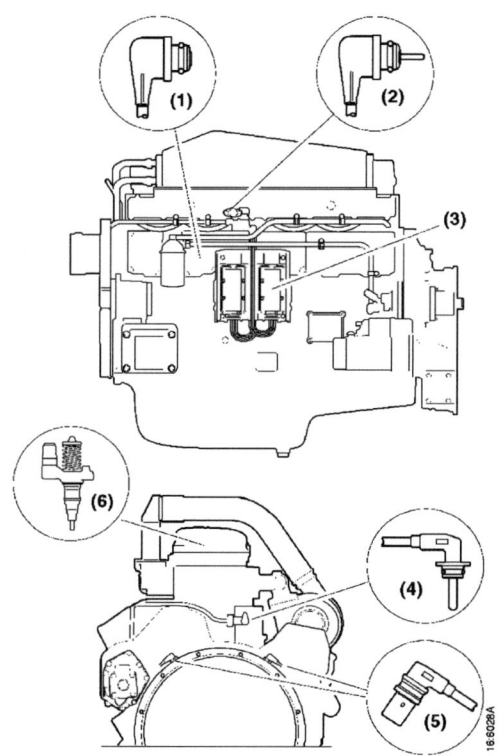

1 – Oil Pressure Sensor
2 – Charge Air Pressure and Temperature Sensor
3 – EMS S6 Control Unit
4 – Coolant Temperature Sensor
5 – Engine Speed Sensor
6 – Unit Injector Solenoid Valves

Figure 12-2

EMS

Function Description - Engine Management System (EMS S6)

8SY Engines

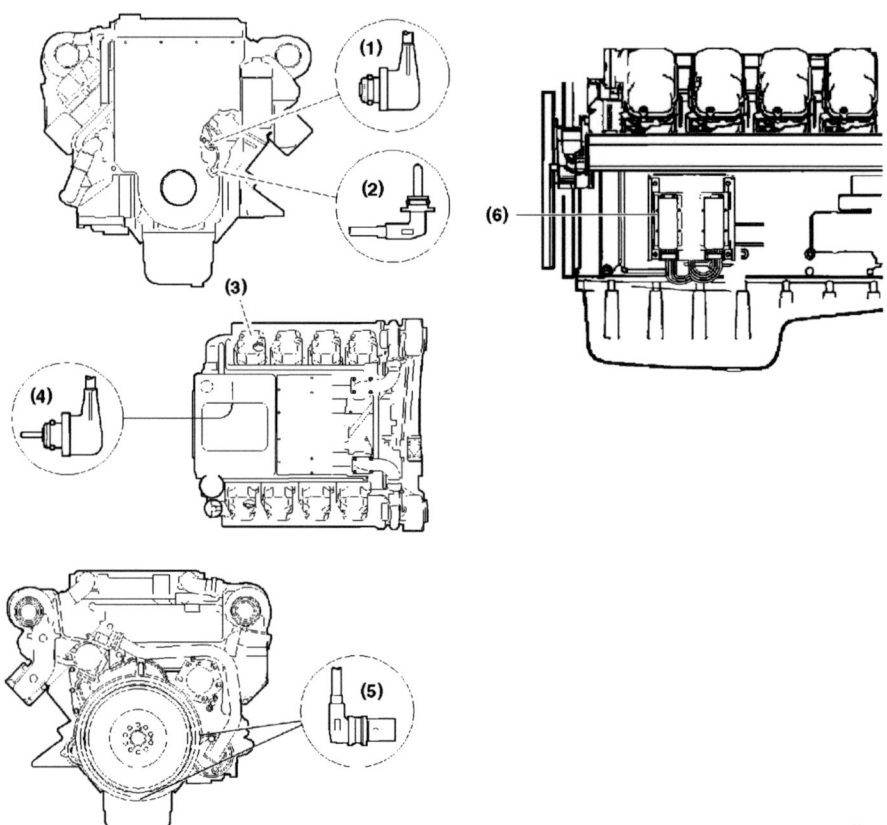

1 – Oil Pressure Sensor (Optional Combination Oil Pressure and Oil Temperature Sensor Available)
2 – Coolant Temperature Sensor
3 – Unit Injector Solenoid Valves
4 – Charge Air Pressure and Temperature Sensor
5 – Engine Speed Sensor
6 – EMS S6 Control Unit

Figure 12-3

Function Description - Engine Management System (EMS S6)   EMS

Engine Speed Sensors - T28 and T29

6SY Engine

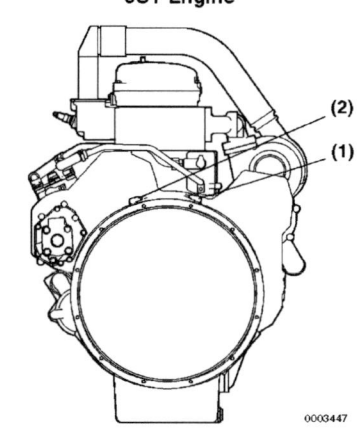

1 – Engine Speed Sensor 1, T28
2 – Engine Speed Sensor 2, T29

Figure 12-4

8SY Engine

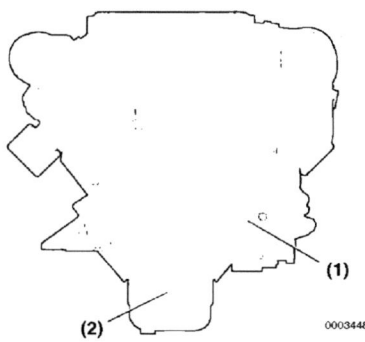

1 – Engine Speed Sensor 1, T28
2 – Engine Speed Sensor 2, T29

Figure 12-5

There are two engine speed sensors in the EMS S6 system; Engine Speed Sensor 1 and Engine Speed Sensor 2. The sensors are inductive, meaning they only produce signals when the engine is running. The signal strength varies significantly depending on the air gap between the sensors and the flywheel, as well as engine speed. The EMS S6 system performs an assessment of the signal strength at different engine speeds. If the signal strength becomes too low, a fault code is generated.

Both engine speed sensors read the position of the flywheel. This means that the system cannot determine which of two possible revolutions the engine is at: for example, whether cylinder 1 or cylinder 6 is at the ignition position. Every time the engine is stopped and the voltage removed, the crankshaft position is stored. Next time the voltage is switched on, the stored position of the crankshaft is used to determine which revolution the engine is at. When the engine has started, a system check is performed to verify that the stored position is correct.

The EMS S6 control unit receives signals from both engine speed sensors. If the control unit receives a faulty signal or no signal from either of the engine speed sensors, the engine torque is limited for safety reasons. If the control unit receives a correct signal, the engine will operate normally again.

If the control unit receives a faulty signal or no signal from both engine speed sensors, the engine cannot be started. If the engine is running, it will stop.

EMS

Function Description - Engine Management System (EMS S6)

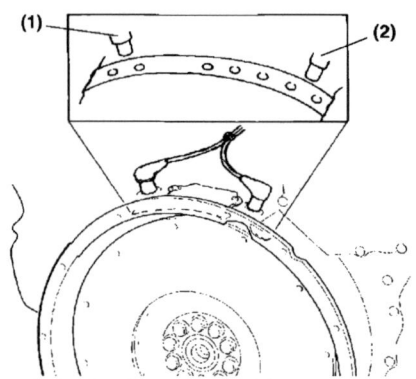

1 – Engine Speed Sensor 1, T28
2 – Engine Speed Sensor 2, T29

Figure 12-6

The engine speed sensors detect the holes in the flywheel when the flywheel rotates and send pulses to the control unit at every hole. This allows the control unit to calculate where in the operating cycle the engine is. The control unit senses and compares the engine speed at combustion in each cylinder. The control unit attempts to keep the engine speed constant by adjusting the fuel volume individually for each cylinder.

The interval between two of the holes is greater than that between the remaining holes. When the control unit senses that this larger interval passes the sensor, it knows that the flywheel is in a specific position in relation to top dead center (TDC up).

If the control unit detects any faults, one or more fault codes are generated.

Sensor Connections to EMS S6

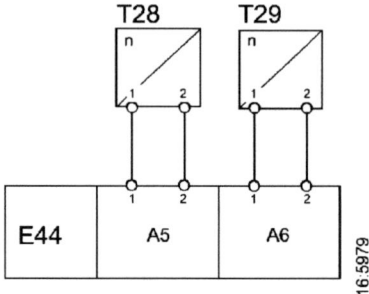

Figure 12-7

Charge Air Pressure and Temperature Sensor - T26

6SY Engines

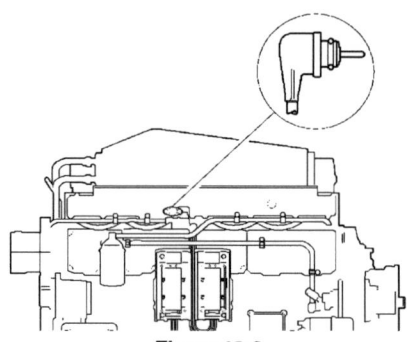

Figure 12-8

Function Description - Engine Management System (EMS S6) EMS

8SY Engines

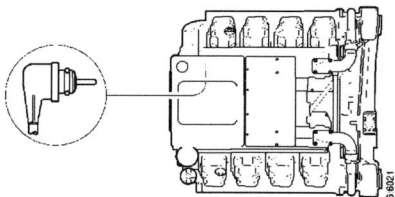

Figure 12-9

The sensors for charge air pressure and temperature are integrated into one single component.

Charge Air Pressure Sensor

The charge air pressure sensor detects the absolute pressure in the intake manifold, which consists of the atmospheric pressure plus the overpressure provided by the turbocharger.

The EMS S6 control unit uses the signal from the sensor to limit the fuel volume when the charge air pressure is below a certain level. The lower the pressure, the less fuel the control unit allows to the unit injectors, avoiding black exhaust smoke.

The control unit reads the voltage from the sensor. The signal voltage is directly proportional to the charge air pressure. High pressure gives high voltage and vice versa.

Depending on factors such as throttle actuation, engine speed, engine acceleration and charge air temperature, the control unit will expect a certain value for the charge air pressure.

If there are any faults in the signal, the control unit will operate according to a preset pressure value. As a safety precaution, the engine torque is then limited.

Charge Air Temperature Sensor

The charge air temperature sensor detects the intake air temperature. The control unit uses the signal from the sensor to finely adjust the fuel quantity so that black smoke is not produced. The warmer the charge air, the less fuel the control unit allows to the unit injectors.

The sensor is of the NTC type, meaning its resistance is temperature dependent. If the temperature increases, the resistance in the sensor drops.

If the voltage is outside a certain range, the control unit will operate according to a preset temperature value.

The engine will then react more slowly than normal when actuating the throttle in cold weather, as the control unit thinks that the air is warmer than it actually is.

Sensor Connection to EMS S6

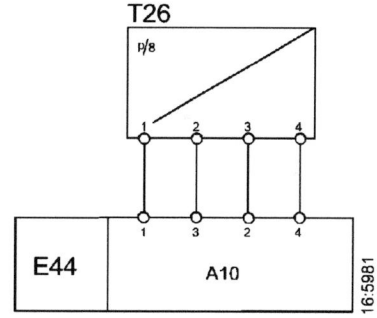

Figure 12-10

EMS

Function Description - Engine Management System (EMS S6)

Coolant Temperature Sensor - T27

6SY Engines

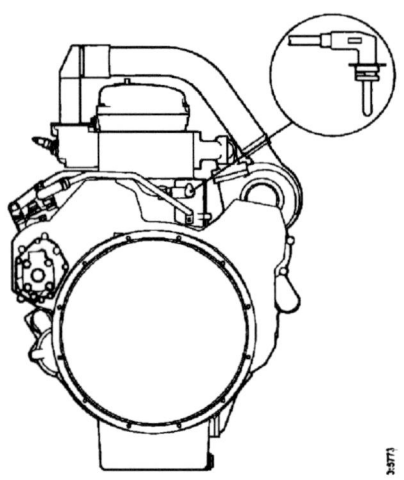

Figure 12-11

8SY Engines

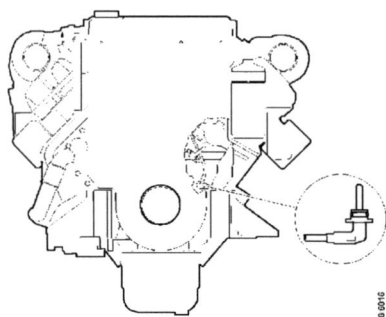

Figure 12-12

The coolant temperature sensor affects the fuel volume and injection timing when starting the engine and when the engine is cold. It also affects the engine idling speed and maximum engine speed when the engine is cold and the engine power when it is too warm.

If the coolant temperature sensor senses that the engine is cold when attempting to start (cold start), the engine will make a few turns without any fuel being injected to heat up the cylinders and then the amount of fuel injected will gradually increase until the engine starts.

Directly after a cold start, the engine speed is limited to 1000 rpm to protect the engine.

The length of time engine speed limitation is engaged varies depending on the coolant temperature:

Below -10°C (+14°F)	30 seconds
Above +20°C (+68°F)	1 second
Between -10° to +20°C (+14° to +68°F)	Linear 1-30 seconds

The engine idling speed returns to normal when the coolant has reached +20° to +60°C (+68° to +140°F). The temperature limits will differ between engine types.

Sensor Connection to EMS S6

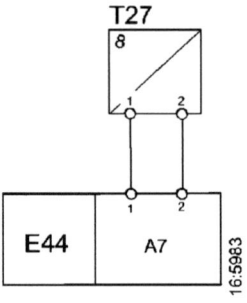

Figure 12-13

Function Description - Engine Management System (EMS S6)

EMS

The control unit reads the voltage from the sensor. If the voltage is outside a certain range, the control unit will operate according to a preset temperature value. The engine will then have poorer cold start characteristics and will emit more white smoke in cold weather.

Power vs. Engine Temperature

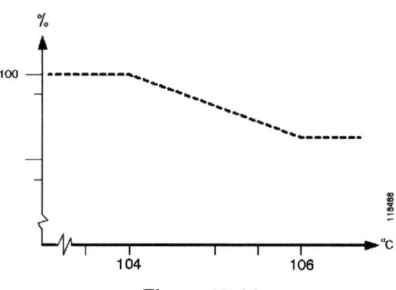

Figure 12-14

On certain engines, the engine power is limited when the coolant temperature exceeds 104°C (219°F). Engine power is limited to prevent further engine overheating, and a fault code is generated at the same time **(Figure 12-25)**.

Oil Pressure Sensor - T25

6SY Engines

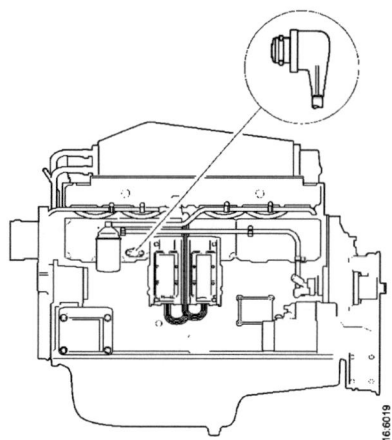

Figure 12-15

8SY Engines

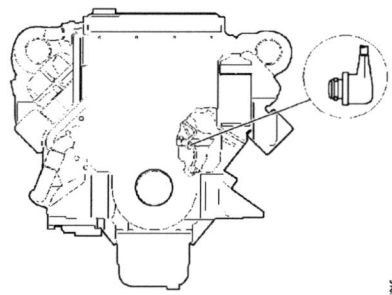

Figure 12-16

The oil pressure sensor measures engine oil pressure.

EMS

Function Description - Engine Management System (EMS S6)

The control unit reads the voltage from the sensor. If the signal voltage is outside a certain range, the oil pressure gauge on the instrument panel will show 2.5 bar (36 psi), regardless of engine speed, and a fault code will be generated at the same time.

The control unit expects a certain oil pressure depending on the engine speed. Below 1000 rpm, the oil pressure should be at a certain level. Above 1000 rpm, the oil pressure should be at a higher level, in order to provide sufficient oil pressure for piston cooling, etc. If the oil pressure is below the expected value, a warning alarm is sounded. The oil pressure warning alarm will sound at different pressure levels depending on the engine speed.

As an option on 8SY marine engines, a dual-purpose sensor is available that measures both oil pressure and oil temperature. It is located in the same place as the oil pressure-only sensor.

Connection to EMS S6

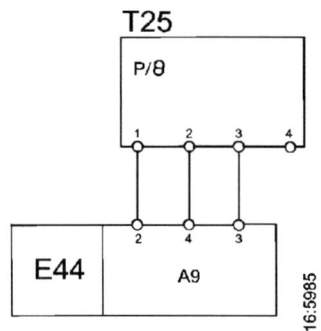

Figure 12-17

EMS S6 Control Unit E44

Function of EMS S6 Control Unit

6SY Engines

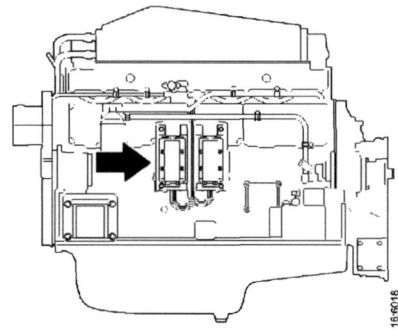

Figure 12-18

8SY Engines

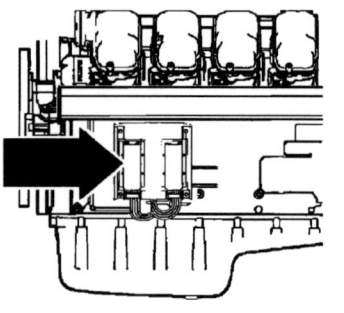

Figure 12-19

The EMS S6 control unit collects information which it processes into signals that control the fuel volume and injection timing.

The control unit converts the system voltage to a voltage of approximately 5 V, which it supplies to sensors, etc. These sensors are always grounded through the control unit.

Function Description - Engine Management System (EMS S6)

EMS

EMS S6 Control Unit Connections

The EMS S6 control unit is connected to other components and systems via connectors A and B **(Figure 12-31)**. The following graphic and table show the pin locations and assignments.

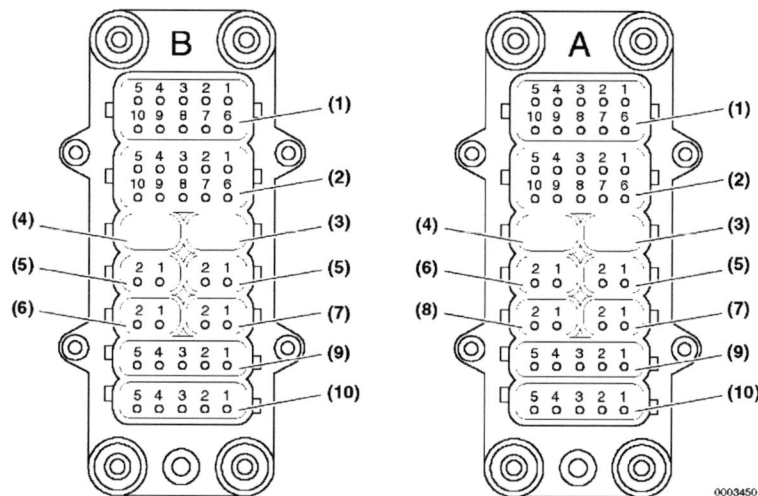

Figure 12-20

EMS

Function Description - Engine Management System (EMS S6)

EMS S6 Control Unit Pin Assignments

Connector	Pin	Assignment	Detail
A1 (6SY / 8SY)	1	Voltage supply, +24 V to unit injectors	8SY cylinder 8 6SY cylinder 4
A1 (6SY / 8SY)	2	Voltage supply, +24 V to unit injectors	8SY cylinder 7 6SY cylinder 5
A1 (6SY / 8SY)	3	Not used	
A1 (6SY / 8SY)	4	Voltage supply, +24 V to unit injectors	8SY cylinder 6 6SY cylinder 6
A1 (6SY / 8SY)	5	Voltage supply, +24 V to unit injectors	8SY cylinder 5
A1 (6SY / 8SY)	6	Ground for unit injectors	8SY cylinder 8 6SY cylinder 4
A1 (6SY / 8SY)	7	Ground for unit injectors	8SY cylinder 7 6SY cylinder 5
A1 (6SY / 8SY)	8	Not used	
A1 (6SY / 8SY)	9	Ground for unit injectors	8SY cylinder 6 6SY cylinder 6
A1 (6SY / 8SY)	10	Ground for unit injectors	8SY cylinder 5
A2	1	Not used	
A2	2	Not used	
A2	3	Not used	
A2	4	Not used	
A2	5	AUX_AN_0, Extra analog input (Ground)	
A2	6	Not used	
A2	7	AUX_AN_1, Extra analog input (+5V)	
A2	8	AUX_AN, Extra analog input (Signal)	
A2	9	Not used	
A2	10	Not used	
A3	1 - 2	Not used	
A4	1 - 2	Not used	
A5	1	Input signal from engine speed sensor 1	
A5	2	Ground for engine speed sensor 1	
A6	1	Input signal from engine speed sensor 2	
A6	2	Ground for engine speed sensor 2	
A7	1	Input signal from the coolant temperature sensor	
A7	2	Ground for coolant temperature sensor	
A8	1 - 2	Not used	
A9	1	Input signal from the oil temperature sensor. The control unit detects the voltage level between pins 1 and 4 (8SY marine engine only).	
A9	2	Voltage supply, +5V to the oil pressure sensor	
A9	3	Input signal from the oil pressure sensor. The control unit detects the voltage level between pins 3 and 4.	

Function Description - Engine Management System (EMS S6) — EMS

Connector	Pin	Assignment	Detail
A9	4	Ground for oil pressure sensor	
A9	5	Not used	
A10	1	Voltage supply, +5V to the charge air pressure sensor	
A10	2	Input signal from the charge air pressure sensor. The control unit detects the voltage level between pins 2 and 3.	
A10	3	Ground for charge air pressure sensor	
A10	4	Input signal from the charge air temperature sensor. The control unit detects the voltage level between pins 3 and 4.	
A10	5	Not used	
B1	1	Voltage supply, +24V to the control unit	
B1	2	Ground connection for the control unit to chassis	
B1	3	Input signal +24V, from the ignition lock (when the key is in the drive position)	
B1	4	Not used	
B1	5	Not used	
B1	6	Voltage supply, +24V to the control unit	
B1	7	Ground connection for the control unit to chassis	
B1	8	Not used	
B1	9	CAN communication, H lead	
B1	10	CAN communication, L lead	
B2 (6SY / 8SY)	1	Voltage supply, +24V to unit injectors	8SY cylinder 1 6SY cylinder 1
B2 (6SY / 8SY)	2	Voltage supply, +24V to unit injectors	8SY cylinder 2 6SY cylinder 2
B2 (6SY / 8SY)	3	Not used	
B2 (6SY / 8SY)	4	Voltage supply, +24V to unit injectors	8SY cylinder 3 6SY cylinder 3
B2 (6SY / 8SY)	5	Voltage supply, +24V to unit injectors	8SY cylinder 4
B2 (6SY / 8SY)	6	Ground for unit injector	8SY cylinder 1 6SY cylinder 1
B2 (6SY / 8SY)	7	Ground for unit injector	8SY cylinder 2 6SY cylinder 2
B2 (6SY / 8SY)	8	Not used	
B2 (6SY / 8SY)	9	Ground for unit injector cylinder 3	8SY cylinder 3 6SY cylinder 3
B2 (6SY / 8SY)	10	Ground for unit injector cylinder 4	8SY cylinder 4
B3	1 - 2	Not used	
B4	1 - 2	Not used	
B5	1 - 2	Not used	
B6	1 - 2	Not used	
B7	1	Not used	

EMS

Function Description - Engine Management System (EMS S6)

Connector	Pin	Assignment	Detail
B7	2	Not used	
B8	1 - 2	Not used	
B9	1 - 5	Not used	
B10	1 - 5	Not used	

Repair   EMS

REPAIR

Replace the EMS S6 Control Unit

6SY Engines

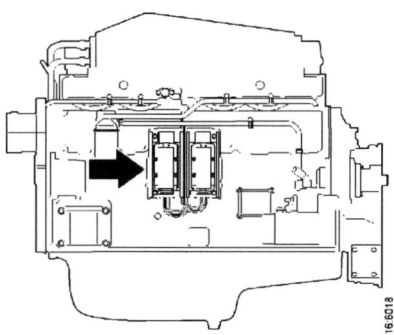

Figure 12-21

8SY Engines

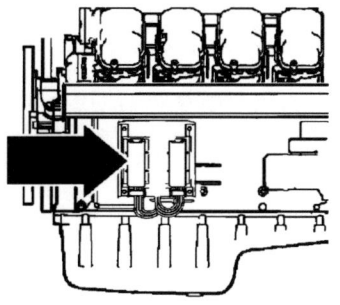

Figure 12-22

1. Remove the covers over the connectors on the control unit and unplug the connectors.
   NOTICE: The EMS S6 control unit may be damaged if it is powered when you unplug it. Before removing the control unit, the key switch must be turned off before removing harness connectors.

2. Remove the control unit attaching screws and remove the control unit.

3. Install the new control unit and tighten the screws to 22 N·m (195 in.-lb).

4. Plug in the connectors on the control unit.

5. Perform the necessary programming with the diagnostic tool. Start the engine. Check the fault codes and delete them.

Remove the EMS S6 Wiring

1. Drain coolant from the engine. **WARNING!** *Wait until the engine cools before you drain the engine coolant. Hot engine coolant may splash and cause burns.*

2. Remove upper rocker covers. *See Remove and Install Rocker Covers on page 5-23.*

3. Disconnect the connectors from the control unit.

4. Mark the cables with the respective cylinder numbers.

5. Disconnect the cables from the unit injectors. The screws cannot be removed, but they should be unscrewed as far as possible.

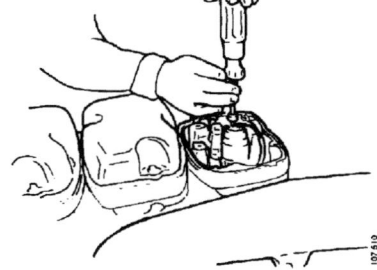

Figure 12-23

6. Remove cables from each cylinder head **(Figure 12-34).**
   - **6SY:** Remove the cable duct to which the cables are attached. Remove the cable bushings in the lower rocker covers and remove the cables.

- **8SY:** Remove the bushings from the lower rocker covers. Pull out the cables from the rocker covers and lift off the cable ducts.

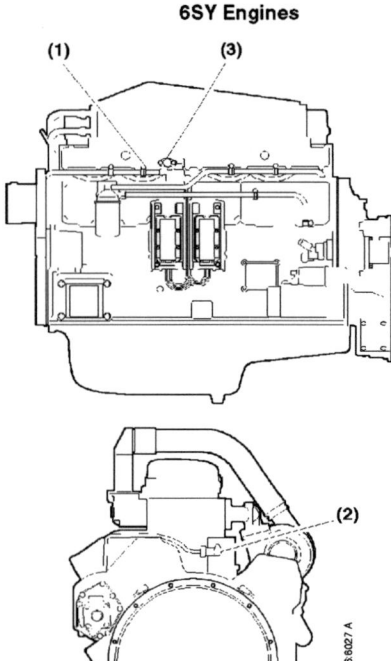

6SY Engines

8SY Engines

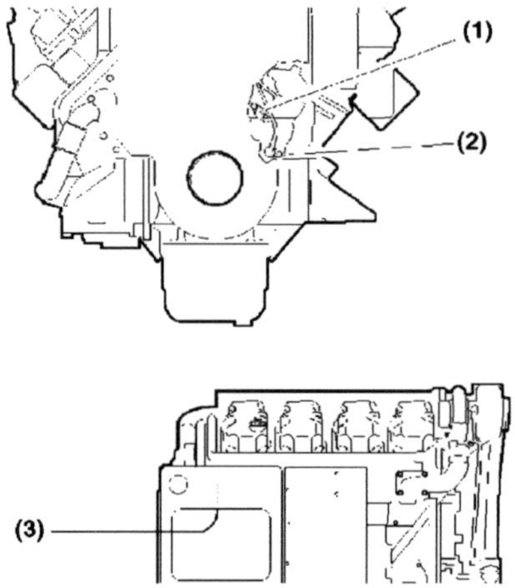

Figure 12-25

Figure 12-24

7. Remove the charge air sensor **(Figure 12-24, (3))** or **(Figure 12-25, (3))** and clamps.
   NOTICE: Handle the engine sensors with care. They are magnetic and are sensitive to impacts.

8. Remove the oil pressure sensor **(Figure 12-24, (1))** or **(Figure 12-25, (1))** and clamps.

9. Remove the coolant temperature sensor **(Figure 12-24, (2))** or **(Figure 12-25, (2))** and clamps.

Repair   EMS

6SY Engines

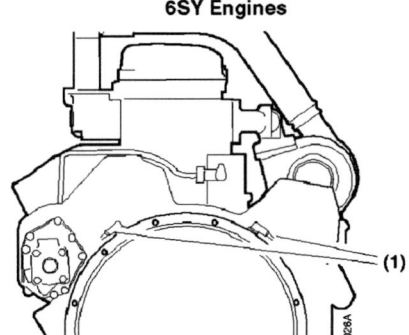

Figure 12-26

8SY Engines

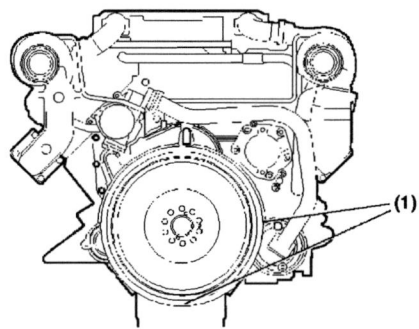

Figure 12-27

10. Remove both engine speed sensors **(Figure 12-26, (1))** or **(Figure 12-27, (1))** and clamps.

EMS Repair

Installing EMS S6 Wiring

Wiring and Cable Duct - 6SY

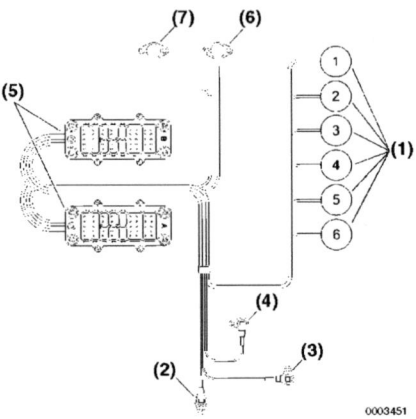

1 – Cylinders 1 - 6
2 – Coolant Temperature Sensor
3 – Engine Speed Sensor 1
4 – Engine Speed Sensor 2
5 – Connector to Control Unit
6 – Charge Air Pressure and Temperature Sensor
7 – Oil Pressure Sensor

Figure 12-28

Wiring and Cable Ducts - 8SY

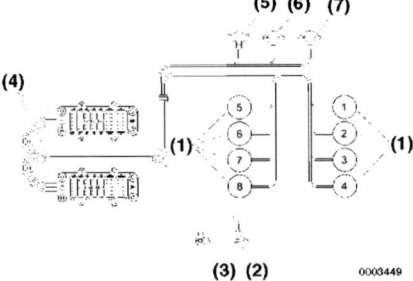

1 – Cylinders 1 - 8
2 – Engine Speed Sensor 1
3 – Engine Speed Sensor 2
4 – Connectors to Control Unit
5 – Coolant Temperature Sensor
6 – Oil Pressure Sensor
7 – Charge Air Pressure and Temperature Sensor

Repair

- Make sure that the inlet pipe between the turbocharger and the air cleaner has been removed.
- Install the cable ducts. Schematic illustrations of of the cable ducts and their components on each engine are shown in **Figure 12-26** and **Figure 12-27**.

1. Run the cables to the unit injectors.
2. Check that the correct cable is connected to each unit injector by testing the cables with a multimeter as shown in the tables below.

6SY Engine

Cylinder	Connector	Pin
1	B2	1 and 6
2	B2	2 and 7
3	B2	4 and 9
4	A1	1 and 6
5	A1	2 and 7
6	A1	4 and 9

8SY Engine

Cylinder	Connector	Pin
1	B2	1 and 6
2	B2	2 and 7
3	B2	4 and 9
4	B2	5 and 10
5	A1	5 and 10
6	A1	4 and 9
7	A1	2 and 7
8	A1	1 and 6

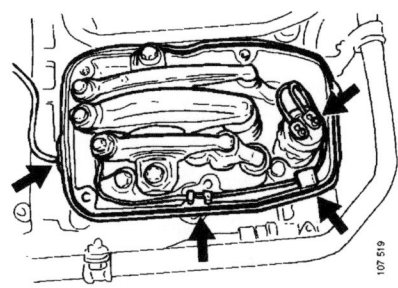

Figure 12-30

3. Press the cables into the groove in the lower rocker cover (**Figure 12-30**).

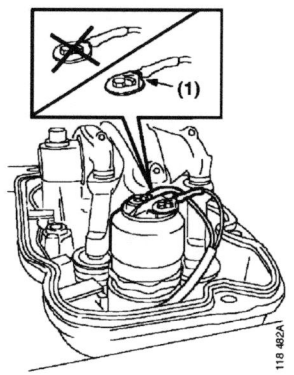

Figure 12-31

4. Install wire terminals. *NOTICE: Ensure injector wire terminals are installed with the bosses (**Figure 12-31, (1)**) facing up.*

6SY Engines

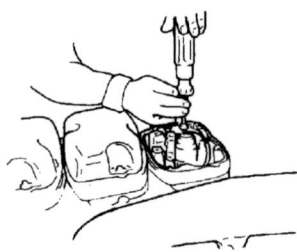

Figure 12-32

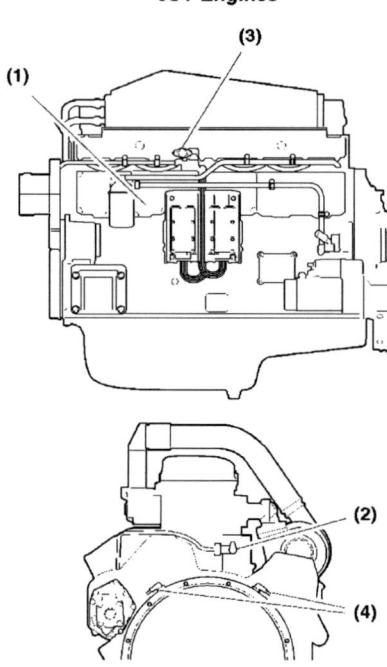

Figure 12-33

5. Connect wires to the unit injectors. Their relative position is not important. Use torque screwdriver OEM Part No. *588 179* (or similar tool) to tighten screws to 2 N·m (283 in.-oz) **(Figure 12-32)**. *NOTICE: Do not over-tighten the cable connection screws on the unit injector. If a screw breaks, the unit injector must be replaced.*

6. **8SY engines**: Attach the bushings and cable ducts to the lower rocker covers.

Repair EMS

8SY Engines

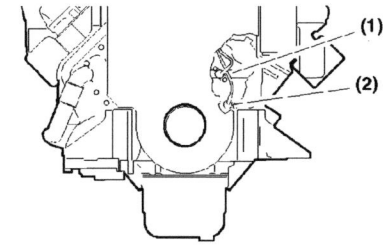

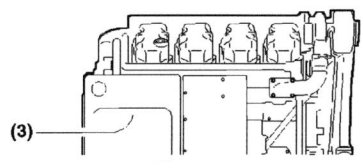

Figure 12-34

7. Install the oil pressure sensor **(Figure 12-33, (1))** or **(Figure 12-34, (1))** and clamps.
   NOTICE: *Handle the engine sensors with care. They are magnetic and are sensitive to impacts.*

8. Install the coolant temperature sensor **(Figure 12-33, (2))** or **(Figure 12-34, (2))** and clamps.

9. Install the charge air sensor **(Figure 12-33, (3))** or **(Figure 12-34, (3))** and clamps.

10. Install the engine speed sensors and clamps.

11. Connect ECOM to the engine and check the unit injectors by activating them. Also check that the values from the sensors are correct.

12. Connect the wiring harness connectors into the control unit.

13. Install the upper rocker covers. *See Remove and Install Rocker Covers on page 5-23.*

14. Install the inlet pipe between the turbocharger and the air cleaner.

15. Fill engine with coolant.

This Page Intentionally Left Blank

Section 13

TROUBLESHOOTING

	Page
Introduction	13-3
Troubleshooting Chart	13-3
Fault Codes	13-18
Working Procedure	13-18
After Troubleshooting or Repair	13-18

TROUBLESHOOTING

This Page Intentionally Left Blank

Introduction

TROUBLESHOOTING

INTRODUCTION

This section contains information and diagnostic troubleshooting charts to accurately diagnose and engine, starter, or alternator problem.

TROUBLESHOOTING CHART

White Smoke

Effect	Cause	Troubleshooting	Action
Incompletely burned fuel	Cold engine	The white smoke starts to turn blue and disappears when the engine is warmed up	If possible: reduce engine speed or put the engine under load. Install a white smoke limiting device (exhaust brake). Install flame heater. Install an engine heater.
Too much fuel in relation to air at low combustion temperatures	Injection timing too late	Unit injectors misadjusted	Adjust unit injector rocker arms.
	Intake valve does not open properly	Incorrect valve adjustment	Adjust valve clearance.
	Faulty unit injector		Replace
	Leaky injector, dripping		Replace

White Smoke, Water Vapor

Effect	Cause	Troubleshooting	Action
Water in the combustion chamber	Leaky charge air cooler	Test pressure (air - 0.5 bar [7.25 psi]; liquid - 4 bar [58 psi])	
	Leaky cylinder head gasket	The fault is also present when the engine is hot	
	Cracked water-cooled exhaust manifold		
	Cracked cylinder head (not cracks between valve seats)	If the fault is hard to trace: Change all cylinder heads for exchange cylinder heads or pressure test all cylinder heads. Heat the cylinder heads before pressurizing them.	
	Crack in cylinder liner		

TROUBLESHOOTING Troubleshooting Chart

Black Smoke when Running / Under Load

Effect	Cause	Troubleshooting	Action
Too much fuel in relation to air at high combustion temperatures	Injection timing too late	Unit injectors misadjusted	Adjust unit injector / rocker arms
	Intake valve does not open properly	Incorrect valve adjustment	Adjust valve clearance.
	Faulty unit injector		Replace unit injector
	Leaky injector, dripping		
	Nozzle tip jams		
	Incorrect spray pattern from nozzle		Clean or replace unit injector
	More than one gasket under injector		
	Fault in turbocharger	Check charge air pressure	
	Clogged air filter		Replace
	High exhaust backpressure		Remove exhaust restriction
	Worn intake valves		Grind or lap valves
	Clogged intake port		Clean

Blue Smoke

Effect	Cause	Troubleshooting	Action
	Worn piston rings and / or cylinders		Repair as necessary
	Oil leakage in turbocharger	Check for oil in the intake manifold after the turbocharger	
	Damaged piston cooling nozzles		Change damaged nozzles
	Gasoline in diesel oil		

Fuel in the Oil

Effect	Cause	Troubleshooting	Action
Dilution of oil in sump	Unburned fuel passing the piston	Worn piston rings	Normally about 1% of fuel in the lubricating oil per 200 hr of operation
	Defective injector		Replace
	Frequent cold starts		
	Worn engine	Check "blow-by" in crankcase: Correct value for new engine: 0 - +10 mmAq (0 - +0.014 psi) (flow rate 60 - 100 l/min.) Closed crankcase ventilation:-50 - +20 mmAq (-0.071 - +0.028 psi)	
	Intake valve not opening	Misadjusted valve or worn camshaft lobe	Adjust valve or replace camshaft

Troubleshooting Chart

TROUBLESHOOTING

Oil in Coolant

Effect	Cause	Troubleshooting	Action
	Internal oil cooler leak with engine running	Pressure test the oil cooler Note: oil cooler test pressure: 10 bar (145 psi) oil on the oil side, 0.5 bar (7.25 psi) air on the water side, immersed in water 25 - 27°C (77 - 81°F)	
	Defective cylinder head gasket		Replace
	Crack in cylinder head (not between valve seats)	If the fault is hard to trace: Replace all cylinder heads or pressure test all cylinder heads. Heat the cylinder heads before pressurizing them.	

Coolant or Water in Oil

Effect	Cause	Troubleshooting	Action
Dilution of oil in sump	Internal oil cooler leaks when engine is not running	Pressure test oil cooler	
	Leaky O-rings at cylinder liner	Leakage in telltale hole	Change liner O-rings
	Water is condensed in crankcase ventilation and runs down into the sump	Engine does not reach normal operating temperature	
	Crack in cylinder head	Run the engine until warm. Remove the oil sump and all side covers. Pressure test the cooling system. If coolant seeps out behind side covers or at the camshaft bearing, there is probably a crack in one of the cylinder heads. As a rule, it is possible to see which cylinder head or heads are leaking.	Change the cylinder head for an exchange cylinder head. If no leakage is found, change all cylinder heads for exchange cylinder heads
	Crack in water jacket on cylinder block/cylinder head. (Coolant runs down through the pushrod hole)		
	Crack in water jacket on cylinder head. (Coolant runs down via the oil duct for rocker arm lubrication.)		
	Cracked cylinder liner		
	Cracked water-cooled exhaust manifold		
	Leakage in charge air cooler core	Test pressure (air - 0.5 bar [7.25 psi]; liquid - 4 bar [58 psi])	
	Water enters via the exhaust/intake system		Install a self-closing cover on the exhaust pipe Position the air cleaner so that water cannot run into it

TROUBLESHOOTING

Troubleshooting Chart

Low Oil Pressure

Effect	Cause	Troubleshooting	Action
Gauge shows low pressure	Defective sensor/instrument	Test the oil pressure on warmed-up engine using a mechanical pressure gauge directly on the engine	
	Incorrectly adjusted oil relief valve		1 shim = 0.2 bar (2.9 psi)
	Broken spring in oil relief valve	Low max. oil pressure of 2 bar (29 psi) at 2000 rpm	Check / repair relief valve
	Oil relief valve piston stuck in open position		
	Incorrect crankshaft bearing/main bearing size has been installed on reground crankshaft	Maximum oil pressure 2 bar (29 psi) even with cold engine	Change to bearings of the correct size. Check the bearing seats before assembly
	Worn main or rod bearings	Low oil pressure at idle - possibly accompanied by a knocking sound	Rebuild engine
	Seizing in camshaft bearings	If the bushing slides all the way out of the bearing seat, the oil pressure gauge reading will be very low. The engine throws out oil through the crankcase ventilation	
	Loose piston cooling nozzle		
	Loose suction pipe to oil pump, the pump sucks air		
	Engine too hot	-	
	Extremely low lubricating oil viscosity		Choose a viscosity that is suitable for the ambient temperature
	Worn bushings or loose shaft in oil cleaner		Change rotor if bushing is worn oval. Change worn/damaged shaft
	Broken O-ring on cyclone part of oil cleaner		
	Defective oil pump drive		
	Internal leakage in oil cleaner	Check that the oil centrifugal cleaner is correctly assembled	
	Loosened guide plates in the oil cooler preventing passage of the oil		
	Worn/damaged oil pump		
	Clogged oil cooler		
	Loose screws in intermediate timing gear		

Troubleshooting Chart

TROUBLESHOOTING

Effect	Cause	Troubleshooting	Action
Gauge indicates low pressure at maximum speed but not at idling speed	The main oil passage (to piston cooling nozzles) plug in the rear of the engine is loose	Oil pressure at idle / low engine speed is not affected since the delivery valve closes at 3 bar (43.5 psi)	

High Oil Pressure (Warm Engine)

Effect	Cause	Troubleshooting	Action
Gauge indicates high pressure	Defective sensor / instrument	Test the oil pressure on the warm engine using a mechanical pressure gauge directly on the engine	
	Oil viscosity too high		Choose a viscosity that is suitable for the ambient temperature
	Incorrectly adjusted oil relief valve		1 shim = 0.2 bar (2.9 psi)
	Piston in oil relief valve jammed in closed position		
	Valve in oil duct to piston cooling nozzles is binding		

Abnormal Piston / Cylinder Wear

Effect	Cause	Troubleshooting	Action
Short service life	Unclean induction air due to inadequate filtering (wrongly dimensioned air filter)	Wear ridge (ring travel shoulder) at piston top dead center	Install a more efficient air filter
	Unclean intake air due to leakage in intake piping		
	Wrong grade of oil, polishing damage		
	Changing of filters and oil has been neglected		
	Low coolant temperature (cold engine)		
	Excessive sulphur content in fuel		Change the fuel Change to oil with a higher base number Shorter oil change intervals
	Defective injector (causes oil film to be washed off)		

TROUBLESHOOTING

Troubleshooting Chart

Vibration - No Driven Components Engaged

Effect	Cause	Troubleshooting	Action
	Incorrect injection timing		Adjust unit Injector
	Individual injectors not operating	Diagnose per separate EMS manual	Replace defective component
	Flywheel has come loose		
	Crankshaft hub loose		
Vibration or unusual noise at 1500 - 1700 rpm	Defective vibration damper		
Drive belts run off pulleys			
	Unsuitable rubber suspension and location		Change to rubber elements of different hardness
	Weak engine bed	Movement at engine attachment points	Reinforce the engine bed

Vibration - Transmission Engaged

Effect	Cause	Troubleshooting	Action
	Engine and propeller shaft misaligned	Check engine alignment	Align
	Bent propeller shaft		Replace
Maximum boat speed is reduced	Bent propeller		Replace
	Slipping transmission		Repair

External Corrosion on Cylinder Liner

Effect	Cause	Troubleshooting	Action
	Unsuitable corrosion protection agent, glycol or water in coolant		Flush the cooling system and fill with coolant as described in *Engine Coolant on page 3-13*

Troubleshooting Chart

TROUBLESHOOTING

Engine is Hard to Start

Effect	Cause	Troubleshooting	Action
Air in fuel system	Leak in suction pipe		
	The highest fuel level in the tank is lower than the feed pump. If the engine is not operated for several days, the fuel in the suction pipe may run back to the tank because of a leaky overflow valve		Install a "daily supply tank" at a higher location than the feed pump
	Leaky overflow valve		
	Low battery voltage		
	Ambient temperature too low		Starting aids are not normally needed at temperatures above -15°C (5°F)
	Oil viscosity too high		
	Paraffin precipitation in the fuel		
	Blocked intake or exhaust system		
	No fuel		
	Wrong injection timing		
	Faulty injector		

Hydraulic Lock

Effect	Cause	Troubleshooting	Action
Starter motor not powerful enough to pull the piston over the compression stroke (if the engine fires, a connecting rod could be bent)	Leaky charge air cooler	Test pressure (air 0.5 bar (7.25 psi), liquid 4 bar (58 psi)	
	Leaky cylinder head gasket		
	Crack in cylinder head	If the fault is hard to trace: Change all cylinder heads for exchange cylinder heads or pressure test all cylinder heads. Heat the cylinder heads before pressurizing them.	
	Crack in cylinder liner		Replace
	Water has entered the engine via the exhaust or intake system		Install a self-closing cover on the exhaust pipe Position the air cleaner so that water cannot run into it
	Crack in water-cooled exhaust manifold		
	Injector open		

TROUBLESHOOTING

Troubleshooting Chart

Knocking

Effect	Cause	Troubleshooting	Action
Exhaust valves close too late and strike the piston crowns	Timing gears incorrectly meshed	Check the valve timing	
	The crankshaft gear has come loose		
	Valve mechanism not operating		
Rapidly increasing valve clearances	Oil flow problem to the rocker arms		
The piston strikes the cylinder head	Loosened big end cap (wrong tightening torque after repair)		Tighten to the proper torque
	Foreign objects in the piston crown		
	Piston seizure (may be caused by clogged piston cooling nozzles)		
	Wrong injection timing		
	Worn collets on exhaust valves		
Broken upper piston rings	Incorrectly adjusted injectors		
	Connecting rod bearing seizure		
	Faulty injector (seized, worn, incorrect or cracked tip, fatigued spring)		
	Incorrectly adjusted injector		
	More than one washer under injector		
Melting damage on piston crown	Injection timing extremely advanced, 30° BTDC or more	Check the injection timing	
	Incorrectly adjusted injector		

Troubleshooting Chart

TROUBLESHOOTING

Excess Oil Consumption

Effect	Cause	Troubleshooting	Action
Blue smoke under load	Piston ring seizure		
	Piston seizure	Combustion temperature too high	
	Liner wear	Unclean intake air	
	Carbon polishing (in patches)	Poor grade of oil	
	Piston ring wear		
	Piston rings stuck		
	Tapered piston rings installed wrong way		
	Broken piston rings	Individual piston rings broken = incorrectly fitted Several upper rings broken = start spray used wrongly, wrong injection timing (too early) Several intermediate rings broken = worn rings or grooves	
	Worn valve guides	Check the clearance between valve and guide. High exhaust temperature? Poor grade of oil?	
	Oil level too high		
	Defective shaft seals in turbocharger	Check whether oil is present in the compressor or intake manifold	
	Clogged air filter		
	Excessive vacuum in the air intake before the turbocharger	Measure the vacuum (max. 500 mmAq [1.45 inHg]) Check the air filter	
	Oil viscosity too low		
	Deformed/incorrectly directed piston cooling nozzles		
	External leakage		

Excess Fuel Consumption

Effect	Cause	Troubleshooting	Action
	Faulty injector		
	Low charge air pressure		
	Manner of driving, operating/load conditions		

TROUBLESHOOTING

Troubleshooting Chart

Low Cylinder Compression

Effect	Cause	Troubleshooting	Action
Rough engine operation or low power output	Worn piston rings and cylinder	Perform compression test	
	Broken piston rings		
	Incorrectly adjusted/ defective valves		
	Hydrostatic lock/bent connecting rod		

Low Engine Output

Effect	Cause	Troubleshooting	Action
	Low fuel supply pressure (below 0.3 bar)	Check the feed pump and overflow valve for leakage Check for leakage in the suction pipe between tank and feed pump Clogged fuel filter/paraffin precipitation in fuel	
	Faulty injector		
	Fuel too hot		
	Incorrect fuel specification	Check density and viscosity	
	Low charge air pressure	Check charge air pressure	
	Abnormal pressure drop in intake piping	Check the vacuum before the turbocharger, maximum 500 mmAq Check the air filter	
	Worn engine	Check "blow-by" in crankcase Correct value for new engine: 0 - +10 mmAq (0 - +0.014 psi) (flow rate 60 - 100 l/min.) Closed crankcase ventilation: 50 - +20 mmAq (-0.071 - +0.028 psi)	
	Leaky valves	Take compression readings and compare those of the different cylinders	
	Incorrect injection timing		Adjust unit injectors
	Intake air temperature too high	Check the temperature of the air before the engine. Above +25°C (77°F) will reduce engine power	
	Exhaust backpressure too high	*See Principal Engine Specifications on page 3-15.*	
	Intake counter-pressure too high	*See Low Charge Air Pressure on page 13-15*	

Troubleshooting Chart

TROUBLESHOOTING

Engine Overheat

Effect	Cause	Troubleshooting	Action
Instrument shows high temperature	Defective sensor/instrument	Check that sensor and instrument match each other (120° and 150°C [248° and 302°F]) Check using a test thermometer	
	Low coolant level		
	Clogged seawater filter		
	Clogged freshwater/seawater cooling system		Clean the cooling system internally and externally
	Pressure cap not operating	Pressure test	
	Impeller on closed cooling or seawater pump worn or damaged		
	Incorrect comb / worn cover on seawater pump		
	Restriction in coolant flow, e.g. pieces of rubber from seawater impeller		
	Cooling capacity too low	Take a reading of the cooling capacity	
	Combustion gas leakage (causes loss of coolant)	Test compression	
	Defective thermostats	Check opening temperature of thermostats	
Reduced coolant flow	Drive belts slip or pump pulley loose on pump shaft		
	Air pockets in engine cooling circuit		Vent at the cooling system's highest point Check that the ventilation piping to the coolant recovery tank is not clogged
	Excessive pressure drop in the external cooling system	Check with forcibly opened thermostats	
	Clogged heat exchanger		
	Cavitation damaged impeller in coolant pump		
	Leakage in charge air cooler		

Engine Runs Too Cold

Effect	Cause	Troubleshooting	Action
Instrument indicates low temperature	Defective sensor/instrument	Check that sensor and instrument match each other (120° and 150°C [248° and 302°F]) Check using a test thermometer	
	Thermostat jammed in open position	Check operation of thermostat	

TROUBLESHOOTING Troubleshooting Chart

Coolant Loss

Effect	Cause	Troubleshooting	Action
	Defective cylinder head gasket (external leakage)		
	External leakage		
Coolant forced out of coolant recovery tank	Turbocharging pressure enters cooling system via leaking charge air element	Test pressure (air - 0.5 bar [7.25 psi]; liquid - 4 bar [58 psi])	
White smoke when engine hot indicates water vapor	Crack in cylinder head (not cracks between valve seats)	If the fault is hard to trace: Change all cylinder heads for exchange cylinder heads or pressure test all cylinder heads. Heat the cylinder heads before pressurizing them.	
	Cracked cylinder liner	Grey oil = coolant in oil	Locate the leak by removing the oil sump and pressurizing the cooling system while turning the engine over by hand
	Leaking cylinder head gasket	Check for warped cylinder head	Replace cylinder head gasket

Contaminated Coolant

Effect	Cause	Troubleshooting	Action
	Faulty inhibitor		Flush the cooling system and refill with coolant as described in *Engine Coolant on page 3-13*
	Overdosed corrosion inhibitor		

Engine Heater

Effect	Cause	Troubleshooting	Action
Boiler scale on engine heater	Incorrect mixture or type of glycol and/or corrosion inhibitor. Antifreeze with phosphate-based inhibitor must not be used		Flush the cooling system and fill it with coolant as described in *Engine Coolant on page 3-13*
Short service life	The heater is not designed for continuous use. Suitable temperature for thermostat control = 40° - 60°C		

High Oil Temperature

Effect	Cause	Troubleshooting	Action
Instrument indicates too high temperature	Defective sensor / instrument	Check using test thermometer	
	Poor water flow in oil cooler		

Troubleshooting Chart   TROUBLESHOOTING

High Exhaust Temperature

Effect	Cause	Troubleshooting	Action
	Wrong injection timing	Check the injection timing	Adjust unit injectors
	Nozzle drips	Check type, opening pressure and general condition	Clean / replace unit injector
	Exhaust backpressure too high	See Principal Engine Specifications on page 3-15.	
	High inlet air temperature	Faulty intake air cooler	
	Low charge air pressure		
	Clogged air filter		

Low Charge Air Pressure

Effect	Cause	Troubleshooting	Action
	Dirty / damaged turbine/compressor wheel in turbocharger		Check/clean
	Leakage between turbocharger and cylinder head		Check/change gaskets
	Bearing seizure in turbocharger	Check bearing play	Recondition/change turbocharger
	Clogged air filter	Check the vacuum before the turbocharger. See Principal Engine Specifications on page 3-15.	
	Exhaust backpressure too high	See Principal Engine Specifications on page 3-15.	
	High fuel temperature		

Low Fuel Pressure

Effect	Cause	Troubleshooting	Action
	Clogged fuel filter		
	Defective overflow valve		
	Defective feed pump		
	Air leakage in suction pipe		
	High pressure drop in suction pipe		

TROUBLESHOOTING Troubleshooting Chart

Low System Voltage

Effect	Cause	Troubleshooting	Action
Normal charging voltage: 27 - 28 V	Broken alternator drive belt		
	Slipping alternator drive belt		
	Batteries in poor condition		
	Alternator fault		
	Voltage regulator fault		
	Battery charger fault		

High System Voltage

Effect	Cause	Troubleshooting	Action
Normal charging voltage: 27 - 28 V	Voltage regulator fault		
	Battery charger fault		

External Oil Leakage

Effect	Cause	Troubleshooting	Action
	Crankcase pressure too high	Check "blow-by" in crankcase. Correct value for new engine: 0 - +10 mmAq (0 - +0.014 psi) (flow rate 60 - 100 l/min.) Closed crankcase ventilation: -50 - +20 mmAq (-0.071 - +0.028 psi)	
	Leaky crankshaft seal		
	Leakage at liner seal via overflow hole in cylinder block		
	Defective cylinder head gasket		
Leakage in manifold joint	Low load		

External Coolant Leakage

Effect	Cause	Troubleshooting	Action
	Leakage in cylinder liner seal		
	Cold leakage		Replace hoses using better quality hoses (preferably silicone)
	Defective cylinder head gasket		
	Coolant pump leakage	Check at the water pump housing's weep hole	
	Leakage at charge air cooler connection		

Troubleshooting Chart

TROUBLESHOOTING

Oil Forced Out Crankcase Ventilation

Effect	Cause	Troubleshooting	Action
	Hole in piston crown	Increases when white smoke limiting device is engaged or exhaust brake applied	
	Bearing seizure in turbocharger		
	Oil seepage via pistons - liner		

Turbocharger Failure

Effect	Cause	Troubleshooting	Action
Loss of power	Excessive bearing play in turbocharger		
	Lubrication piping between turbocharger and filter incorrectly connected		Check the connections

TROUBLESHOOTING

FAULT CODES

Fault codes will be displayed on the digital display. Interpretation of those codes can be found in publication supplied with the unit.

Working Procedure

Try to form a comprehensive view of the problem. Start by asking the user the following:

- Fault symptoms
- Conditions in which the fault occurs
- How often the fault occurs
- If the fault codes have been erased

Then, present all the stored fault codes.

Compare them and try to conclude the probable cause of the fault before taking any other measures. The fault codes are stored in the order they were registered.

AFTER TROUBLESHOOTING OR REPAIR

The engine control unit may have generated fault codes due to the current fault or during troubleshooting. Do not forget to check and clear any fault codes.